# Children and Their Parents in Brief Therapy

# Children and Their Parents in Brief Therapy

### Edited by
### Harvey H. Barten, M. D.
Medical Director,
The Guidance Center of New Rochelle
Clinical Associate Professor of Psychiatry,
Cornell Medical College, New York
and
### Sybil S. Barten, Ph.D.
Assistant Professor of Psychology,
State University of New York,
College at Purchase
Clinical Assistant Professor of Psychology,
Department of Psychiatry,
Albert Einstein College of Medicine, New York

**Behavioral Publications**          New York
**1973**

Library of Congress Catalog Card Number 72-10161
Standard Book Number 87705-082-1
Copyright © 1973 by Behavioral Publications

BEHAVIORAL PUBLICATIONS, 2852 Broadway—Morningside Heights,
New York, New York 10025

Printed in the United States of America

**Library of Congress Cataloging in Publication Data**

Barten, Harvey H      1933-        comp.
   Children and their parents in brief therapy.

   1.  Child psychotherapy.  2.  Parent and child.
I.  Barten, Sybil S., 1933-    joint comp.  II.  Title.
[DNLM:  1.  Family therapy.  WM 430 B283c  1972]
RJ504.B39              618.9'28'914            72-10161
ISBN 0-87705-082-1

TO OUR CHILDREN AND PARENTS

# CONTENTS

## GROUP AND FAMILY
## APPROACHES

# BEHAVIOR MODIFICATION TECHNIQUES

## PHARMACOTHERAPY

# ACKNOWLEDGEMENTS

We should like to express our appreciation to all of the authors and publishers who generously consented to have their articles reprinted. We also want to thank Betty Atkins and Daisy Moritz for their valuable secretarial assistance.

# 1. INTRODUCTION

## Harvey H. Barten, M.D.
## Sybil S. Barten, Ph.D.

### NEW PERSPECTIVES IN
### CHILD MENTAL HEALTH

This collection of readings has been assembled to complement a recently published volume on brief therapies for adults.[4] While based on similar basic concepts, brief therapy with children and their parents confronts the therapist with technical problems of a different nature for which specific strategies must be developed. The treatment of children's disorders is complicated by the diversity of their problems at different developmental levels and the difficulties in distinguishing pathological reactions from growing pains. Clinical syndromes at most age levels are less well defined than they are for adults. Diagnostic categories are still notoriously inadequate, with large numbers of children lumped together in "wastebasket" diagnoses such as "Adjustment Reaction." In evaluating a child's problem, data often must be obtained from multiple, sometimes contradictory, sources. The origins of a problem may be concealed within a multidimensional social context. The child himself frequently sidesteps a direct investigation of the presenting problem, which initially he may be unable to acknowledge.

Until now, these complicating factors have discouraged those who might otherwise have been disposed to condense and shorten therapeutic procedures. Faced with problems obscured by the child's reticence and the family's defensiveness, as well as by the variability or ambiguity of observable behaviors, therapists, particularly those lacking substantial clinical experience with all age levels, were understandably inclined to play it safe. They proceeded slowly, cautiously and thoroughly, obtaining mountains of information and incorporating as much of their data as possible into highly complex, sophisticated, but unwieldy formulations.

Indeed, cases often were not sharply formulated until completion of the process of multidisciplinary data-gathering and conferencing by the "holy trinity" of psychiatrist, psychologist and social worker. The assumption that a child's problems could only be unscrambled and corrected by labyrinthine endeavors stifled the search for alternative, more pointed explorations, perhaps directed primarily toward key adult figures. But this in turn hinges upon a conceptualization of behavior patterns that permits more direct, focused, action-oriented interventions.

Child psychiatry has thus lagged behind other branches of psychiatry in streamlining its techniques to meet contemporary demands for service. The inadequacies of therapeutic resources for children are increasingly a source of public and professional concern. This has been eloquently articulated in several recently published national studies, particularly the Joint Commission on Mental Health of Children[17] and the Ad Hoc Committee on Child Mental Health.[1]

To those who have followed the oft-reiterated (and largely unheeded) calls for action in community-oriented journals such as the American Journal of Orthopsychiatry, these findings hardly come as any great surprise. Nor have professionals in child guidance clinics been unaware of the increasingly large discrepancy between the demand for children's treatment services and available therapy hours. But tradition dies hard; some of the special problems noted above have discouraged those who otherwise might have sought more efficient techniques earlier. Moreover, in working with what are perceived as innocent, vulnerable children, it is difficult for many dedicated workers to justify to themselves using a limited approach which leaves some problem areas unresolved. In part sentimental, in part overcautious, this viewpoint tends to look with skepticism or disdain upon those who take shortcuts. But for each child who receives exhaustive therapy, many others, for reasons of the implacable laws of supply and demand, receive nothing. Given the always insufficient resources to resolve the bulk of every troubled child's problems, overall community needs are ignored by attempts to meet all the needs of only those children or families who have become the responsibility of a given agency because it has thoroughly delineated their problems.

With the emergence of the Community Mental Health movement, many professionals are adopting a different perspective, which suggests that limited therapeutic resources must be deployed in such a manner as to inject change-inducing elements into faulty family and social systems as early as possible. This may avert the need for later, more extended therapeutic endeavors, which are less likely to be successful.

Not only is there a growing movement to broaden the scope of psychiatric practice so that it will encompass an increasing portion of the total community, but the tempo and strategies of child psychiatry, like other branches of psychiatry, are themselves changing irrespective of patient populations. Private practitioners are now also questioning prior assumptions and are adopting a more pragmatic approach, utilizing modest interventions before committing themselves to more complex therapies, and often selecting time-limited therapy as the treatment of choice. Private insurance plans[15] are increasingly oriented towards short-term therapy; many of the proposals for federally supported national insurance visualize short-term approaches. Thus, both in response to shifting professional attitudes and to mounting pressure from public and private funding sources, it will be more and more difficult for mental health professionals to adhere only to stereotyped therapeutic orthodoxies, or to continue to serve only a limited, selected caseload. The "good treatment candidates" are too often children from highly motivated, cooperative, intact, middle-class families.[14,17] Meanwhile the rest of the population has become increasingly informed and vocal about their needs, and now they are knocking more insistently on our doors.

The papers included in this volume represent a sampling of innovative experiments with a variety of techniques for the short-term treatment of children and their parents. These include emergency or crisis therapy, a spectrum of brief approaches including family and group therapies, behaviorally-oriented approaches, classroom techniques, and the use of psychotropic drugs. We have selected several papers on the brief therapy of school phobia because this is a particularly well defined maladaptive syndrome, generally responsive to short-term strategies and illustrative of some basic concepts. Clearly, further progress in the field of short-term children's therapy should be facilitated by the sharper demarcation of additional maladaptive syndromes, so that therapists may rapidly identify them and immediately employ tested therapeutic strategies. The current state of the art is such that we can only present isolated therapeutic experiments rather than a comprehensive and systematized compendium. Fortunately, the present decade is one of experimentation and innovation. The Child Guidance movement, once in the forefront of leadership, has become bogged down by institutionalization; there is growing dissatisfaction with timeworn practices[2] and increasing interest in innovation and change.

## SHORT-TERM STRATEGIES

Traditional techniques tend to be cautious, non-directive, comprehensive in scope and relatively indirect in method (e.g., play therapy). But the orientation of short-term therapy must be precisely the opposite. Rather than slowly and systematically collecting information on all facets of the child's experience, the therapist rapidly delineates a problem area. Active, focused, incisive interventions are communicated to parent, child, or both. Rather than waiting for solutions to emerge, the therapist urges the child and/or his parents to explore and define available options for correcting the difficulty. The therapist proceeds on the assumption that the child has some awareness about why he has been brought to the clinic, and that efforts will be made to communicate directly and straightforwardly about his problems, even though he may initially resist or deflect these probes. The therapist hopes that in the process of helping the child explore alternative behaviors, or convincing the family to realign forces that negatively affect the child's behavior, solutions will emerge which interrupt vicious cycles, instill more positive expectations, and lead to further experimentation and change in other areas, even after the therapeutic process has been concluded.

Obviously, short-term techniques will not be the answer in every case. They must be an expansion of the therapist's repertoire rather than a universal substitute for long-term therapy. However, major interventions (if available) must be reserved for children with major needs. At the start, children's problems often involve relatively superficial or circumscribed behavioral disturbances, which are unwittingly exacerbated by the reactions of parents, teachers and others. Whether acting out of ignorance, insensitivity, frustration, or anxiety, and however exemplary their intentions, these adults may intensify problems rather than help resolve them. Short-term therapy is often a means of making adult figures aware of how they may perpetuate problems and how they can deal more effectively with the behavioral disturbances.

## WHO IS THE PATIENT?

Since the attitudes and actions of adults are so critical in setting the stage for a child's problems, or subsequently—even if unknowingly—maintaining them, and since it is frequently simpler to appeal to reason or to suggest behavior modification techniques and other kinds of concise interventions to adults, the latter often are the major participants in short-term therapy. (Rosenthal and Levine[29], for example, worked with family members as often or more often than the child in 85 percent of their cases.) The therapist attempts to delineate pathogenic forces that operate within the social milieu and possibly contribute to the child's problems by injuring feelings, threatening his sense of security, providing contradictory cues for behavior, or setting rules which are vague or unworkable. Parents, siblings, or teachers are challenged to interrupt vicious cycles.[35] Once the therapist succeeds in prevailing upon a family member to change his behavior toward the child, this person must accept the responsibility for supporting rather than sabotaging the child. Phillips and Johnston (Chapter 2) attribute the problems of most of the children they have treated to the parents' failure to provide sufficient structure. The major thrust of their time-limited therapy is to remedy this deficiency. "Change the system and you change the child."

Bolman[5] applies *systems theory* more generally in describing the complex interactions within a social milieu that give rise to a child's problems. He describes a systems approach as follows: "1. Attempting to estimate ... the relative contribution of the different system levels. These include: the child and the sublevels of neurological and psychological structure; the family and its various patterns of parental roles and communication; the school and its relationships among child, teacher, principal, and pupil services; the community and its various competencies; and the influence of regularized societal ... patterns of education and medicine on the preceding age, sex, temperament, family, school, and community variabilities. 2. After a rough estimation of the contribution of these levels has been made, deciding which levels or interfaces provide the most likely point(s) of leverage for change. This might include drugs, individual therapy, behavior modification, family counseling or therapy, mental health consultation in the schools, curricular changes ... improved school-community relations. ... 3. After a decision about which point(s) of leverage look most effective has been made, approaching them in a manner that is most likely: a) to evoke cooperation from the primary level; b) to minimize noncooperation or antagonism from other levels; and c) to keep communications open so that errors or misjudgments may be corrected by feedback from any of the other levels." (pp. 30-31)

Sometimes, of course, the child is the primary focus,

but there should be specific indications for this. These would include the child's capacity and motivation to participate, as well as the nature of his problem. Thus, a therapist might elect to focus on the child, if the child were able and willing to talk about his problems and the therapist wanted the child to unburden himself of feelings such as grief or anger. Short-term therapy with the child himself also allows for modeling, behavior rehearsal, sanctioning alternative behaviors which the child has hesitated to employ, or helping a child to discover alternative methods for dealing with problems that he has already attempted, unsuccessfully, to resolve. With increasing maturity, children become more amenable to direct therapy.

In utilizing *behavior modification techniques,* the therapist either can work directly with the child or indirectly through parents or teachers, as illustrated by Wagner (Chapter 19). These strategies deal explicitly with overt, readily observable behaviors. Behavior therapists assume that maladaptive behaviors are learned and can be corrected by the application of principles derived from learning theory. Their procedures (Chapter 18) attempt systematically to eliminate selected symptoms in the child which "are either most distressing to the patient or to those in his social environment, or most suitable for treatment. As such, problem definition is likely to be simple and practical." Werry and Wollersheim (Chapter 18) state that behavior therapy is the treatment of choice when symptoms or problem behaviors are discrete and easily recognized; when the patient and/or family are symptom- rather than insight-oriented; or when experienced child therapists are in short supply, since behavior therapy can be performed, under supervision, by relatively unskilled therapists (p. 365). Werry and Wollersheim's overview is included to introduce the reader to this rapidly growing field, the specifics of which are beyond the scope of this volume.

In deciding who is the patient, the therapist must always bear in mind which system changes are most practicable and most likely to lead to sustained benefits. If the social milieu continues to seriously undermine the child, it is futile for the therapist to concentrate his efforts primarily upon him, since any benefits will at best be of transient value and the situation likely to revert quickly back to its previous state.

## EDUCATIVE ASPECTS OF SHORT-TERM THERAPY

For brief therapy in general, the line between education and treatment can be difficult to draw. In the case of brief therapy of children and their families, treatment frequently consists of imparting and demonstrating healthy and effective child-rearing patterns. Parents are often woefully ignorant about how to handle areas of conflict and difficulty in their children. Particularly when adequate models were absent in their own families, new parents learn how to raise children by trial and error, often reaching faulty and self-defeating conclusions. Parents who fail to profit from experience and act on the basis of continuing misconceptions are all too common. Short-term therapy thus requires a substantial measure of parental education. Many of the critical "lessons" that parents must learn in order to modify their children's behavior and attitudes can be effective in a remarkably short period, unless the parents' practices are sustained by their own neurotic needs. For example, parents can be made aware of those normal developmental changes that cause a transformation in familial and social relationships. When parents learn to anticipate maturational crises[30] and turbulent transitional periods, their reactions can be calmer and less dictated by the shock or defensiveness that only compounds the child's problems.

Other educative efforts sensitize parents to their use of language and its effect on the child. For example, a mother can be made aware of the danger of negatively labeling a child's behavior so as to perpetuate it. For certain parents, it is helpful to remind them to observe and listen to the child rather than to judge or attempt to inhibit undesirable behavior. Listening, they discover, need not signify assent. Frequently in this context, the issue of the boundary between child and adult comes up. It is necessary to point out that the child's behavior does not always represent a personal assault on the parent. It is often a surprise to parents that positive reinforcement actually obtains better results than negative reinforcement and, paradoxically, that excessive criticism maintains the behavior it seeks to suppress. Indeed, some of the child's difficulty may stem from his despair of doing anything to offset previous errors in order to earn parental esteem and love.

On a more structured level, programmed texts on child management[26,33] have been developed as a means of encouraging parents to question and redefine child rearing practices. These texts can be utilized in behaviorally-oriented group therapy for parents.[23] The very process of responding to a questionnaire that has no therapeutic motivation whatever[28] has unexpectedly influenced subsequent parental behaviors—probably because it identified or crystallized some key issues that forced parents to reflect upon some of their practices.

Short-term family therapy[18,19]   (Chapters 16 and 17) deals with these issues in other ways, such as clarification of family roles or the reinvolvement of a family member who has emotionally distanced himself from the group. Sometimes parents must be confronted with the displacement of their problems upon their children.

In their classic longitudinal studies of early childhood, Chess, Thomas and Birch[7,8] have provided invaluable documentation of the origins of pathological interactions between parents and their children. The authors challenge the widely held assumption that pathology in the child generally reflects pathology in the parents. Instead, they attempt to demonstrate that the difficulty often stems from dissonance between parental expectations and the child's inborn temperamental characteristics. In the reprinted summary (Chapter 7) of their book, *Temperament and Behavior Disorders in Children,* they describe some of the difficulties emerging from a "poor fit" between parents and child. Their findings are particularly germane to brief psychotherapy, which is oriented toward modifying destructive interactions between parents and child and increasing understanding of the child's disposition, capabilities, and limitations.

## LEARNING SHORT-TERM TECHNIQUES

Particularly for those with different experience and traditions, the mastery of short-term techniques requires considerable reorientation. Rather than mapping the child's total environmental field, ascertaining all his levels of functioning, and inventorying all areas of weakness, the therapist must focus immediately on the current problem. (When therapists inexperienced with short-term techniques discuss their first cases, it is clear that some find this shift in emphasis very difficult.) Even after a therapist has defined a central problem area, he may feel compelled to pursue other areas of conflict as they emerge, blurring the focus both for those being counseled and for himself. Furthermore, many therapists find it difficult to refrain from dealing with all problem areas which have been uncovered. Implicitly, they assume that the child and his family are incapable of handling these remaining conflicts, even after the child's confidence or the family's competence is bolstered by the successful resolution of the presenting problem. On the contrary, short-term therapy assumes a *health-oriented* outlook that is more concerned with delineating and communicating the child's and his family's assets and strengths, in order to encourage them to seek their own solutions for many of the problems that time-limited therapy cannot resolve. Students of short-term therapy must accept this premise or they will inevitably convert the majority of their short-term cases into extended therapy.

Kerns (Chapter 6) describes other difficulties that therapists have in accepting an abbreviated form of treatment which they may initially regard as second-best. "The workers' concerns that improvement . . . was a 'flight into health' rather than a real working through of the problem, made them reluctant to terminate."

*Time limits* are clearly established at the start, so that

both patient and therapist are aware of what should be happening at every phase of treatment. More frequently than not, the goal is of a problem-solving nature rather than the uncovering and resolution of internal conflicts, though the therapist develops hypotheses for himself about the latter, which he uses in formulating a treatment plan. The basic elements of short-term therapy, including its focused, circumscribed, health-oriented, problem-solving character have been discussed in greater detail in previous publications.[3,4]

## COMMON PATTERNS OF DISORDER

The delineation of a problem area is greatly facilitated by schemata that classify maladaptive patterns in relation to developmental crises and to frequently encountered life stresses and traumata. Anthony[2] has outlined one such classification in which three categories of crisis are described. Under *maturational crises,* he includes the shift from large muscle to small muscle usage upon entering school, "neurological" learning unreadiness, growth spurts, pubertal development, and the shift from preoperational to operational thinking. *Psychosocial crises* include the transition from home to school, and from a lower-level school to a higher-level school, as well as the new social dimensions of adolescence, and the adolescent child's rejection of family values. Under the category of *life crises,* Anthony includes birth of a sibling, family illness, parental disharmony, father's unemployment, home disasters, and death in the family.

## GROUP APPROACHES

Epstein (Chapter 14) describes groups for parents which meet for a total of six weekly sessions, during which problems are defined and clarified and parental misconceptions modified. "A major undertaking is to help the parents to become more accepting of a wide range of behaviors without reacting to their children as pathological specimens." A great deal of teaching goes on in these sessions, and the parents learn from each other's experiences. Group members are expected to devise alternate responses to the child. In dealing with drug abuse problems among children and adolescents, Gottschalk et. al. (Chapter 15) utilized separate groups of children and parents, who joined each other at the end of the session to provide an opportunity for children to interact with other parents before eventually resolving issues with their own parents.

## PATIENT SELECTION

While it is clear that some patients are better candidates for brief therapy than others, this may be difficult to establish at the start. Intact families, who present relatively circumscribed problems and are willing to make efforts to solve their problems, certainly are more likely to be favorable candidates than families with complex, chronic or pronounced difficulties, or families with resistive or hostile attitudes towards therapy. Yet it has been a rather curious paradox that those patients, who would most likely respond to any therapy—short or long, generally tend to be selected for long-term therapy, while less promising patients are assigned to short-term therapy. This reflects many therapists' preference to devote their major efforts to the most receptive and promising cases.[14,21,29] One could argue that, on the contrary, long-term therapy should be reserved for the most difficult or disturbed patients. One can utilize short-term therapy as an initial procedure, during which the need for more extended procedures will become apparent in the more difficult cases.

Short-term therapy is not viewed as a panacea, but as one of a spectrum of interventions. As described more thoroughly in a previous publication,[4] we must view each child's hierarchy of needs in terms of what therapy makes the most sense for him at this particular time in his life, what his family or social context can accept and support, as well as what is available within the limited pool of therapeutic resources. In some cases, short-term therapy will be a regretted expedient because nothing else is available. In other cases, it may be the treatment modality of choice, even when family or community resources could provide more. Small successes can provide models for problem-solving and catalyze the individual's and/or family's independent experimentation and change without risking the dependency or passivity that longer therapy sometimes engenders. Whether short-term therapy is chosen for reasons of expedience or preference, the choice should be made in a non-dogmatic, pragmatic fashion which does not cast aspersions on other methods and which measures outcome against intention, acknowledges oversimplifications and shortcomings, and seeks new strategies when faced with inadequate results.

## PREVENTION AND EARLY INTERVENTION

Since parental errors of omission and commission may have a cumulatively detrimental effect, and failures in navigating developmental nodal points and attaining essential social and academic skills expose the child to pyramiding difficulties, early case-finding and treatment have become major community mental health goals. For example, we believe that mental health specialists could perform yeoman service in pediatricians' offices by periodically surveying the child's development. Busy pediatricians can seldom take the time to do this in more than the most cursory fashion. A few words of encouragement or advice to parents often would suffice. Areas of concern could subsequently be monitored without the necessity of a formal psychiatric referral. Augenbraun, Reid and Friedman (Chapter 9) describe just such an approach with preschool children. Evaluation and short-term therapy in pediatric and well-baby clinics can achieve similar objectives.[6,16] For that matter, unresolved parental conflict during pregnancy and the perinatal period can set the stage for subsequent mother-child problems.

In Caplan, Mason and Kaplan's (Chapter 8) classic investigation of the crisis of premature birth, the authors delineate some of the adaptive mechanisms which enable the parent to weather the crisis. An analysis of how mothers handle these tasks provides remarkably accurate predictions of outcome. If the mother does not resolve some of her own conflicts and misconceptions about prematurity, "a mother-child relationship may be established which will interfere with healthy personality development in the child." Their findings may presage the development of preventive interventions at the very start of an unhealthy interaction between parent and child (Chapter 7). Caplan, Mason, and Kaplan's paper provides a discussion of the concept of crisis, from which many of the principles of crisis intervention have been developed (Chapters 4 and 16).

## COUNSELING IN SCHOOL SETTINGS

Entry into preschool or kindergarten programs is the point at which most children with emotional difficulties become visible to the community. The school is a vital and still under-utilized resource in identifying and modifying children's problems.[34] In this volume, Kelleher (Chapter 10) surveys multiple points of possible intervention in the school. Kennedy (Chapter 12) and Waldfogel, Tessman and Hahn (Chapter 11) describe the need for early intervention in the treatment of school phobia. The latter emphasize the advantages of having the therapist present in the school, where the child can obtain direct support in the feared situation and the school personnel can be guided in handling the crisis optimally. Minuchin (Chapter 13) deals with learning and behavior problems that stem from students' misperceptions of teachers as attempting to impose unreasonable control. These often seem to be a projection of intrafamilial conflict. Minuchin has developed innovative approaches, which attempt to teach the ghetto child to differentiate the classroom from the home. The children are urged to assume more appropriate pupil roles and use the classroom as a place to learn, rather than a battleground in which power struggles occur and integrity is at stake.

Guidance personnel within the school system are expanding their roles as therapeutic agents, often working closely with teachers and administrators in brief therapeutic interventions. A faltering child with a weak ego structure craves support and reinforcement, yet often receives criticism and threats from his dissatisfied teacher. Kelleher provides some cogent examples of how teachers unwittingly reinforce behaviors they would like to eliminate. Parents as well as teachers can be taught to apply behavioral principles in fostering more desired attitudes toward school and in motivating children to learn. Counselors and teachers, without attempting to probe the complex, intimate details of the child and his family's inner dynamics, can seek means of promoting adaptive behavior, e.g. by utilizing selective, positive reinforcement. Easily mastered behavioral and communications approaches have the additional advantage of allowing school personnel to deal with behavior, which all can observe, without feeling constrained by such real concerns as invasion of family privacy or the utilization of more complex psychotherapeutic procedures, which neither their training nor their job mandate has sanctioned. Group counseling in the schools can focus upon here-and-now issues such as the child's interaction with peers or authority, his expectations about the school, or his presentation of self.

## HOW EFFECTIVE IS BRIEF THERAPY WITH CHILDREN AND PARENTS?

Existing studies of the effectiveness of brief psychotherapy with children are few and the conclusions that can be drawn are limited by methodological inadequacies which the authors readily acknowledge. Among other things, controls are lacking or imperfect and population samples are determined by the idiosyncrasies of catchment areas and admission practices of particular agencies. Particularly dissatisfying is treatment evaluation, which is primarily based upon global assessment of symptomatic and behavioral improvement without assaying changes in the psychological functioning of the child and his family or their vulnerability to subsequent stress. This is attempted in the elegant studies of brief psychotherapy with adults conducted by Sifneos[32] and Malan.[22]

When evaluated by superficial criteria, the results of brief psychotherapy for children compare favorably with those of long-term therapy. Nonetheless, our guess is that the gains of long-term therapy, measured by more rigorous criteria, would be more impressive. For that matter, brief therapy should not be expected to accomplish *as much* as long-term therapy with its more ambitious goals. However, brief therapy should at least achieve specific objectives related to the resolution of immediate problems which might otherwise become more intractable; or it should begin to unscramble dilemmas, which families can then persist in solving on their own. Another evaluative dimension involves measuring the gains of therapy against the costs to the individual family, and in the context of the totality of community needs.

Most of the studies which we surveyed have obtained results far beyond the minimal requirements specified above. They report a range of 50–80 percent of patients improved (a range which appears to reflect the success rate of any form of psychotherapy). Rosenthal and Levine[29] (Chapter 3) found a 55 percent rate of improvement for unselected patients. Treatment *failures* are characterized by severe symptoms, or by severe parental discord or pathology. The number of disintegrated families is striking, as compared to families of the improved cases. In further analyzing treatment failures, the authors note that not only were the families unmotivated, but the therapists for these families were ambivalent or even opposed to brief therapy.

In Hare's study of outcome in unselected cases in a child guidance clinic, 72 percent were improved at the time of discharge, and most had sustained this improvement at follow-up two years later. Eisenberg, *et al.*[13] studied a group of neurotic children who received brief therapy for a period of eight weeks. Evaluations obtained from teachers, as well as from therapists and parents, indicated that this treatment was highly effective.

Phillips[27] found that children and parents seen in time-limited, structured sessions actually tended to do better than those seen in "depth" therapy, as measured by a number of parameters assessing behavior in the home and school. His therapy was focused largely on the parents, attempting to provide them with simple explanations of the child's behavior and ways of setting limits and "developing a success pattern in daily relationships, rather than being bogged down with failures and impasses." "The therapy is characterized by a widespread, alert set of relationships with people important to the child, rather than an intensive, personally involved, long-lasting therapy with the child alone." In another study done by Phillips and Johnston (Chapter 2), the results are even more impressive as compared to long-term therapy.

Attempting to describe favorable responders more precisely, Shaw, Blumenfeld and Senf[31] found that neurotic children tended to respond better than children in other diagnostic categories, particularly when there had been a short duration of symptoms, a problem related to a crisis, or a school phobia. Seventy-three percent of neurotic children were rated improved after short-term treatment. Inhibited, constricted children had a better prognosis than aggressive children, perhaps because they accept therapeutic intervention more readily. The authors also speculate that parents who allow the development of aggressive behavior show a greater abnegation of their role responsibilities. Similarly encouraging rates of improvement are reported by Nebl[25] and Lessing and Schilling.[20]

In Levitt's comprehensive and thoughtful overview of research on psychotherapy with children, he summarizes studies of school phobia, concluding that school phobia responds particularly quickly and easily to therapy. Naturally, the treatment of the more severely disturbed phobic child is more complicated. Both Kennedy (Chapter 12) and Waldfogel, Tessman and Hahn (Chapter 11) specify criteria for determining whether limited intervention in cases of school phobia will be sufficient. The latter paper underscores the distinct relationship between prompt therapeutic intervention and successful treatment outcome.

In the conclusion of his review, Levitt notes that fewer than one-third of the children referred to child guidance clinics receive any therapy, and that these children are chosen on the basis of favorable prognosis, suggesting that they might have improved even without therapy. Eisenberg[11,12,14] also has made this point repeatedly, challenging professionals to devote a greater portion of therapeutic resources to those children who are the greatest source of concern to the total community. Levitt's final words deserve quoting:

> Few conditions have been definitely established as requisite or even advisable for the treatment of the child patient. Innovation in therapy is the order of the day; rigid orthodoxies find scant empirical support. Finally, there seems to be no substitute for the *long-range* follow-up study of the procedure for investigating either therapy outcome or therapy process when the patients are children.[21]

## CONCLUSION

The papers in this volume range from discussions of conflicts arising at crises of the perinatal period, or those stemming from unwarranted parental expectations, to the brief treatment of problems such as drug abuse and other difficulties of adolescents. Effective short-term therapy with children and their parents demands a wide range of skills and a thorough knowledge of normal and abberant patterns of behavior at different developmental levels. The therapist must be versatile and pragmatic, and he must not shun experimental or unorthodox procedures if they hold promise of introducing elements of health into a troubled family system. Only by breaking out of traditional molds will mental health professionals find new ways of conceptualizing and correcting faulty behavioral constellations, and diversify their therapeutic skills. We must, as Eisenberg[11,12,14] urges, make our practice relevant to widespread community needs; and we must, as Mechanic[24] cautions, beware of those who preach dogma. It is only in this spirit of taking a fresh, critical look at still inadequate practices that we can meet the challenge of our present, community-responsible era.

# REFERENCES

1. Ad Hoc Committee on Child Mental Health. Report to the Director. National Institute of Mental Health, Public Health Service Publication No. 2184, 1971.

2. Anthony, E. J. Primary Prevention with School Children. In H. H. Barten and L. Bellak (Eds.), *Progress in community mental health.* Vol. 2. New York: Grune and Stratton, 1972.

3. Barten, H. H. The coming of age of the brief psychotherapies. In L. Bellak and H. H. Barten (Eds.), *Progress in community mental health.* Vol. 1. New York: Grune and Stratton, 1969.

4. Barten, H. H. *Brief therapies.* New York: Behavioral Publications, 1971.

5. Bolman, W. M. Systems theory, psychiatry, and school phobia. *American Journal of Psychiatry,* 1970, **127,** 25-32.

6. Bruch, H. Brief psychotherapy in a pediatric clinic. *Quarterly Journal of Child Behavior,* 1949, **1,** 2-8.

7. Chess, S., Thomas, A., & Birch, H. G. Behavior problems revisited: findings of an anterospective study. *Journal of the American Academy of Child Psychiatry,* 1967, **6,** 321-331.

8. Chess, S. Temperament and learning ability of school children. *American Journal of Public Health,* 1968, **58,** 2231-2239.

10. Donner, J., & Gamson, A. Experience with multifamily, time-limited, outpatient groups at a community psychiatric clinic. *Psychiatry,* 1968, **31,** 126-137.

11. Eisenberg, L., & Gruenberg, E. M. The current status of secondary prevention in child psychiatry. *American Journal of Orthopsychiatry,* 1961, **31,** 355-367.

12. Eisenberg, L. If not now, when? *American Journal of Orthopsychiatry,* 1962, **32,** 781-793.

13. Eisenberg, L., Conners, C. K., & Sharpe, L. A controlled study of the differential application of outpatient psychiatric treatment for children. *Japanese Journal of Child Psychiatry,* 1965, **6,** 1-8.

14. Eisenberg, L. Child psychiatry: the past quarter century. *American Journal of Orthopsychiatry,* 1969, **39,** 389-401.

15. Goldensohn, S. S., Fink, R., & Shapiro, S. The delivery of mental health services to children in a prepaid medical care program. *American Journal of Psychiatry,* 1971, **127,** 1357-1362.

16. Hare, M. K. Shortened treatment in a child guidance clinic: the results in 119 cases. *British Journal of Psychiatry,* 1966, **112,** 613-616.

17. Joint Commission on Mental Health of Children. *Crisis in child mental health: challenge for the 1970's.* New York: Harper & Row, 1970.

18. Langsley, D. G., Fairbairn, R. H., & De Young, C. D. Adolescence and family crisis. *Canadian Psychiatric Association Journal,* 1968, **13,** 125-133.

19. Langsley, D. G., & Kaplan, D. M. *The treatment of families in crisis.* New York: Grune and Stratton, 1968.

20. Lessing, E. E., & Shilling, F. H. Relationship between treatment selection variables and treatment outcome in a child guidance clinic: an application of data-processing methods. *Journal of the American Academy of Child Psychiatry,* 1966, **5,** 313-348.

21. Levitt, E. E. Research on psychotherapy with children. In A. E. Bergin & S. L. Garfield (Eds.), *Handbook of psychotherapy and behavior change.* New York: John Wiley and Sons, 1971.

22. Malan, D. H. *A study of brief psychotherapy.* London: Tavistock Publications, 1963.

23. McPherson, S. B., & Samuels, C. R. Teaching behavioral methods to parents. *Social Casework,* 1971, **52,** 148-153.

24. Mechanic, D. Sociological issues in mental health. In L. Bellak & H. H. Barten (Eds.), *Progress in community mental health.* Vol. 1. New York: Grune & Stratton, 1969.

25. Nebl, N. Essential elements in short-term treatment. *Social casework,* 1971, **52,** 377-381.

26. Patterson, G. R., & Gullion, M. E. *Living with children: new methods for parents and teachers.* Champaign, Illinois: Research Press Co., 1971.

27. Phillips, E. L. Parent-child psychotherapy: a follow-up study comparing two techniques. *The Journal of Psychology,* 1960, **49,** 195-202.

28. Rae-Grant, Q., & Stringer, L. A. Mental health programs in schools. In M. F. Shore & F. V. Mannino (Eds.), *Mental health and the community.* New York: Behavioral Publications, 1969.

29. Rosenthal, A. J., & Levine, S. V. Brief psychotherapy with children: a preliminary report. *American Journal of Psychiatry,* 1970, **127,** 646-651.

30. Scherz, F. H. Maturational crises and parent-child interaction. *Social Casework,* 1971, **52,** 362-369.

31. Shaw, R., Blumenfeld, H., & Senf, R., A short-term treatment program in a child guidance clinic. *Social Work,* 1968, **13,** 81-90.

32. Sifneos, P. E. Learning to solve emotional problems: a controlled study of short-term anxiety-provoking psychotherapy. In R. Porter (Ed.), *The role of learning in psychotherapy. International Psychiatry Clinics,* Vol. 6, No. 1. Boston: Little Brown, 1969.

33. Smith, J. M., & Smith, D. E. P. *Child management: a program for parents and teachers.* Ann Arbor: Ann Arbor Publishers, 1970.

34. Stickney, S. B. Schools are our community mental health centers. *American Journal of Psychiatry,* 1968, **124,** 1407-1414.

35. Wender, P. H. Vicious and virtuous circles: the role of deviation amplifying feedback in the origin and perpetuation of behavior. *Psychiatry,* 1968, **31,** 309-324.

# Concepts and Strategies

# 2. THEORETICAL AND CLINICAL ASPECTS OF SHORT-TERM PARENT-CHILD PSYCHOTHERAPY*

### E. Lakin Phillips, Ph.D. and
### Margaret S. H. Johnston, M.A.

Nearly everyone who has thought seriously about psychotherapy has entertained notions of how to shorten it. In the outpatient child guidance clinic the interest in short-term treatment and flexible treatment methods is usually heightened because of public demands on the time and skill of professional clinicians. At a meeting of the association of clinics in the metropolitan area of Washington, it was reported that waiting lists for child treatment vary from a few months to over two years in various parts of the United States. In the Washington,

Reprinted from *Psychiatry,* 1954, **17,** 267–275, by special permission of The William Alanson White Psychiatric Foundation, Inc., and the authors. Dr. Phillips is Professor of Psychology and Director of the University Counseling Center, George Washington University, Washington, D. C. and Director, School for Contemporary Education, McLean and Falls Church, Virginia. Mrs. Johnston is in private practice in Rockville, Maryland.

* The data for this paper were collected at the Arlington County Guidance Center and the Fairfax County Child Guidance Clinic which are conducted by the State Department of Mental Hygiene and Hospitals, Richmond, Va. The ideas and practices expressed herein are the authors' and do not necessarily represent those of the Department.
The authors are indebted to Drs. David McK. Rioch, Ardie Lubin, and Harold M. Skeels for their helpful comments during the preparation of this report. Mrs. Gloria B. Gelfand worked with many of the parent-child cases at the Arlington County Guidance Center.

D.C. area, waiting lists range from a few months to over one year.

Two factors contribute to the feasibility of flexible treatment methods and short-term treatment in child guidance clinics. First, children are highly amenable to psychological treatment; because they are growing and changing, the forward surge can be made use of to heighten participation, to lessen pathology, and to shorten treatment. Second, parents probably respond better *as parents* than they do simply as adults seeking help. Since a child's problems tend to reflect in various ways the problems of the parents,[1] the child's need for help means in most instances that the parent, too, needs help.

This paper reports an experience with the use of short-term therapy at two child guidance clinics, and it attempts to compare the results with those obtained at the same clinics by conventional therapy. Short-term therapy in this instance consisted of a stated number of interviews—subject, in some cases, to extension which was also of defined length. This plan was based on a somewhat different rationale than that of conventional therapy and, in turn, brought about a somewhat different type of therapy. In general, therapy was directed not at retrospective self-examination, but at the child's pattern of interaction in current situations.

We have been encouraged to explore short-term treatment by the experience which has been reported from the general field of social psychology. It has, in certain situations, been amply demonstrated that improvements in human relations, and the subsiding of internal stresses in schools, factories, neighborhoods, and so on, can be brought about by short-term contacts with the persons concerned, by group opinions and pressures, and by a general atmosphere of interpersonal acceptance.[2] Thus this experience has led us to stress, as a part of short-term treatment, group and situational factors. Such approaches have sometimes been dismissed scornfully on the basis that they bring about only superficial attitude changes, leaving the deep wellsprings of human motivation untapped. But while the exploration of deep motivation undoubtedly has its place, those who work in clinical settings cannot afford to overlook the realistic benefits which have been obtained by social psychologists with alternative treatment practices stressing group interaction.

Allport, in a discussion of motivation theory, has commented on this question as follows:

> This prevailing atmosphere of theory has engendered a kind of contempt for the "psychic surface" of life. The individual's conscious report is rejected as untrustworthy, and the contemporary thrust of his motives is disregarded in favor of a backward tracing of his conduct to earlier formative stages. The individual loses his right to be believed. And while he is busy leading his life in the present with a forward thrust into the future, *most psychologists have become busy tracing it backward into the past* [italics added].[3]

Cameron in a discussion of modern methods of therapy says:

> The newer approach to therapy is relativistic, elastic, and plastic. The old is doctrinaire, essentially fundamentalistic and deterministic. . . . In dealing with the living organism you are dealing with a continually emergent situation and, as often as not and sometimes oftener, the newly established conception has, within a short period of time, developed sufficient powers of inhibition, to prevent the reestablishment of the less effective blueprints which previously governed his behavior.[4]

## SETTING OF THE STUDY

The experience with short-term therapy described here took place in two outpatient child guidance clinics in the Washington, D. C., area—Fairfax and Arlington.[5] At the Fairfax clinic, short-term therapy has been in use for about two years, and a follow-up study of 16 parent-child pairs treated at this clinic has been included in the data presented in this paper. Fourteen conventional cases have also been included. During one period of time, the conventional method was used by all therapists for all cases; and during another period, the short-term method was used exclusively. Thus there was no selection of method for any particular case. In short-term therapy, treatment has usually terminated at the tenth interview.

At the Arlington clinic, short-term parent-child treatment has not been in progress long enough to provide follow-up data. Thus while many of our general statements on short-term treatment are based on experience at both clinics, we have included no data on this method from the Arlington clinic. Data on the conventional method at this clinic have been included. Short-term therapy has not at any time been mandatory for all cases at the Arlington clinic, but it has usually been accepted when offered. Following the tenth interview, the clinic has adopted the practice of extending another block of treatment in those few cases where more help is required.

In considering setting a limit for therapy, we first explored the experiences of other outpatient clinics in the Washington area and found the average number of contacts for parent-child pairs to be between 12 and 18 interviews. This average, however, included extreme variation, from two or three interviews in aborted cases up toward a hundred interviews in other cases. In essence, there was no correlation between the length of therapy and its success. Therapy might be short either because it was abortive or because it was incisive; and therapy might be long either because the problems were formidable or because the therapy failed to be incisive.

# THEORETICAL ORIENTATION AND METHODS

In attempting explicit statements of our rationale, we are confronted with a difficulty which has been noted by Ruesch and Bateson:

> For the present we observe that psychiatry is predominantly concerned with the perception and description of the abnormal and undesirable and that the technical vocabulary is almost entirely focused upon the pathological aspects. ... It is a science rather inarticulate about its operations and with its theoretical focus concentrated upon the diagnosis of abnormality and the analysis of normal dynamics in abnormal circumstances. The dynamics of normal cir-

cumstances and the methods of implementing the therapeutic process are comparatively little studied.[6]

*To whom does short-term therapy apply?*  In our experience, most of the children who come to the outpatient
child guidance clinic present no problems of a deep nature. Moreover, when such problems do occur, we feel
that the outpatient clinic is not the place to provide the
intensive treatment which is required. The common core
of the problems brought to the clinic is a too loose structure of interpersonal relations, seen most clearly in disciplinary and management difficulties encountered by the
parent or teacher. The child is at odds with significant
adults, largely because these adults do not set appropriate limits for the child. The recognition that many parent-child problems are those of management entails the
adoption of different goals from those of therapies which
require retrospective self-examination, the uncovering of
severely repressed feelings, and so on. The therapist is
concerned with the structure of the child's interpersonal
relations and the setting of appropriate limits for him,
and he endeavors to obtain clarity about this in a concrete way with the child and also with the parent. It is because these problems are amenable to help, without requiring exhaustive exploration, that short-term therapy
is applicable and helpful. Moreover, this viewpoint affords an opportunity for flexible arrangements—for
example, either parent or child can be treated alone.

*The notion of structure and the importance of lim-
its.*  We use the term structure in the sense that Lewin uses it in referring to the shaping-up, forming, and
delineating of experience as it progresses from a vague
and undifferentiated condition to a more highly articulate
one. Seemingly, man finds it necessary to structure
vague, formless, rootless experiences, so that he is better
able to cope with them. Theoretical support for this notion of structure can be drawn from Sherif's findings[7] in
his study of the autokinetic phenomenon, showing the
social influences of perceived motion, and from the elec-
trical study of the brain showing the seeking for structure
by means of "scanning operations":

... the alpha rhythms are a process of scanning—searching for a pattern—which relaxes when a pattern is found. It is as if you were looking for one particular word in a page of print; you scan the page, line by line, until you come to the word; then the scanning movement ceases; anyone watching your eyes could tell when you had found what you were looking for.[8]

The parallel in the parent-child situation is that the parent fails to structure the relationship with the child in emotionally acceptable ways: the parent is inconsistent, expects too much or too little, vacillates, is too easily cajoled, and so on. The child's scanning of the behavioral and interpersonal field yields a different pattern from that which the parent's scanning yields, and hence conflict and emotional involvement ensue. In this relative interpersonal chaos, the child seeks clearer structure and more validity for his pattern; but since he is a child he cannot seek it in the most mature and productive ways.

Nor can the parent, who, by the time the child begins testing everyone, is herself beginning to wonder if there is or ever can be any order in the universe of children. The mother often reports that the child seems to take advantage of her inability to say yes or no, her inability to stick by her guns on disciplinary matters, and her inability to follow through on a restriction, regulation, or expectation, and to resist giving in to the nagging, whining child. In these instances, she characteristically presents a picture of exhaustion, of being at the end of her rope, of having "tried everything," and of feeling victimized by an unscrupulous child (in the most perplexing cases). Often she has grossly overexercised a rational, persuasive, reasoned, verbal approach to the child, until the point is reached where words and threats mean nothing and both the parent and the child are gripped by emotion.

From the child's point of view, he is faced with a parent who cannot maintain a stable position, wrong or right, and who cannot offer him security and safety. The child keeps pushing, seeking to delimit his areas of operation, seeking to find out what is related to what. He learns that the parent's words do not mean what they are supposed to mean, that there is always a way of getting around them on an impulse of the moment. But the child is also made anxious by the indefiniteness and the insecurity of the relationship; he feels cast adrift, and he may experience the parent's feeble stand as disinterest, as license, or as simple confusion and inadequacy, all of which are far from comforting to the child.

Thus a basic idea in our approach to short-term therapy is the importance of the firmness of the interpersonal structure—or, in other words, the importance of limits. This view of the nature of the parent-child problem is also the core of the treatment practices. Confusion for both the clinician and the parent arises when these testing episodes are interpreted as wholly id-dominated, as signifying deep, underlying problems, as entirely representing hostility and belligerence, or something of the sort. What they signify, from our viewpoint, is clumsy, inarticulate, and immature ways of wanting to know where one stands, of wanting to have a dependable relationship to an adult. Such acting out is a self-system characteristic, not a matter of the alleged *id*.[9]

This, then, is roughly the theme of the therapy hours with the parent, characteristically pursued in verbal and other symbolic ways. The child learns more mature ways of relating to people in the therapeutic exchange by means of the limits set in verbal, physical, and other activities; depending upon the child's age and other particulars, he may act out his problems.

*Structuring the treatment situation.* Just as a certain firmness of structure is needed in the child's other interpersonal relations, so it is needed in the treatment situation itself. This conception is one of the most important contributions which the use of short-term therapy has made to our clinical approach. While treatment usually consisted of a block of ten interviews, it would have been equally valid to set the interview limit at eight, 12, 15, or some other number; for the actual number, within reason, is not the important matter. What is important is that the interview series has a beginning, an end, and other discernible features—in other words, that the treatment experience itself has a structure. While at first the sheer time limits of short-term therapy were uppermost, this same consideration is now fitted into a larger theoretical framework. Time is still important, but it now fits into its proper place in the total treatment setting. It is as if time considerations forced the issue; the issue, then, receives at least a temporary solution in the terms outlined in this paper. The structure has now been made larger; the time element, as such, is not given as close attention, yet the result is that treatment remains short-term although the load is carried by the *total* treatment milieu rather than by and through time limits alone.

*The child's patterns of interaction.*    We regard the child as a shifting point in an interaction matrix, in accordance with Sullivan's comments on personal individuality.[10] The child is part of the interpersonal system of family, neighborhood, school, and so on. *Change the system* (as one does in therapy with varying degrees of success) *and you change the child.* Thus we consider the child's patterns of interactions with others to be the key to his problems and to be more important, in understanding his difficulties, than his areas of repression. The child is not an historical or developmental capsule that has to be explored for its own sake. His relationship with others is the important facet of the therapeutic enterprise—not extraction, not recovery of repressed materials or of the lost past. The child in our experience—Klein[11] to the contrary notwithstanding—is largely incapable of such historical, retrospective self-examination and is developmentally unable to comprehend it when it is carried on in monologue form by the therapist.

Children, like adults, suffer more from what they *affirm* (or assert) than from what they deny. The role of affirmation in anyone's psychological space is clearly seen in his relationships; the role of denial derives from psychic isolation and psychic autonomy. The notion of interaction places emphasis on the child's ability to relate and on his growth capacities, both of which are important in treatment.

Relatedness is not a one-way street, but depends upon reciprocal capacities in the therapist, as Sullivan,[12]

Rogers,[13] and Allen[14] have stressed. Treatment is "reflex-
ive" in the sense that Ruesch and Bateson have described it;[15] that is, it includes therapist as well as patient, and even includes the theorist. There is feedback to
patient and therapist as each talks, gestures, and so on.
The feedback from patient to therapist has affected our
attitudes, practices, and theory. In general, replacing assumptions about repression and denial with assumptions about relationships helps to free the therapist to
work more realistically with parent and child and helps
to establish working relationships in therapy without
placing all the burden of readiness on the client.

*The starting of a self-healing process.*   Emphasis is
placed on the patient's own forward direction in treatment. The criticism which has sometimes been made
that short-term therapy is perforce superficial and eva-
sive we find to be unsubstantial and to be in conflict with
the idea of the part played by self-healing processes. The
person "is not passive, but a participant in his own universe," as Ruesch and Bateson have said in developing
the idea of "negative entropy."[16] Therapy is a continuous
exchange between client and therapist—an open system
of codification, evaluation, hypothesis formation, and so
on—making possible the development of new or alternative attitudes or hypotheses on the client's part. The fact
that a person is not a closed energy system, but an open,
ongoing one, gives the therapeutic interaction its opportunity to effect behavioral and attitudinal changes. This
ongoing exchange is another way of talking about such
clinical notions as growth potential, forward surge, and
so on. Casting thoughts into quasi-communication
theory helps to make more explicit the seemingly esoteric
clinical notions and helps to point up the interpersonal
processes of therapy in their more constructive modes.

*Concurrent stimulation versus serial causation.*   We feel
that the child in therapy is placed in the context of what
might be termed concurrent stimulation from all sides; although we expect a degree of change, we are willing to let
changes come as they will, when they will. We do not feel

## TABLE 1
### Outcomes of Short-Term
### and Conventional Therapy
### for Three Treatment Samples
### in Two Clinics

| | Fairfax Clinic | | | | Arlington Clinic | |
| | Short-Term Cases | | Conventional Cases | | Conventional Cases | |
| Judged Results | No. | Per-cent | No. | Per-cent | No. | Per-cent |
|---|---|---|---|---|---|---|
| Successful .............. | 2 | 13 | 1 | 7 | 4 | 13 |
| Improved ................ | 14 | 87 | 8 | 57 | 19 | 64 |
| Failure ................. | 0 | 0 | 5 | 36 | 7 | 23 |
| Total ................. | 16 | 100 | 14 | 100 | 30 | 100 |

that our patients "must see their hostility before they can relax," "must recover the past before they can control the present," and so on. There is no necessity to "get at this before tackling that," because the total relationship is the focus. If the relationship is near optimal, then the child will change at the rate and in the ways he finds available to him. Many changes occur concurrently or in nondiscernible ways; the patient and therapist are not running up and down a psychic ladder which has incontrovertible steps in an incontrovertible order, nor are they dealing with a psychic filing system in which everything has a specific place. *Whatever is basic gets tested out in living; it does not have to be pursued for its own sake.*

## DATA

*Outcomes of cases treated by short-term therapy.* This study included 16 short-term parent-child cases and 14 conventionally treated cases at the Fairfax clinic, making a total of 30 pairs.[17] Thirty conventionally treated cases at the Arlington clinic were used as a second control group.[18] Table 1 presents three categories of outcome for these cases—*successful, improved,* and *failure*—giving the number and percentage of cases falling within each category. These evaluations of outcomes were made on an over-all basis, including the written case records, consultation with the psychiatrists, psychologists, or social workers, and follow-up interviews with the mothers about one year after termination of treatment. So far as possible, all cases were treated alike in the judgment process; bias, if any, was more apt to be against short-term treatment because of its newness and its challenge to old assumptions.

When the frequencies of the short-term and conventional cases falling within the three categories are compared with those frequencies which would be expected by chance, a Chi Square of 5.546 results. For two degrees of freedom, this figure is just short of significance at the .05 level (.05 level = 5.991). In other words, the difference in outcome between the short-term and conventional methods would be, by chance, as great as shown in Table 1 only five to six times in a hundred. This level of significance is high enough to warrant further study.

*Types of endings.*   The types of endings associated with the two treatment methods are shown in Figure 1. The classification of types of endings was: *mutually agreed* (that is, the ending of the therapy was mutually planned and agreed upon by parent and therapist); *return for more therapy* (that is, the therapy was considered successful to a point, but it was agreed that more help was required); endings brought about by *outside circumstances;* and *premature withdrawal* (that is, the therapy was abortive because of premature withdrawal of either the therapist or the parent and child).

It may seem obvious that in short-term therapy, where a block of ten interviews was planned from the beginning, mutually agreed endings would be much more frequent than in conventional therapy, as shown in Figure 1. The significance of the number of mutually agreed endings is more apparent when one compares it with the

## FIG. 1
## Types of Endings for
## Short-Term and Conventional
## Parent-Child Treatment Cases
## (Fairfax Sample Only)

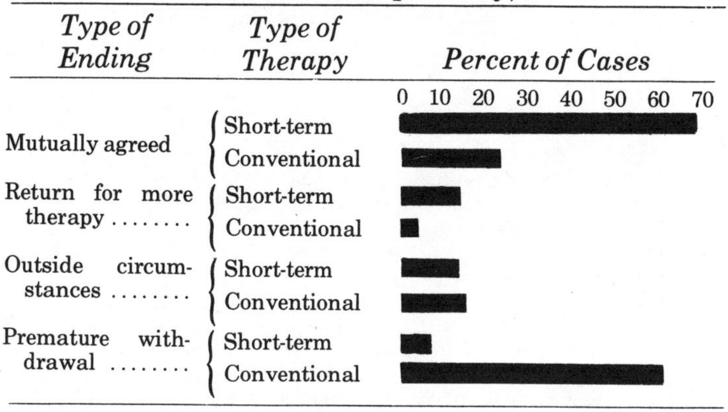

| Type of Ending | Type of Therapy | Percent of Cases |
|---|---|---|

number of premature withdrawals. In other words, it was presumably more feasible for all concerned to carry through a limited, planned program to some kind of goal without discouragement and withdrawal, than it was to carry through an indefinite program to some unspecified point where it could be agreed that some goal had been reached.

*Number of interviews and use of staff time.*   While short-term therapy was based on the block of ten interviews, the actual mean number of interviews for the 16 Fairfax short-term cases was 11.43, because of the inclusion of four cases which continued beyond the tenth interview or returned for more help. The Fairfax conventional group showed a mean of 12.1 interviews, but this figure includes four failures, one coming for nine interviews and three for six or fewer interviews. Thus the difference between these two means is unreliable. However, among the successful and improved cases, the mean of 11.43 visits for the short-term group is to be compared with a mean of 14.10 visits for the conventional treatment cases, netting a $t$ value of 1.15 ($P = .04$). The difference is great enough to have arisen only four times in 100 by chance.[19]

Two examples of short-term therapy drawn from our case material are presented below to give some qualitative idea of the nature of the work. Case 1 is abstracted from a series of ten interviews with a mother-child pair. Case 2 is abstracted from five interviews with a mother whose three preschool children were not seen.

### Case 1

When Frank, age four, was first brought to the clinic, his mother reported that he was aggressive and "seems to feel the need to hit or push children without warning and without provocation—same at home and at school." He was reluctant to leave his mother on the first visit, broke away from the therapist who was interviewing him, and interrupted his mother's interview with another therapist. He had been in and out of three nursery schools, and the parents were at that time considering placing him in an all-day treatment home. The clinic approved this plan, and the case was closed at the clinic. These plans did not materialize, and a year later the parents reapplied to the clinic for help. We gave the child psychological tests, reinterviewed the mother, and offered them a series of 10 interviews, which was accepted.

*Interview 1, with child.* Frank was hyperactive, overly verbal, restless, and interested in various play material for short periods but tired quickly. After 20 to 25 minutes in the playroom, he began to cry and to yell that he wanted to leave; he finally left the playroom and interrupted his mother's interview with her therapist.

*Interviews 2, 3, 4 (weekly intervals).* During these interviews, Frank became less obstreperous and more conversational; the therapist anticipated emotional storms, but these were truncated at each interview by a firm refusal to let Frank leave the playroom before the time was up, although Frank would contest this several times.

*Interview 5 (one-week interval).* Frank began to express his aggression with toys and did not spread himself out emotionally as much as before. After one bout of acting out with his toys, he said, "Whew, there I feel better," then sat down in the chair as if to recuperate from strenuous physical and emotional exertion. The therapist reported that the child was "over the hump."

*Interviews 6, 7 (weekly intervals).* Frank played more quietly and seemed more conversational and matter-of-fact. Compared to earlier hours, Frank was contented, happy, and self-contained. He discussed his feelings and relationships with others in a more considered, less emotional and bombastic way than before. He no longer converted his feelings into immediate, impulsive demands or aggressive action.

*Interview 8 (two-week interval).*  The child brought his own games along today to share with the therapist; he invited the therapist to play checkers and other games with him, and played with finger paints some. He was conversational and matter-of-fact.

*Interview 9 (one-week interval).*  Frank brought some more games today and again wanted to play checkers and to paint. He talked about an impending vacation trip. His conversation was matter-of-fact.

*Interview 10 (nine-week interval).*  Frank came back today, tanned and exuberant about his trip and his new experiences. He appeared very normal, outgoing, comfortable, and conversational. He obviously enjoyed his "visit" to the therapist and felt no need to release tension or work off anything. He reported that he liked school now.

*Interviews with mother (same dates as child's interviews).*  During the period of the interviews, the mother moved from a position of guilty, self-accusing attitudes—in which she felt that she had "rejected" and mistreated Frank—to a feeling that she had greatly overindulged him and had let him be "cock of the walk" without any bounds or limits. This insight gave her a new view of the boy's needs and made it possible for her to exercise more judgment and more control over emotionally provocative situations. In this way she could overcome her exhaustion, her bewilderment, and her lack of resourcefulness in respect to Frank's demandingness.

At the last interview, the mother reported that she was very pleased with Frank's progress and with her own newly found ability to enjoy the boy and relax with him; she reported that Frank was doing well at school and that he no longer struggled so much with members of the family or with his peers.

## Case 2

Mrs. D's initial contact with the clinic was over the telephone. During this conversation with the therapist, she complained of her plight, despaired of doing anything about it, and cursed. She had three children, ages five, three, and one.

*Interview 1.*  Mrs. D clenched her fists and pounded on the arms of the chair during this interview. Although she admitted that her problem with her two oldest children, ages five and three, was her own, she continued to express exasperation and despair. They would not mind her, she said, and they never took no for an answer. They kept her breathless from morning to night, and she wondered if they would not turn out to be "real problems as adults."

*Interviews 2, 3 (weekly intervals).* The nature of the parent-child involvements became more manifest in these interviews. The children would contest the mother's discipline and involve her in a tug-of-war; she would become exhausted, act childish herself, hate herself for this, and fail to follow through on her requests and admonitions; and in this way a cyclic pattern of interaction was maintained. We discussed her failure to follow through and her fear of hurting the children by making them do something after they had protested.

*Interview 4 (two-week interval).* Mrs. D seemed more relaxed today and reported that she was beginning to "get my point over to the boys and to get them to do *some* of the things I request." She began to see how she could "mean 'no' when I say 'no.'" In discussing problems about child rearing and her own remaining problems, she seemed much less pushed, less angry, and less urgent.

*Interview 5 (two-week interval).* Mrs. D came in and said, "My problem is over—I've solved it. Stevie is really much better because I'm better, and Jon is really a darling—he's so little trouble now." She reviewed her behavior with the children over the past four or five weeks and the changes in her attitude. She had seen some signs of jealousy in the older child over the baby, but she understood this and felt it was temporary, and she gave additional evidence of being on the way toward solving her practical difficulties as they arose with the children.

## CONCLUSION

The evaluations of the results and the types of endings of the two therapy procedures suggest a reasonably clear advantage for the short-term practice, within the limits specified herein. The suggestion is evident that the short-term structure helps to create a more clear-cut and decisive treatment milieu and to bring about more favorable treatment outcomes. Although conventional treatment may often be short, the very feebleness of its structure and its lack of self-consciousness, as it were, often obfuscates the results, and the clinician often fails to know wherein he succeeded or failed. When short-term methods are used, the associated firmness and clarity of structure allow each person concerned to know where he is most of the time, and the whole process has more tonus. It is this aspect of short-term therapy which we believe is beneficial to the patient and which is an aid in his assimilating help from the therapeutic relationship, rather than the number of interviews.

Our case material shows many instances of, for example, children who had been dismissed from school because of the seeming enormity of their problems, but who were able to return to school within two or three months after beginning treatment and have since been able to adjust satisfactorily. In many cases, parents who were at the end of their ropes were able to see what the child's lack of being properly controlled was doing to them and to the child, and were able, sometimes within a very few interviews, to gain new perspective and to give firmness, assurance, and dependability to the disciplinary situation. In general, we have found that the kind of help most usually required is the setting of limits for the child and the firming-up of parent-child relationships.

We do not wish to give the impression that results comparable to these could not be duplicated by other therapists using different methods based on different philosophies. The point is that our findings illustrate, in part, the results of a set of attitudes or expectancies that the persons concerned can handle their own difficulties with a small amount of judicious help. When such cases occur in more conventional therapy practice, their real significance is lost, because current problems and attitudes of the parent-child pair are regarded as resistance, or as examples of repression, or are otherwise dismissed from scrutiny; and the improvement of management and current relationships is viewed as superficial.

The approach which we have described fits into the public health framework of helping many people gain better mental health rather than spending inordinately long periods of time treating a very few. By relying on self-corrective processes, aided and abetted by a few interviews, the child guidance clinic can permit and foster a wider service to the general population.

# REFERENCES

1. See, for instance, C. M. Loutitt, *Clinical Psychology;* New York, Harper, 1947. E. L. Phillips, "Parent-Child Similarities in Personality Disturbances," *J. Clin. Psychol.* (1951) 7:188-190. Merrill Roff, "Inter-Family Resemblances in Personality Characteristics," *J. Psychol.* (1950) 30:199-228. P. M. Symonds, *The Dynamics of Parent-Child Relationships;* New York, Columbia Univ. Press, 1949.

2. See, for instance, D. Cartwright and Alvin Zander, *Group Dynamics: Research and Theory;* Evanston, Ill., Roe, Peterson, 1953. A. W. Gouldner (ed.), *Studies in Leadership;* New York, Harper, 1950. Kurt Lewin, *Resolving Social Conflicts;* New York, Harper, 1948. Lewin, *Field Theory in Social Science;* New York, Harper, 1951. Elton Mayo, *The Social Problems of an Industrial Civilization;* Cambridge, Harvard Univ. Press, 1945. Mayo, *The Human Problems of an Industrial Civilization;* New York, Macmillan, 1946.

3. Gordon W. Allport, "The Trend in Motivational Theory," *Amer. J. Orthopsychiatry* (1953) 23:107-119; p. 108.

4. D. C. Cameron, "Unorthodox Working Concepts for Psychotherapy," *Med. Ann.* D. C. (1953) 22 (May) :226-234, 278; see especially pp. 228-229.

5. The type of short-term therapy described here was begun at the Fairfax clinic by Dr. Thomas A. Harris, who calls it the "block" method. It has been adopted at the Arlington clinic at the instigation of the senior author, on the stimulus of Dr. Harris' work.

6. J. Ruesch and G. Bateson, *Communication: The Social Matrix of Psychiatry;* New York, Norton, 1951; pp. 234-235.

7. Muzafer Sherif, "A Study of Some Social Factors in Perception," *Arch. Psychol.* (1935) no. 187.

8. W. G. Walter, *The Living Brain;* New York, Norton, 1953; p. 109.

9. The theoretical question can be raised as to *why* the parents are unable to set appropriate limits, with the implication that this question requires extensive answering, thus forcing the therapist outside the position promulgated here. Questions asking *what* (the parent does or does not do that leads to difficulties) and *how* (the parent perceives the parent-child impasse) are relevant and answerable in the clinic treatment, whereas *why* questions are not; the former are heuristic, the latter is not.

10. H. S. Sullivan, "The Illusion of Personal Individuality," *Psychiatry* (1950) 13:317-332.

11. Melanie Klein, *The Psycho-Analysis of Children;* London, Hogarth Press, 1932.

12. H. S. Sullivan, *Conceptions of Modern Psychiatry;* Washington, D. C., William Alanson White Psychiatric Foundation, 1947. Sullivan, "The Theory of Anxiety and the Nature of Psychotherapy," *Psychiatry* (1949) 12:3-12.

13. Carl R. Rogers, *Client-Centered Therapy;* Boston, Houghton Mifflin, 1951.

14. Frederick Allen, *Psychotherapy with Children;* New York, Norton, 1942.

15. Reference footnote 6; pp. 253-256.

16. Reference footnote 6; p. 250; see also pp. 177-183.

17. Mean ages of the children were 8 years 4 months for the 16 short-term cases, and 8 years 3 months for the 14 conventional cases; in both groups the age ranges were from preschool age up to adolescence.

18. While short-term treatment is now being used at the Arlington clinic, it has not been in progress sufficiently long to provide follow-up data. The 30 conventional Arlington cases used here as a second control group were treated before the advent of short-term practices.

19. Durham's study, carried out on a similar outpatient child guidance population, shows how varied treatment practices may be within the conventional framework. Although the mean number of visits in her study was 13.74, the standard deviation was 13.38 visits, and the range varied from two to 67 visits. The short-term structure permits as good if not better results concerning treatment outcomes without incurring the limitations of conventional practices. Mary S. Durham, "Some Observations Concerning External Criteria of Success in Psychotherapy," *J. Psychol.* (1952) 33:175-181.

# 3. BRIEF PSYCHOTHERAPY WITH CHILDREN: PROCESS OF THERAPY

Alan J. Rosenthal, M.D.,
and Saul V. Levine, M.D.

The use of brief psychotherapy as one attempt of many in the mental health field to meet the growing challenges of the untreated emotionally disturbed has aroused increasing interest in the past decade. Use of this treatment modality with adults has achieved general acceptance, and its well-described methodology is utilized by many practitioners (1); it is losing the stigma of an inferior or second-class method of treatment. Brief psychotherapy with children, on the other hand, although it has been utilized by some centers for many years, has developed more slowly and has not achieved the same recognition or acceptance.

The authors have undertaken the present study to test the efficacy of brief psychotherapy with children, to develop indications and contraindications for its use, and to delineate the treatment methods and techniques most useful in its practice. This report describes the latter as-

Reprinted from *The American Journal of Psychiatry,* 1971, 128, 141-146, by permission of the publisher and the authors. Copyright 1971, the American Psychiatric Association. Dr. Rosenthal is Assistant Professor of Psychiatry and Director of Child Psychiatry, Stanford University Medical Center, Stanford, California. Dr. Levine is Assistant Professor of Psychiatry, University of Toronto and Staff Psychiatrist, Hospital for Sick Children, Toronto, Ontario, Canada.

The authors wish to acknowledge the help of Elizabeth S. Bing, Ph.D., in defining process and content categories in this study.

pect of the study and will detail the treatment techniques and the process and content of brief psychotherapy with children.

## The Study

This study, which is described in more detail in a previous report (2), was conducted in the child psychiatry clinic of a university medical center. Patients and families who applied to the clinic for treatment were assigned, in a completely blind manner, to either the experimental (brief therapy) group, or to the control (long-term therapy) group. The only patients excluded from the study were children who were grossly psychotic, were significantly mentally retarded, were 13 years of age or more, or had had psychotherapy within the prior year. In this study, brief psychotherapy was defined as a maximum of ten calendar weeks. Long-term therapy could be as lengthy or as brief as the individual therapist felt was indicated for each case in the control group. The therapists—psychiatric residents, psychologists, and social workers—each treated equal numbers of cases from the experimental and control groups. Each patient and family was evaluated as they entered therapy and at three months, six months, and one year following this. Detailed evaluation forms containing information about the child's symptoms, his general adjustment at home and at school, his degree of improvement during and following therapy, treatment outcome, prognosis, and recommendations were completed by the child's parents, his schoolteachers, and his therapist at these intervals, with the final evaluation at the one year follow-up.

The authors have previously reported a comparison of the treatment outcomes for the two groups of patients in therapy (2). In brief, of the experimental group (completely unselected for brief psychotherapy), 55 percent demonstrated marked improvement at the one-year follow-up. Less than 25 percent were referred for further therapy at the termination of the brief therapy period; three-quarters of these were referred by therapists who had expressed, prior to the onset of the study, ambivalent or oppositional feelings about the use of brief psychotherapy. Of those patients and families who received brief therapy *only*, 76 percent demonstrated marked improvement at the one-year follow-up. This compared with a 79-percent improvement rate for the same time period for the control (long-term therapy) group. Perhaps most significantly, however, the length of therapy for the control group was five to seven times greater than that for the brief therapy group (see table 1).

## Therapeutic Methods

The successful results of brief psychotherapy become meaningful only if the therapeutic techniques can be transmitted to and are adopted by other practitioners. We attempted, therefore, to analyze in detail the process of brief psychotherapy and the treatment techniques we employed in its use. The structural elements of our brief therapy process, which we will describe here, include the time limit of the therapy, the definition of a treatment focus and goals of the therapy, the development of rapport, the issue of termination, and the activity of the therapist.

*Time limit.* During the initial interview each family was informed that the therapy would be limited to

### TABLE 1
### Comparison of Experimental Group
### with Control Group

| Breakdown of cases | Experimental Group | Control Group |
|---|---|---|
| Total patients to date | 31* | 35 |
| Insufficient follow-up | 2 | 1 |
| Referred elsewhere | 8 | 0 |
| Definite to marked improvement | 16 | 27 |
| Mean length of therapy | 8.1 weeks | 39.9 + weeks** |
| Range | 4-10 weeks | 10-50 + weeks |

\* Two patients have not completed therapy.

\*\* After one year, 16 out of 34 patients are still in therapy. To date the mean length of therapy in this group is 53.5 + weeks (range: 10-145+ weeks).

eight visits within ten weeks, and that an attempt would be made to accomplish as much as possible in alleviating the family's difficulties during that time. Because of the relative brevity of the therapy period, the family was requested to take an active role and to assume some responsibility in the therapy process, under the therapist's guidance. Families were explicitly asked, for example, to continue discussions of certain issues raised in the therapy hour at home, or to attempt to consciously change aspects of their own behavior after the therapy hour and to discuss the results of these in the following hour.

This time limit, and the family's participation and responsibility in the therapy, appeared to place a certain pressure or expectation for improvement upon both the therapist and the family. We have referred to this elsewhere as "therapeutic pressure" (2); if it is guided appropriately by the therapist, it appears to enhance the therapeutic process. Others have noted the apparent productive and beneficial effects of such an external time pressure (3); in fact, in one report knowledge of a time limit was significantly associated with a favorable treatment outcome, fewer patient dropouts from therapy, and greater patient motivation (4). As was the case in that study, very few of our patients or families were displeased about the time limit; they did not feel that this was deficient or "second-class" therapy.

*Treatment focus and goals.*   Given the time-limited period of therapy, a rapid evaluation and case formulation were essential. This was attempted during the initial interview and was followed by a definition of the focus of therapy and the setting of realistic treatment goals, based on that formulation. In addition, the family was informed—either in a general or specific sense—of the formulations, focus, and goals in the process of enlisting their collaboration in the therapy. Although therapists also attended to these matters with their long-term cases, they tended to be much less specific and definite in their formulations and treatment goals; the explicit time limitation of the brief therapy probably demanded a more definitive therapeutic strategy. We attempted to deal with presenting symptoms and "here-and-now" problems in the brief therapy cases, but we also approached and confronted underlying psychopathology as we felt appropriate and therapeutic. The importance of this treatment focus and the goal in brief psychotherapy is referred to frequently in the literature (3-7).

*Rapport.*    The development of rapport, or even positive transference, is an important feature of most psychotherapy but is an essential of brief therapy. With limited time, the early establishment of rapport and a therapeutic alliance are necessary if the collaborative work of the therapist and family is to occur. The sharing of a focus and treatment goals was the beginning of the therapeutic alliance, and the therapist attempted to maintain this positive relationship throughout the therapy. Others have also noted the importance of this positive therapeutic relationship in brief therapy (3, 6).

*Termination.*    The issue of termination arose during the initial interview as the ten-week limitation was explained. Interestingly, for many of the patients in our study loss was a central dynamic feature of their presenting problems, and termination became a prominent focus in the course of their therapy. This was handled with the patient both as a reality issue and as a representation of previous significant loss. Termination as a focus in brief psychotherapy has also been discussed elsewhere in some detail (5).

*Activity of the therapist.*    In this study, the process of therapy was an active, often a directive one. Appropriate interventions by the therapist based on his formulations, treatment focus, and goals, were frequent; they included observations, reflections, and interpretations as well as reassurance, advice, and direction.

In addition, the therapist emphasized the psychological strengths of the child and parents, helping them to utilize these strengths in coping with their difficulties. One nine-year-old girl, for example, had great difficulty in her relationships to peers because of resentment, frustration, and low self-esteem. In the second interview it was discovered that this girl, in her loneliness and isolation, had taught herself quite a number of current songs on the piano, something about which she was appropriately proud. The therapist suggested that she might find some opportunity to display this talent, and after some exploration of her concerns about it, she did play the piano in an informal setting at school. Fortunately, a conversation evolved between her and two other girls about music, and this at least was a beginning of a positive interpersonal relationship for her.

In another case, a seven-year-old boy's mother, who could display a great deal of genuine warmth, concern, and empathy when she felt someone was in need, nevertheless was angered and disappointed at her son's aggressiveness and school problems. As she began to understand—with the therapist's help—that he was reacting to deeper feelings of anxiety, fear, and helplessness, her view of him changed, and she could begin to relate to him more positively, utilizing her capacity for warmth and empathy. The active search by the therapist for the family's strengths and his encouragement to use these in coping with the internal and interpersonal aspects of their lives was a process strongly emphasized in the brief psychotherapy setting.

## Content of the Therapy

The individual family members who participated in the brief therapy naturally influenced the content of the therapy itself. In 85 percent of the brief therapy cases, family members other than the identified "patient" were seen as often or more often than the patient in the brief therapy time period. Next to the patient himself, the most frequently involved other family members in therapy were the mother alone, the entire family together, and, less frequently, the mother and father together. This family orientation of the brief therapy was reflected in its content. We devised a list of six "content categories" and rated the amount of therapy time spent on each type of content. The categories of content occupying the most time in the brief therapy setting were, in order of frequency: child rearing practices, communication within the family, intrapsychic conflicts of the patient and/or parent, and sibling rivalry. The other two categories were marital relationship and environmental manipulation.

Obviously, in formulating therapeutic goals the therapists emphasized family dynamics, and the content of the therapy appeared well suited to frequent conjoint family or parent-child sessions.

The following case account will illustrate many of the features of the brief psychotherapy process that we have described.

## Case Report

*Case 1.*    Carrie is a ten-year-old girl whose father and stepmother brought her to the clinic because of her insomnia, nightmares, poor peer relations, and a number of fears, all of which had been present for three years. She had lived with her natural mother following the parents' divorce when she was four years of age, but her mother was ruled unfit by the court and she was awarded to her father and stepmother a month prior to their appearance at the clinic.

In the family's first visit it became apparent that Carrie was a bright, precocious child whose mother had demanded independent and adult-like behavior of her, was inconsistent in providing for her physical needs, and offered little emotional warmth in their relationship. This left Carrie repeatedly disappointed and frustrated, yet she vigorously defended her mother and even cried upon leaving her.

During the second portion of this visit the therapist talked with Carrie, who announced she would soon be returning to live with her natural mother. The therapist observed that she must think a great deal about her mother, at which point Carrie burst into tears. As she could not verbalize the reasons for her tears, the therapist commented that it was sometimes difficult to talk about very deep feelings—that she probably had a good many feelings about leaving someone with whom she had lived for many years and coming to live in a strange house and family. Carrie's tears slowed and she managed a barely perceptible nod and smile.

The therapist's initial formulation of the problem was as follows: Carrie was undergoing a grief reaction due to her sudden separation from and loss of her mother, about whom she had acutely ambivalent feelings. Her fears and sleep disturbances had most likely developed as a reaction to her natural parents' marital difficulties, their divorce, and the subsequent demands and relative emotional deprivation she experienced. These symptoms had continued as she experienced both the present disruption and separation in her life and the grief and guilt from her ambivalent ties to her mother. Some ambiguity also existed in Carrie's mind about the permanence of her present living situation due to conflicting messages she received from her natural mother.

With the aid of the family, the therapist developed the following focus and goals for the brief therapy period: to help Carrie recognize her ambivalent feelings about her mother; to help her begin to work through her feelings toward her new parents and her adjustment in her new home, school, and peer group; to help Carrie's parents understand her feelings and their relationship to her symptoms; to help them to develop sympathetic, consistent management and positive ways of relating to her and to their own difficulties; and to encourage more open channels of communication among family members so that they might continue to provide mutual support for each other in the future.

Following the family's initial clinic visit, the therapist spent a total of three and one-half hours each with Carrie and with her parents over the next eight weeks. He actively offered observations, interpretations, and direction based on his formulations and goals and attempted to prepare the parents to cope with the present difficulties and those that might arise. Although Carrie did not indicate agreement with all of the observations and interpretations made, her parents reported that she seemed to be improving. They simultaneously began to modify their views and management of her. By the end of the nine-week therapy period, they reported that her fears had disappeared or diminished markedly, that she was sleeping through the night without disturbance, and that she had improved considerably academically, although she was still having some difficulties in her peer relationships.

Carrie's termination with her therapist was verbally compared to her separation from her mother, but her strengths in coping with her difficulties now and in the future were stressed. The parents were advised that Carrie's difficulties might continue to some extent and that their consistency in handling them would be essential for her continued improvement. At the one-year follow-up they reported that Carrie was free of all symptoms except for occasional mild anxiety, and she was now playing with other children regularly. Although, as she informed her parents, she did not always like her therapist, who was "stern and never smiled," she missed seeing him, as "he was the first person she ever had a chance to sit and talk with." Obviously her parents now fulfilled that function, and their communication and mutual support were much enhanced.

## Conclusion

The process of psychotherapy we have described here comprises a brief therapy "set," which has been referred to previously (2). The elements of this set, which we feel are important features of successful brief psychotherapy, are: therapist motivation for brief therapy, the "therapeutic pressure" of time-limited therapy and the expectation of improvement, the collaborative effort of therapist and family in defining a focus in therapy and working toward specific treatment goals, rapid development of the therapeutic alliance, termination as an issue from the onset of therapy, a family-oriented approach in therapy, the active definition and utilization of the family's strengths in coping with their difficulties, and encouraging the family to return for further consultation if additional stress or crises arise.

If this treatment modality receives acceptance by the child psychotherapist, we will be able to reach many more of the large numbers of disturbed children and families not now receiving care.

# REFERENCES

1. Wolberg, L. Methodology in short-term therapy. Amer J Psychiat 122:135-140, 1965.
2. Rosenthal, A. J., Levine, S. V. Brief psychotherapy with children: a preliminary report. Amer J Psychiat 127:646-651, 1970.
3. Shaw, R., Blumenfeld, H., & Senf, R. A short-term treatment program in a child guidance clinic. Social Work 13:81-90, 1968.
4. Parad, L. G., Parad, H. F. A study of crisis-oriented planned short-term treatment: part II. Social Casework 49:418-426, 1968.
5. Mackay, J. The use of brief psychotherapy with children. Canad Psychiat Ass J 12:269-279, 1967.
6. Proskauer, S. Some technical issues in time-limited psychotherapy with children. J Amer Acad Child Psychiat 8:154-169, 1969.
7. Heinicke, C. M., Goldman, A. Research on psychotherapy with children. Amer J Orthopsychiat 30:483-494, 1960.

# 4. CRISIS INTERVENTION AND SHORT-TERM THERAPY: AN APPROACH IN A CHILD-PSYCHIATRIC CLINIC

Irving N. Berlin, M.D.

Ego psychology (A. Freud, 1936 and Erikson, 1959, 1963, 1968) and crisis theory (Lindemann, 1944; Caplan, 1959; Parad and Caplan, 1960; Klein and Lindemann, 1961) have given rise to formal teaching and application of a methodology once used intuitively by many teachers in child psychiatry. Inherent in these efforts is the systematic use of the energies mobilized by a crisis to deal with the emerging problems on a reality level, utilizing the latent ego strengths of the family members involved. Most effective crisis and short-term therapy is based upon psychodynamic understanding of the underlying unconscious motivation which has kept the family both in an impasse and together (Gilman, 1965; Parad, 1965; Wolberg, 1965). It addresses itself to relevant interventions which will not arouse individual resistances or exacerbate unresolved conflicts that might lead to further decompensation. Thus, the healthiest parts of the ego in each family member are engaged in a goal or task-oriented effort to achieve attainable ends (Rapaport, 1962 and Erikson, 1963).

It has become clear that in this process some durable

Reprinted from *Journal of the American Academy of Child Psychiatry*, 1970, **9,** 595-606, by permission of International Universities Press, Inc. and the author. Dr. Berlin is Professor of Psychiatry and Pediatrics and Head, Division of Child Psychiatry, University of Washington School of Medicine, Seattle, Washington.

personality changes occur in individuals which, with support to the family, result in more integrative relations and more effective individual capacities for dealing with both internal conflicts and external realities (Lindemann, 1944; Parad, 1965; Kaplan and Mason, 1960; McGuire, 1965). In our efforts to teach such interventions we have used the model developed in mental health consultation and especially in crisis intervention. This model permits the statement of several hypotheses and often their stepwise testing for validity before advancing to the next step. In each instance we ask ourselves not only what brings the family for help, but we also ask those questions which emerge from the crisis model. These questions are: What is the crisis, whom does it affect, why is it disorganizing, what were the individuals' or family's resources and plans for coping with it prior to intervention? How can the issues around the crisis be opened for discussion, what are the unsaid or unspoken issues which are not shared by the family members concerned? What are the ego strengths to be mobilized, how can one involve these individuals in their own behalf, what are the specific tasks to be carried out to help resolve or reduce the crisis? What help and support do they need, and finally, how can one consolidate the gains made (Sarvis, DeWees, and Johnson, 1959; Cadden, 1964)? In this process the therapist or team forms some tentative ideas about which family member seems most vulnerable as a result of the current crisis and how we can quickly engage that person or persons in a way which will enable him to feel less helpless (Kalis, 1961). Our dynamic hypothesis about the roles played by family members in their previous equilibrium helps us to utilize each family member's competencies. Effective intervention enables the entire family to function better with some alteration in individual roles, but usually not at the expense of any one family member.

Such interventions require a good deal of activity on the part of the therapist, primarily an honest sharing of his clearly labeled speculations concerning the unspoken feelings and needs which the crisis has brought into the open. As he requests validation from the family or cites what has seemed to be true in other instances with other families, he tries to help the family members feel relatively free to disagree with him. Thus, some of their hurts, fears, anger, and longing for closeness and tenderness are stated and heard. Therefore, despite initial denial that these unspoken feelings are important in the current problem, subsequent behavior by family members and their descriptions of their interaction may validate these speculations.

Inherent in the method is that the urgency of the situaation permits the family to agree on several tasks they will mutually undertake to reduce the problem for which they sought help. In the course of such an endeavor, the evaluation of why these efforts did or did not succeed often brings to light some of the serious conflicts in the family, and within each of the members, which have led to the present exacerbation of troubles. As one understands these conflicts and modifies the tasks to be attempted by the various family members, one begins to assess the validity of the original hypotheses and to engage the healthy aspects of each family member in the direction of more effective resolution of his conflicts. Since most of the time the family comes for help because of pressures from an outside agency or because of acute internal disequilibrium, one can usually keep the family engaged until some fairly clear resolution of the acute problem occurs.

Experience in a public health well-baby clinic and other experiences common to many consultants show that a warm, effective, mothering public health nurse is able to reverse the failure-to-thrive process when the mother is young, depressed, etc. This experience has led us to define more clearly certain aspects of this approach. The following vignettes describe some of these learning experiences as well as their application to an adolescent crisis.

## AN INFANT PROBLEM IN A WELL-CHILD CLINIC

In a public health well-child clinic, a nurse called my

attention to a young mother with a six-month-old infant
boy. The baby was crying, and his mother held him
away from her like a tuba. The nurse relayed her feeling
that the mother was depressed, unhappy, and estranged
from the child. When the nurse held the baby he immediately stopped crying as he was cuddled and patted.
The history obtained from the 19-year-old mother revealed she was married to escape from home, experienced a few months of marital bliss and carefree living,
and then became pregnant which was accompanied by
much nausea and fatigue. After the birth of the baby, his
constant crying was a terrible drain on the mother. He
didn't seem to eat or to gain weight well, and he kept her
up nights. As a result, she said, she felt tired and depressed.

With my accompanying comments, the nurse demonstrated some easier ways to hold the baby and some
burping and feeding procedures. Then, with the nurse's
encouragement, the mother practiced them. She said the
baby wiggled so much when he took the bottle that she
usually propped it in the crib. Again, with my explana-
tory comments, the nurse illustrated how holding him in
a comfortable position during feeding was important as
it allowed patting, talking to the baby, and getting bub-
les up, which not only resulted in less colic, but also provided the necessary stimulation for development. I suggested that all this might save wear and tear on mother.

The nurse made a home visit to help mother organize
her day. She played with the baby as she and mother
talked over the day's schedule, and made several suggestions that might help mother feel more effective, especially around how to introduce new foods. Mother seemed
much more comfortable with the baby, but still talked
and played very little with him.

On the next clinic visit I complimented the mother on
the baby's weight gain, and the nurse and I engaged in
conversation about the need for regular stimulation by
talking, singing, and playing with the baby as important
to his development. The nurse commented that some
play times after his nap and before his bath were often
most convenient. While the nurse did the routine mea-

surements, the mother and I chatted about how hard it was to know what to do with the first baby, and how playing, talking, singing, etc. seemed kind of silly at first. Several home visits in the next month found the mother spending more time playing with the baby and receiving much more enjoyment from this.

On the second visit, mother told the nurse of her anger at father who spent lots of time roughhousing with the baby on Sundays and little time with her. When the nurse mentioned how hard it was for us as adults to say, "I want to be played with too," the mother agreed and said she had felt this way, but that no words had occurred to her. This mother and many others in the clinic, who were identified as emotionally distant from their infants and usually depressed, were helped by sympathetic listening and clear specification of tasks that were within their emotional capacity and which altered their infants' behavior. Some demonstration and follow-up in the home increased mother's readiness to talk, play, and cuddle with the infant. The physician's and nurse's encouragement and praise for a job of mothering increasingly well done was clearly important. Many mothers learn to enjoy their infants who might otherwise be neglected and prone to emotional and psychophysiological disorders.

## A CHILD WITH ASTHMA

Those of us involved with psychosomatic problems in a pediatric or public health clinic are often struck with the fact that parents seem to miss the premonitory signs of the onset of an acute episode. Then, over and over, they relate with anger their frantic efforts to deal with the full-blown episode of asthma, epileptic attack, diabetic coma, or insulin reaction.

We were asked to see Linda, a 13-year-old asthmatic girl, whose continued severe attacks were leading to emphysema. The anger evident between mother and daughter was so great that long-term psychotherapy had been suggested for both of them, but after two years they had stopped. When the family was seen, father gave the impression of being a passive bystander who supported mother's angry tirade about the daughter's use of asthma to avoid chores, schoolwork, etc. The parents reported that these episodes usually messed up their vacations, holidays, and their social life. Linda smiled tolerantly at her mother during the interview, commenting that she had no control over her attacks. We then tried to reconstruct her most recent attack. It became clear that mother first noticed heavy wheezing when Linda was studying for a test. Mother's thought, "She will probably to too sick to go to school," was not followed by any action on her part, and at bedtime the wheezing increased. She gave Linda some Tedral, but the wheezing escalated until she had to be taken to the emergency hospital at midnight for an injection of adrenaline. They returned home at 3:00 a.m. This was a frequent sequence.

The parents and daughter were told that to tackle this problem all three had to be involved in early detection of breathing difficulties, and that the adrenaline mist early in the game, followed by Tedral, might avoid the trip to the emergency hospital. We asked all three to spot the early discomfort, report it to the others, and take prompt action. The next several weeks revealed mother and daughter each pushing on the other the responsibility for early detection. Father stayed out of it all. After our analysis of the situation and father's avoidance of responsibility, although he noted clearly the sequence, we all agreed that he should be assigned the role of the dispenser of medication, to whom mother and daughter could turn to help validate the respiratory distress.

In the next three weeks several incipient attacks were aborted. Several others were not, and the midnight trip to the emergency hospital was repeated. Each failure was examined as objectively as possible in terms of who missed the cues and how they could have been picked up and acted on. In one instance Linda wanted mother to noticed; she therefore said nothing to either parent, both of whom missed the signs. In another instance mother noticed labored breathing; however, Linda denied this, became angry, and father joined her in saying that mother imagined it. This was one of the few father-daughter alliances. Later came the wheezing and its aftermath.

The successful instances resulted from collaborative efforts by all concerned. Father became more attentive to the problem, and he, mother, and daughter each cited instances when one or another spotted the onset and initiated prompt treatment.

It became clear from these detailed investigations that Linda often did not notice her own labored breathing, as if she were not involved, so that she did not heed its portent. However, as both parents became more vigilant and called the breathing difficulties to her attention, she became more aware of them and began to take more responsibility for medication. Thus, their next vacation trip was the first not marked by emergencies. Father became more assertive about what needed to be done at the signs of an early attack, and the steps to be taken to abort the attack were repeatedly spelled out. He later became more assertive in other family matters.

Of interest also is that mother was able to offer Linda help with school work when it became clear that she was the one best equipped to help. This resulted in greater closeness between them. Thus, as the parents were helped to do their job as parents more adequately, Linda could also assume more responsibility. This altered many of the circular problems and anger between parents and between perents and child. Their relationship gradually improved. Father later admitted that he had been afraid of the anger between his wife and daughter and that because he did not want any anger focused on him, he left Linda's care to his wife. Our emphasis on his importance in the family finally altered his function, especially when he was given a specific task to fulfill in the service of his family.

## AN ADOLESCENT ON PROBATION

We were asked to see Fred in an emergency interview. He was a large 14-year-old boy who had been caught trying to sneak his grandfather's rifle out of the car under his father's eyes. This was the last of a series of thefts and brushes with the law over a two-year period which began when he entered junior high school. Mother had gone to work at this time, and a 16-year-old girl took care of Fred and his nine-year-old sister after school. His grades had been D's and E's during the last year after having previously been A's and B's. Each theft was executed so as to call attention to him. For example, he stole the family car, drained the tank, and left the car stranded in the middle of a downtown intersection so that the police had to bring him home. He collected money on a friend's paper route from family friends. Thus, in a variety of ways, he had been signaling for attention and help.

We first saw Fred on referral from the local psychologist who reported a very psychotic Rorschach. There was question of emergency hospitalization for psychosis. Fred interacted shyly but appropriately. In response to questions about sexual feelings and masturbation, he did not withdraw as adolescent schizophrenics often do, and he was able, with encouragement, to talk about his feelings. He gave us some sense of his predicament. In emotional maturity he was on the 14-year-old level, but his size led him to associate with 16- to 18-year-olds. Neither parent was available to talk to him, except when he got into trouble.

Father, a robust city engineer, was puzzled by Fred's behavior and the fact that they had not been close in recent years. Hunting and fishing were spoiled by the boy's stubbornness and unwillingness to follow father's lead, and they rarely spoke to each other now. Mother appeared tense, frozen, and distant. She complained that these problems reduced their status in their small community. She enjoyed her work as a legal secretary and expressed pleasure that father and she now did more together during the evenings. However, she was unable to get Fred to talk to her about anything and commented that her opinions were worthless because she was a woman. Every week they battled over Fred's straightening his messy room.

We talked with both parents and Fred around the problems of an adolescent's need for both independence and closeness, the particular dilemma raised by Fred's size, and the possible meaning of his behavior in terms of needing the attention for himself. We also discussed his need to find a male model and to deny his sexual feelings toward girls and toward his attractive mother.

I suggested that, in order to spend time together, father teach Fred to drive the family car, inasmuch as he was stealing it anyway. Father's goal would be to increase Fred's driving competence and indicate his approval and pleasure when Fred performed well. I also hoped that when they went hunting or fishing, father would let Fred take the lead, since by this time he should have learned something from father. At the same time Fred would also receive needed recognition for his competence. Other areas of possible mutual interchange were discussed. Mother could think of no way to initiate discussions with Fred. Her angry remark, "What about that filthy room—he always leaves the door open to taunt me," prompted me to suggest that Fred wanted her involvement and that often if one offered to help with a chore, it not only got done, but it also provided an opportunity for talking together. I asked mother if she would try this, and she muttered she guessed so.

I reviewed with Fred and his parents our discussion of the relevant issues related to his behavior and his parents' disjunctive interaction with him. We went over the agreement for father and mother to try to spend more time with Fred, and Fred in turn agreed that he would try to reduce his fights with mother, improve his grades, stop the car stealing, etc. At this point Fred mentioned he hoped his parents would not fight so much. Father nodded and said he had been unhappy about mother's working, but knew she enjoyed it. He picked at her about TV dinners, the babysitter's failure to clean house, etc. Mother replied happily that this was the first time she had heard him say he knew she enjoyed her job. We agreed to meet in three weeks when the parents could take a long weekend to come to the clinic.

On the next visit the family members were much more relaxed. Mother's face was softer, and Fred said that things were better at home. He had made up some work in school and was doing better. Father remarked that

Fred was becoming an excellent driver, and he surprised father with his acute and well-thought-out observations and opinions on many things that they discussed during the driving lessons. Mother grinned and said that while she and Fred cleaned his room he wondered why he couldn't babysit for his sister and earn the money. Mother said, "Sure if you will do the whole job of picking up the house, getting the supper, and being home all the time and responsible for your sister." Fred replied that he would like to try, and so far he had done an excellent job. I expressed my pleasure that they had done so well in working things out and recapitulated in detail the changes and the kinds of tasks which they had worked on that had brought the changes about. I emphasized the need for continued effort in these directions. On leaving, Fred said that father was going fishing with him in some streams father had never fished before.

A follow-up letter four months later revealed the family still doing well. Mother answered the letter, observing that she and Fred still did his room together because this was the only time he felt free to talk to her about girls. Father and mother had fewer fights now, and Fred was becoming active in sports where his size was an advantage. This had resulted in a new set of friends his own age and with similar interests.

It might be said that we spelled out for the parents tasks that were opportunities for involvement with their adolescent son at a time when they were feeling helpless, hurt, and angry. In the process one could note that they were able to provide better role models as well as some opportunities for mutual closeness with their son.

## CONCLUSIONS

In these vignettes and other cases we have followed using a basic crisis intervention model, many questions and hypotheses that were generated were not tested in any single case. However, in the long run we feel we have been able to ask and answer the relevant questions and test most aspects of the hypothesis raised by this model and thus modify aspects of the model appropriately. We hope others will be encouraged to do it more fully. For example, the critical issues in teaching such a method center around how one understands a crisis, i.e., what past and immediate interactions and conflicts in and between family members are relevant. In a few instances such awareness is not very relevant, as in the instance of the crisis around prematurity described by Cadden (1964), Caplan (1959), and Kaplan and Mason (1960).

Here the sheer impact of the premature infant on the family, especially the mother, is most effectively met by frequent contacts with the mother by someone trained in helping mother to learn to interact with and to stimulate a premature infant. However, without actual physical help with household chores, cooking, and care for other family members, the mother and others, because of weariness and lack of sleep, may not be able to benefit from the psychological interventions.

In other instances a clear awareness of the long-standing conflicts in and between family members may be essential for effective intervention (Cain, 1961). Thus, our asthmatic girl was caught in a variety of parental problems and conflicts, some of which she internalized and unconsciously used, and others which she appeared to manipulate consciously. The historical data from previous psychotherapy indicated that father's passivity and withdrawal from mother and daughter were a result of early conflicts in the marriage. Mother needed to find a man who could take care of her and nurture her, and father viewed mother as a strong woman with supplies for him. The inevitable result is over-simplified here; however, the effort to help father find a viable and effective role in the family and to reduce some of the mother-daughter conflicts which made them the active pair in the triad, permitted all three to have more pleasurable contact with each other. This stemmed from a dynamic understanding of both the needs and conflicts present. In this instance we did have a good dynamic history of the development of the daughter's asthma. Historical data about the parents' pasts and the material from interviews helped us understand the deep-seated nature of their conflicts and how these had emerged in their relationships.

One of the most prevalent issues in crises and short-term intervention is how to help the family talk together when there has been so much hurt and anger. One method is for the therapist or team to develop aloud some of their ideas about the unspoken issues or messages which appear relevant. Thus, as with adolescent patients, sexual problems between the parents may be talked about when the adolescent is not there. The need for self-fulfillment for mother and her unconscious as well as conscious anxiety about the "mothering" role and possible anxiety about being around a potentially "aggressive" male adolescent with its sexual connotation may be relevant. The father's need to be taken care of by mother was reflected both in his statements and perhaps in the adolescent son's feeling of abandonment when his role model behaved helplessly. Perhaps the continued overt thefts were related to forcing some parental hand. These dynamics are not confirmed.

Time does not permit discussion of the dynamic formulation in each case; however, as we have looked at families in crisis and reviewed their previous capacities to cope with difficult situations, we have sometimes become aware of the *why now* causes. In some instances the present crisis may be the child's recapitulation of a parent's traumatic developmental conflicts during the same developmental stage. These may have remained latent and may now be evidenced in the parental disorganization.

We have observed that some families who have very primitive styles of living, parents who often have had few gratifications in their infancy and childhood life, or families with very sick, i.e., psychotic or antisocial children do not respond well to brief intervention. We may choose to see such families, using a task-oriented approach over a long period of time, at least weekly, and later at monthly intervals, once the family understands how we expect them to work. Here, identification with the authoritative, supportive, parental therapist who expects them to work on problems and helps them achieve clearly discernable ends may be effective.

These methods seem to demonstrate the importance of the therapist's activity—his concerned intention to help and his ability to convince the family that it can be helped. Any gains which bring about increased closeness and less stressful ways of living together are frequently multiplied in unforeseeable ways. The result is often more integrative living by each person and the family as a whole.

## SUMMARY

We have spelled out some efforts in understanding and teaching crisis intervention and brief therapy with families. The case examples illustrate our learning experiences which have led to the development of training in dynamic psychiatry as a basis for understanding and applying lessons from ego psychology developed by Anna Freud, Erikson, Lindemann, and Caplan.

## REFERENCES

1. Cadden, V. (1964), Crisis in the family. In *Principles of Preventive Psychiatry,* ed. G. Caplan. New York: Basic Books, 288-297.

2. Cain, A. C., *et al.* (1961), Interpretation within the metaphor. *Bull. Menninger Clin.,* 25:307-312.

3. Caplan, G. (1959), *Concepts of Mental Health Consultation.* Washington, D.C.: U.S. Children's Bureau.

4. Erikson, E. (1959), *Identity and the life cycle [Psychological Issues,* Monogr. 1] New York: International Universities Press.

5. Erikson, E. (1963), *Childhood and Society.* New York: Norton.

6. Erikson, E. (1968), *Identity, Youth and Crisis.* New York: Norton.

7. Freud, A. (1936), *The Ego and The Mechanisms of Defense* (rev. ed.). New York: International Universities Press, 1966.

8. Gilman, R. D. (1965), Brief psychotherapy: a psychoanalytic view. *Amer. J. Psychiat.,* 122:601-611.

9. Kalis, B. L. (1961), Precipitating stress as a focus in psychotherapy. *Arch. Gen. Psychiat.,* 5:219-226.

10. Kaplan, D. M., & Mason, E. (1960), Maternal reaction to premature birth viewed as an acute emotional disorder. *Amer. J. Orthopsychiat.,* 30:539-552.

11. Klein, D. C. & Lindemann, E. (1961), Preventive intervention in individual and family crises situations. In: *Prevention of Mental Disorders in Children,* ed. G. Caplan. New York: Basic Books.

12. Lindemann, E. (1944), Symptomatology and management of acute grief. *Amer. J. Psychiat.,* 101:141-148.

13. McGuire, M. T. (1965), The process of short-term psychotherapy: I & II; content expectations and structure. *J. Nerv. Ment. Dis.,* 141:83-94; 219-230.

14. Parad, H. J. (1965), *Crisis Intervention: Selected Readings* New York: Family Service Association of America.

15. Parad, H. J. & Caplan, G. (1960), A framework for studying families in crises. *Soc. Work,* 5 (July): 3-15.

16. Rapaport, L. (1962), The state of crisis. Some theoretical considerations. *Soc. Serv. Rev.,* 36:211-217.

17. Sarvis, M. A., DeWees, S., & Johnson, R. (1959), A concept of ego oriented psychotherapy. *Amer. J. Psychiat.,* 20:272-287.

18. Wolberg, L. R. (1965), *Short-term Psychotherapy.* New York: Grune & Stratton.

# 5. THERAPEUTIC INTERVENTION IN A CHILD PSYCHIATRY EMERGENCY SERVICE

## Gilbert C. Morrison, M.D.

Any emergency service presupposes early management of a crisis. Offering such a service in child psychiatry necessitates a study of old problems in our field. When we are faced with a family-in-crisis whose motivation and interest are limited to the immediate crisis, ongoing debates about the value of brief psychotherapy and conjoint family therapy become academic. With the knowledge that the treatment team must effect change not only within the patient's and parents' limited motivation, but also within a limited period of time, we find that questions regarding treatment for symptomatic relief, depth personality change, commitment and self-sacrifice become less relevant. Our goal then becomes finding crisis intervention methods fitting patient-defined prerequisites.

But what are we to consider a crisis or emergency in child psychiatry? Recognizing a psychiatric emergency may be more difficult than defining one in other areas of medicine where evidence of blood loss, trauma or manifestations of impending shock can be quantitatively determined. The point at which "normal" problems of growth escalate into a serious family crisis cannot yet be

Reprinted from *Journal of the American Academy of Child Psychiatry,* 1969, **8,** 542-558, by permission of International Universities Press, Inc. and the author. Dr. Morrison is Coordinator of Graduate Psychiatric Education and Assistant Adjunct Professor of Psychiatry, Department of Psychiatry and Human Behavior, University of California, Irvine, California.

predicted or given status by means of "educated guess." We cannot predict when a boy's runaway will involve a stolen car rather than merely a short stay at a friend's house; when complaints of vague fears of school will be replaced by specific physiological symptoms or frank panic; when a previously unhappy fourteen-year-old girl will add the tragic problem of pregnancy to her troubles; or when the numerous suicidal ruminations, threats, gestures or manipulations of a teen-ager will become a cold mortality statistic.

We note in relation to the latter point the increasing attention paid to suicide threats and attempts in adults, adolescents, and children which can be attributed to impressive statistics, the reevaluation of familiar cliches, and the guardedly hopeful reports from treatment centers such as the Suicide Prevention Center in Los Angeles.

Burks and Hoekstra (1964) reviewed emergency child psychiatric referrals at the University of Michigan Medical Center in 1961. They found that children who had attempted suicide, those developing a psychosis, and those with an acute school phobia presented *bona fide* emergency situations which required prompt clinic intervention. They believed that referrals resulted from family crises rather than from an intrapsychic crisis in the child. The approach of crisis theory and the development of treatment methods to involve the entire family as a unit have stimulated a new look at these familiar problems.

## CHILD PSYCHIATRY EMERGENCY SERVICE

Therapeutic intervention in our Child Psychiatry Emergency Service has been effected by immediate diagnostic evaluation and therapeutic formats utilizing a combination of brief psychotherapy and family therapy methods. The goal of our program is the immediate psychiatric management of child and family crises. An emergency treatment program for children and families can well be viewed as focusing psychiatric attention upon early amelioration of emotional disorders. The following elements of the program were implemented to provide this service: (1) an initial appraisal of the child and his family as quickly as possible; (2) psychiatric emergency treatment methods; (3) the establishment and maintenance of good working relationships with various community agencies, schools, hospitals, and clinics; (4) the provision of sufficient flexibility of schedules within the Child Psychiatry Emergency Service to offer immediate evaluation and follow-up for additional short-term help.

The Child Psychiatry Emergency Service of the Central Psychiatric Clinic was established in late 1964. In preparation for this development, a study was made of "urgent" applications at the Central Psychiatric Clinic since 1959 and of consultations to the emergency room of the Cincinnati General Hospital since 1962. This review revealed that from five to sixteen families applied each month to the hospital emergency room or the outpatient clinic for psychiatric emergency services for their children. The peak months for application occurred January through March and in August. Referrals to both facilities included children with acute anxiety states, school phobia, truancy and school refusal, behavior disorders, adolescent turmoil, hysterical conversions, depressions, suicidal attempts or threats, and mental retardation.

In the emergency room 80 percent of these patients were between thirteen and seventeen years of age; twice as many girls as boys were referred. One half of these patients were diagnosed as adolescent turmoil or adolescent adjustment reaction, and about a third had made suicidal attempts or serious threats of suicide. (Our findings were almost identical with those Mattsson et al. [1967] reported from their studies in Cleveland.) At Central Psychiatric Clinic the "emergency referrals" included a younger group with an average age of twelve years. Patients were frequently referred from the hospital emergency room to Central Psychiatric Clinic. The majority did not follow through and instead returned to the emergency room for intermittent assistance from the psychiatrist on call.

Psychiatric emergencies in children and families have always been seen in emergency services or clinics, but the realities of treatment waiting lists and heavy individual case loads have made the approach to these families other than optimal. Trained professional personnel with some flexibility in their schedules along with a 24-hour emergency room and inpatient facilities are available in few clinics. Even where such services can be offered, many families needing help seem unable to tolerate even a week's delay after the initial contact with an emergency service.

As the studies of Hollingshead and Redlich (1958), Brill and Storrow (1960), and Viola Bernard (1965) have shown so well, the motivation and capacity of some patients to participate in our present methods of individual psychotherapy vary greatly. The need for modification of our therapeutic approach to these families has become clear. The determining factor leading to the request for help is often the individual's or family's interpretation of a crisis in their lives. We recognized that their definition of crisis and its resolution were often quite different from our own. However, we were unable to give them precedence in our already overcrowded clinic with a long waiting list.

The process of establishing a Child Psychiatry Emergency Service then requires that we address ourselves to such factors if the crisis which has led to the initial phone call or emergency room visit is to be treated on an outpatient basis. On our service the child psychiatrist who initially sees the family in consultation in the emergency room or who talks to the family on the phone continues with the treatment team in the role of diagnostician and therapist. The treatment team consists of a child psychiatrist and a psychiatric social worker. The problems associated with scheduling immediate appointments have been managed by previously arranged, flexible psychiatric and social work time with emergency clinic teams. Interviews are immediately recorded and a specific secretary is designated who gives precedence to the typing and distribution of this material.

The treatment approach with these families has in

part been planned along lines formulated from a history of the previous medical experience of our crisis-oriented families. They expected immediate treatment, preferably with medication, in an emergency unit or in a single visit to a doctor's office. Past medical history obtained from these families revealed that they had rarely had a private doctor and seldom went to the same doctor twice. The vast majority had previously been referred for psychiatric evaluation of one or another member of the family, but they had either failed to follow the referral recommendation, had not completed diagnostic evaluation, or had rejected the recommendation for psychotherapy. It seems then that if treatment in an emergency service is to be effective, the service offered must be specific to the symptoms presented and to the limited time available with the families. Additionally, the response can be directed toward establishing a relationship on which longer term treatment can be based.

The initial diagnostic-therapeutic procedure utilized in the Child Psychiatry Emergency Service is a group interview with the child and all significant family members together with the clinical team. This initial family interview focuses on a discussion of the presenting problem and on the formulation of a definition or statement of the nature of the child's or family's problem. The initial goal is to reach some understanding of the problem which is accepted both by the family members and the clinical team. In this interview, methods which might be tried to cope with the crisis are considered and these families usually are helped in this first interview to arrive at some working plan or direction for the immediate handling of the acute situation. Most of the families are seen again as a group from two to ten days later, depending upon their need and the nature of the problem, in order to re-evaluate the family situation and to clarify, if possible, the underlying problems in the family relationships which contributed to the crisis. The team works with the families as long as necessary to alleviate the crisis. The number of family interviews ranges from one to eight; for most families a planned termination occurs after three or four interviews. For some families further therapeutic management includes referral for other types of treatment, such as outpatient collaborative individual psychotherapy for parent and child, inpatient treatment, physical diagnosis and medical management.

## REVIEW OF EXPERIENCE

A review of the first 100 families seen by our service may elucidate more clearly some of the techniques and practices used in the family crisis. The statistical review of the presenting difficulties of the children in these families is similar to the statistical survey of the general hospital emergency unit and the urgent Central Psychiatric Clinic applications for several years prior to the beginning of the Child Psychiatry Emergency Service. Three girls are seen for every two boys (see Table 1). Seventy-five percent of the children admitted to the Service are in the age range of thirteen to seventeen years. School refusal and suicide attempts or threats predominate as the initial causes for referral to the Service, constituting 48 percent of the 100 families.

*Case 1 (school refusal following illness, suicide threat).* Barbara was referred to the Child Psychiatry Emergency Service by her mother's caseworker and the school visiting teacher. She was thirteen, oldest of five children, a high school freshman and near the top of her class scholastically. Three weeks earlier she had a viral illness and following convalescence refused to return to school. In the family and in individual interviews her first day in this

### TABLE 1
### Child Psychiatric Emergencies
### Age and Sex

| Patients' Age Groups In Years | Total | Boys | Girls |
|---|---|---|---|
| 4- 8 | 17 | 10 | 7 |
| 9-11 | 10 | 5 | 5 |
| 12-14 | 31 | 12 | 19 |
| 15-17 | 42 | 13 | 29 |
| | 100 | 40 | 60 |

clinic, Barbara refused to talk, but sat with fixed, downcast face and cried quietly as she had done for many days.

In the interview Barbara's mother told of many separations from her husband and of a divorce two years before. She spoke of her illegitimate baby born four months ago whose father was her employer. At about the time of the birth, Barbara took a plastic bag to bed on several occasions telling her sister that she hoped to smother in the night. She was frequently despondent, preoccupied, and talked about death. Barbara's mother angrily attributed all of the girl's difficulties to the desertion of the family by Barbara's father. She added, calmly, that "at least if Barbara can't return to school, she can care for the young children and have dinner ready for me when I get home." She told of one attempt to return Barbara to school which resulted in both mother and daughter sitting in front of the school and crying all morning and Barbara's promise to take over household responsibilities if she could remain home. The predominant themes discussed in this first interview were the recent pregnancy, which had not been discussed with the children, and the need for Barbara's immediate return to school after the interview that day.

During a phone conversation between interviews, Barbara spoke blandly of school but expressed interest in learning why she could not see her father. Two days later at the next interview she mentioned the same concern and then learned that her mother had blocked the father's attempts to visit the children because of irregular or incomplete child support. An agreement was made to try to find a solution to the problem. With this behind her, Barbara told of her belief that the illegitimate pregnancy was a result of her mother's need to work to support her and the other children. As she talked it became evident that not only Barbara but also her siblings thought they were the cause of the parents' problems and divorce, leading to the mother's work and pregnancy, a conclusion not too different from the mother's projections.

Barbara became progressively guilty and depressed. The school refusal and housekeeping were absolutions for the guilt especially when Barbara found such obvious ambivalence in her mother's determination that she return to school.

The other children were included in subsequent interviews. Their similar confusions and distortions were discussed and arrangements were made for them to visit with their father. Part-time domestic help was obtained for the family. Meanwhile, the mother continued in weekly casework with a psychiatric social worker at the referring agency.

Follow-up six months later revealed that Barbara and her siblings have occasional contact with their father. She successfully completed her school year, dates occasionally, and is teaching in summer church school.

*Case 2 (suicide attempt, sexual promiscuity, pregnancy).* Brenda, a seventeen-year-old high school senior was seen in an emergency child psychiatric consultation in the general hospital emergency unit after ingestion of more than ninety aspirin tablets. The suicide attempt followed an argument with her mother about the purchase of a new dress for the senior prom. Clinical manifestations of depression were evident with expressed feelings of hopelessness, discouragement, and desire for death. This was her first suicide attempt, although she had made threats of suicide for several months. Attempted suicide as a method of dealing with problems was not new to Brenda since her mother had been hospitalized several times in previous years for suicidal attempts with drugs and poison. Each time the mother was referred for psychiatric treatment, but would seem to lose interest and discontinue her appointments.

Brenda's mother frequently disparaged her schoolwork and insisted she was of an age to earn a living. She kept a record of her daughter's menstrual periods and often accused her of pregnancy. Brenda, her mother, and grandmother before her were all the result of illegitimate pregnancies of teen-age mothers.

Brenda's schoolwork was good and she held elective offices in extracurricular activities. She participated in many appropriate peer functions. Her mother, however, actively depreciated her school achievements.

After Brenda's suicide attempt, her mother sent her to live with her grandmother. Consequently, all three were seen in treatment. What evolved was a longstanding history of a family pattern of threats and counterthreats of suicide as well as other manipulative behavior. Brenda increasingly had begun to use the behavior she saw in her home which led to intermittent episodes of guilt and depression. Both her mother and grandmother refused to continue in treatment. Several weeks after Brenda began treatment she reported that she was pregnant and revealed that for several months she had turned to many boyfriends for companionship. She frequently had intercourse during that period. When her mother and grandmother learned of her pregnancy, they readily supported her treatment.

Active and close cooperation with the school visiting teacher, the family's agency caseworker, and a hospital for unwed mothers enabled Brenda to graduate from high school and arrange for adoption of her baby. After the birth of the child, Brenda maintained phone contact with our service and returned to treatment for a short time following her mother's death.

Other patients presenting symptoms in the following order of prominence (Table 2) included conversion reaction with paralysis, sexual promiscuity, acute school phobia, runaway, toxic psychosis from several types of inhalants, fire-setting, manifestations of acute anxiety, incest, killing of pets and symptoms associated with acute psychosis as are exemplified in the following cases.

## TABLE 2
### Predominant Symptoms Precipitating
### Application to the
### Child Psychiatry Emergency Service

| Symptoms | Number |
| --- | --- |
| School refusal (school phobia = 8) | 46 |
| Suicide attempt and threat (SA = 24; ST = 18) | 42 |
| Sexual promiscuity (pregnancy = 7) | 19 |
| Conversion reaction | 19 |
| Physical symptoms (nausea, vomiting, headaches) | 18 |
| Runaway | 12 |
| Anxiety attacks (night terrors = 3) | 12 |
| Bizarre behavior (hallucination, tics, compulsions) | 10 |
| Homicidal attempt or threat (HA = 6; HT = 3) | 9 |
| Incest or result of sexual assault | 7 |
| Drug intoxication | 6 |
| Fire-setting | 5 |
| Killed pets | 4 |

*Case 3 (fire-setting).* Billy Joe, oldest of three children, started setting fires at age four. He began with small brush fires, but the size and damage of the fires increased to include a garage, playhouse, barn, and the steps and porch of a nursing home. This last fire brought him to the attention of the county fire marshal who referred him to the Child Psychiatry Emergency Service. Billy Joe was then five and a half.

The family had migrated from the Southern Appalachian Mountains. The mother in her own words was an "army brat," daughter of a Master Sergeant who had retired to a small town in the mountains. Billy Joe's mother and father married after high school. The closing of the coal mines caused them to move to Cincinnati for the father's employment in an automobile plant. However, they made frequent trips back to their Appalachian home. They looked on Cincinnati as just a place to work, not a home, even though in subsequent years three children were born there.

At the initial interview it quickly became obvious that the mother ran the family. She talked of the father's inadequacies as both husband and father, of marital discord, and of numerous separations from her husband. During these times Billy Joe moved to his mother's bed. She described her husband as a "hell-raiser, gambler, and drinker who I will straighten out."

The mother told of her attempts to dissuade Billy Joe's budding fire-setting by showing him pictures of burned people in a medical book, but to no avail. Another problem of Billy Joe's was stealing. His mother described the way she dealt with the problem as follows: "I put the things he takes away until he is older because I don't know who they

belong to." Billy Joe's fire-setting, stealing, attacks on siblings were evident to the mother for some time, but were ex-
cused with the comment that "he's a little hell-raiser like
his father." During the interview both father and son appeared passive and subdued and sat with bowed heads, the
smaller a carbon copy of the larger. When this was noted,
the mother attributed it to her reminder to them that if they
didn't straighten out, both would go to jail.

It was evident to the clinic team that the parents saw little of a disturbing nature in their son's behavior and that
they were responding only to community pressure in coming to the clinic. Therefore, the team's primary approach to
the family was to help structure the home and neighborhood environment, to support and improve the parents'
relationship, and to decrease the excessive hostile and
sexual stimulation to Billy Joe. With great difficulty, two
later meetings were scheduled and then after changes and
cancellations, reappointments were made. The parents accepted our recommendation that Billy Joe be enrolled in
nursery school and agreed to discuss their marital difficulties with their minister. The county court and fire marshal's office took an active interest in Billy Joe's home
activities, school attendance, and clinic appointments.

Phone follow-ups over a period of eighteen months revealed that Billy Joe settled down when he entered nursery
school and has now completed the second grade. The parents still continue to return to their mountain home at least
monthly, but now express an increasing desire to settle in
the city and buy a home.

*Case 4 (toxic psychosis due to gasoline sniffing).*   About a
month after school started Ronny, age thirteen, oldest of
ten children, freshman in high school, son of a gas station
operator and fundamentalist church minister, was referred
by a social work agency and a school visiting teacher because of a "change in personality." For the previous two
weeks Ronny had "talked out of his head about the boy
scouts and the church"; wore a scout shirt, dirty pants, his
father's shoes and hat to church; then walked out and attended a neighboring church; remained in one classroom
all morning while writing illegible homework; walked
around his room all night, frequently wakened his parents
asking if he could play his bugle or have his toy soldiers.

During summer vacation he had worked at his father's
gas station. He was considered a good worker and was expected to work weekends during the school year. Despite
many siblings, Ronny's home was well cared for and his
parents had ambitions for him to go to college or professional school. His parents' only problem with him during
the summer was his frequently expressed fears about high
school and his wish to transfer to a vocational high school
instead of continuing in an academic program.

A neurological examination was done and revealed no
abnormal findings other than those demonstrated in the
psychiatric interview.

In the psychiatric examination Ronny was rambling and circumstantial; he described grandiose plans. Continuous movement of his legs, alternate standing and sitting, picking at his clothes and drumming on the chair gave evidence of his tension. Occasionally, he was alert and oriented, but he was convinced that the doctor was a school principal. He was aware of his recent behavior, but talked about plots and mistreatments at school. He described visual hallucinations of "little dancing stars and H's and F's that move in front of my eyes." Questioning revealed that he occasionally would kneel to inhale the fumes while pumping gasoline. Additional history a week later confirmed the gasoline intoxication when he told of soaking his handkerchief in gasoline and going to the bathroom to breathe the fumes while masturbating. These activities took place the week before school began.

Ronny's parents wished to care for him at home and to come to the clinic for daily outpatient visits. In family therapy interviews Ronny was encouraged to discuss his school fears and ambitions, and better communication between Ronny and his parents was established. The fundamentalist religion of the family related masturbation, mental illness, and hell. Interviews with the father and son allowed Ronny to see that his father did not consider masturbation unusual even though he objected to the activity.

A two-year follow-up revealed that Ronny has completed his sophomore year in high school with no further difficulty.

Of interest to our Service, and deserving further research and treatment planning for families in crisis, is the fact that 34 of the children experienced the onset of the symptoms which led to their treatment within weeks of the death, illness, or separation of a parent. More than half of the children of the 100 families presented evidence of serious depression associated with self-devaluation, hopelessness, and discouragement underlying the bizarre behavior that led to initial referral. Statistical review shows that (1) three-quarters of the suicide attempts and threats were made by girls; and (2) of all the girls seen between fifteen and seventeen years, three out of four were referred for suicide threat or attempt. Many of these girls were found to have ingested an overdose of their mother's medications as their method of attempted suicide. A finding now under further study was the proportionately large number of teen-age girls presenting with a suicidal attempt associated with evidence of chronic depression, sexual promiscuity, and an actual or feared pregnancy.

No attempt has been made on our service to limit the number of clinic visits so long as the family is intimately involved in the crisis. Some families were seen as many as nine times, but the average contact was for three scheduled appointments. More than 180 other family members were seen with the first 100 children. An attempt was made to see every family within 48 hours of its initial referral to the service. The average elapsed time after the initial request for services was about 36 hours.

Maintaining flexible therapeutic time is one of the more difficult administrative problems of an emergency service. This aspect of our service was studied during the planning stage and several approaches were employed during the first year of the program. Our solution involved several key concepts. These included: designating one or several hours each day for interviewing those families needing urgent consultations; providing flexible treatment "hours" so that families could be seen for a few minutes or several hours, and one or several times a week; scheduling staff conference review of all cases at least weekly; and following through in the transfer of all families that would consider continuing their treatment in long-term programs. We did not claim that the Service could respond to all child psychiatry emergencies in our geographic area, but instead provided consultation to community clinics, agencies, and schools when they requested emergency child psychiatric assistance.

## DISCUSSION

The emergency service has made a continuing study in an attempt to differentiate between those families who will participate only during the acute family crisis and those who will continue for more intensive child psychiatric diagnostic evaluation and treatment. We are interested in distinguishing levels of individual and family motivation. We would like to understand the events that lead to a family crisis and to develop the capacity to understand how the family views its stressful situation. Our impressions lead us to believe that we can make several broad distinctions. Those individuals and families who view the problem as having been stimulated from outside of themselves evidence little motivation beyond a desire for a quick solution. They tend to relate the family's difficulties to unreasonable demands or expectations from the school, neighborhood, or the community. Their initial attitude can be summarized by the expression, "Look what is being done to us." This group comprises the majority of our families, and follow-up studies have revealed that they are least likely to respond to referrals for additional evaluation and treatment.

The second group introduce themselves with comments which imply that they have observed that certain types of problems recur in their family and the transition from crisis intervention methods to an ongoing treatment in the clinic can be expected to follow without difficulty.

More than 80 percent of the children seen by the emergency service have revealed sufficient psychopathology to be recommended for further diagnostic evaluation in our psychiatric clinic or in community agencies. Less than a third, even with careful planning and discussion, have accepted our recommendations for continuing psychiatric treatment or social casework following the alleviation of the crisis. Follow through, by the family's treatment team, was continued for several months after termination of clinic appointments. Follow-up studies in our clinic and with referral agencies have revealed that 9 percent continued in psychiatric or social casework treatment a year after referral.

We have made many attempts to gain a dynamic understanding of these families and their apparent disinterest in studying their own family difficulties leading to crisis referrals. Although our level of understanding still involves some speculation, we believe it is important to try to understand the reasons these families view their problems as transient and external when their descriptions reveal them to be both repetitive and a part of the family style.

Both subtle and overt expressions by the parents reveal the reportedly disturbing behavior of the child to be in part acceptable to the parents' expectations. The parents will complain about their child's runaway, suicide attempt, school refusal, or assaultive behavior, yet will smile, tell of their own belief that education has little importance or describe symptomatic behavior in their own childhood or adolescence that later was "outgrown."

From the first contact we attempt to distinguish those families who have come to the clinic in crisis but will continue with the use of our usual clinic methods from those who will benefit from a modification of more traditional techniques. The former groups are assigned to a collaborative team who will continue with them in ongoing treatment following the diagnostic evaluation. They are not placed on a waiting list for either diagnostic evaluation or treatment and their crisis is viewed as having motivated them to seek treatment rather than to continue procrastination.

Our theoretical understanding of these families is similar to that seen in the phenomenon observed in a flight-into-health in individual psychotherapy. We believe that many families reach the crisis intervention team at a time when the symptom is serving as an attempted, though unsatisfactory, solution. Because of the unsatisfactory nature of the symptom, the individual and family are in a state of flux and receptive to intervention methods. The temporary turmoil caused by the loss or separation of a member of the family or by changes in the family because of changing demands by growing children can be used as a valuable lever in helping the family to gain a different view of themselves. The concepts of symptom formation that involve the shift from relatively stable mental health to agitation and fantasy formation with a new stress are helpful in this theoretical understanding. The use of regression by the family, and individual family members, facilitates the effective intervention of interested professionals. The family temporarily gives authority to the professionals that can be used for counseling or direction, but it is just as effective if the family is encouraged to look at its own situation and derive its own conclusions. Our treatment approach has been to use the latter plan whenever the family is sufficiently intact to observe its dilemma. This emergency service attempts to provide a relatively neutral, objective, but interested setting with experienced professionals in which the family can arrive at its own solutions. Although a follow-up study is in progress, the fact that more than a quarter of the families have made further contact by telephone or subsequent interviews for a new "crisis" implies that this approach is viewed as useful.

The greatest difficulty in understanding the crises of these families, and in teaching crisis intervention methods to our trainees, is the realization that the disruptive family patterns, as we view them, are not considered alien by the family members. Early school dropout, frequent marital separations, impulsive suicide attempts or runaway, and use of the children in parental quarrels are frequently long-established patterns. Modification of these family-accepted patterns is the goal of our service in most cases, and individual insight by the family members at the time of the crisis intervention is unusual. We then are using a goal-limited approach with easy accessibility to the service or clinic during subsequent problems.

## SUMMARY

Our emergency services have provided diagnostic evaluations, family therapy, collaborative psychotherapy, referral for long-term hospitalization, and diagnosis for early access to the outpatient clinic for ongoing treatment. In the emergency service described, the child psychiatrist begins his diagnostic thinking and therapeutic planning at the time of the first phone call or emergency room contact. He continues as a member of the therapeutic team until the family is discharged from the psychiatric emergency service or until further therapeutic contact is established in the outpatient psychiatric clinic. Using this method of psychotherapeutic approach we have been able to formulate a working diagnosis and to begin treatment of the family at the first visit, and within hours of the family's request for psychiatric assistance.

# REFERENCES

1. Alexander, F., & French, T. (1946), *Psychoanalytic Therapy*. New York: Ronald Press.
2. Bernard, V. W. (1965), Some principles of dynamic psychiatry in relation to poverty. *Amer. J. Psychiat.*, 122:254-267.
3. Boaz, W. D. (1965), Conference on Adolescent Medicine, University of Michigan.
4. Brill, N. Q., & Storrow, H. A. (1960), Social class and psychiatric treatment. *Arch. Gen. Psychiat.*, 3:340-344.
5. Burks, H. L., & Hoekstra, M. (1964), Psychiatric emergencies in children. *Amer. J. Orthopsychiat.*, 34:134-137.
6. Gould, R. E. (1965), Suicide problems in children and adolescents. *Amer. J. Psychother.*, 19:228-246.
7. Hollingshead, A. B., & Redlich, F. C. (1958), *Social Class and Mental Illness*. New York: Wiley.
8. Jacobson, G. F., Wilner, D. M., Morley, W. E., Schneider, S., Strickler, M., & Sommer, G. S. (1965), The scope and practice of an early access brief treatment psychiatric center. *Amer. J. Psychiat.*, 121:1176-1182.
9. Mattsson, A., Hawkins, J. W., & Seese, L. R. (1967), Child psychiatric emergencies. *Arch. Gen. Psychiat.*, 17:584-592.
10. Natterson, J., & Grotjahn, M. (1965), Responsive action in psychotherapy. *Amer. J. Psychiat.*, 122:140-143.
11. Shaw, C. R., & Schelkun, R. F. (1965), Suicidal behavior in children. *Psychiatry*, 28:157-168.
12. Wolberg, L. (1965), Methodology in short-term therapy. *Amer. J. Psychiat.*, 122:135-140.

# 6. PLANNED SHORT-TERM TREATMENT, A NEW SERVICE TO ADOLESCENTS

## Elizabeth Kerns, M.S.

Despite the well-documented need for changes in agency delivery of services, little has been published on how these changes can be effected. For example, how does the staff of a traditional casework agency shift its emphasis from long-term therapy to short-term treatment? (It is assumed that such a change is relevant to some of the needs of the agency's clientele and to the community's comprehensive plan for welfare services.) For a staff to evolve a planned short-term treatment (PSTT) approach encompasses much more than consideration of the time element; it makes new emotional and technical demands on the workers. Emotionally, each worker must feel secure and must be sufficiently flexible to examine his current practice and then be prepared to deal with problems which may arise from this examination. Technically, the worker is required to reconsider the philosophy of casework, develop more refined skills in the formulation of diagnostic assessments and treatment plans, reorganize the range of treatment procedures, and terminate at the time mutually agreed upon in initial contacts with clients. Within the framework of these factors, this article describes the experience of the staff of Youth Service of

Reprinted from *Social Casework,* 1970, **51,** 340-346, by permission of the publisher and the author. Miss Kerns is Chief Social Work Supervisor at Cuyahoga County Welfare Department Social Services, Cleveland, Ohio.

Cleveland in learning to deliver services to adolescents through planned short-term treatment.

Youth Service, a voluntary casework agency for over fifty years, offers counseling to young people between the ages of twelve and twenty-one years and their parents living in the metropolitan Cleveland area. It has a small staff of seventeen experienced professional social workers who have specialized skills in treating adolescents. During 1968, 1,315 teenagers were served in individual and group counseling. With the community's growing social awareness—in part a reflection of new federal programs—came an increasing demand for services and a volume of applications which traditional treatment methods could not meet in the foreseeable future. This gap between available services and adolescents' needs for services prompted the agency to hold a one-day meeting to review in depth specific areas of work; to appraise the community resources, the needs of adolescents, and the role of Youth Service within this existing structure; and to decide on the options and priorities for innovation and change. First priority was given to learning short-term treatment as a method of choice to provide more service without sacrificing the quality of treatment.

The formal learning process began with a series of weekly staff development seminars under the leadership of Harry Rubinstein, who was casework director until February 1969. These sessions were used initially for discussion of readings from a selected bibliography and of seminars with Lydia Rapaport on crisis intervention. Because few of the referrals to Youth Service met the criteria of a crisis as defined in the literature, planned short-term treatment was eventually chosen because it seemed applicable to a broader range of case situations. (Although the techniques for planned short-term treatment and crisis intervention are not mutually exclusive, there are differences in the theoretical concepts.)

## Planned short-term treatment

The name *planned short-term treatment* (PSTT) is borrowed from Howard and Libbie Parad.[1] PSTT makes the structured use of time an important treatment variable. In PSTT, the client and worker must reach a mutual agreement to work together toward a specific goal within a given number of sessions. (This agreement constitutes a contract.) During the last sessions, the participants in the contract must evaluate what has been accomplished in relation to the goal. They then decide to terminate or to continue for an additional number of sessions with the same goal or a new goal. (This decision is referred to as renegotiation of the contract.) The terms *contract* and *renegotiation* may or may not be used directly with the clients, but the process and expectations of PSTT must be considered carefully because the client's full understanding and participation are essential.

The seminars on PSTT raised many philosophical and technical questions of which few can be answered fully after only a year of practice. These early questions included the following: (1) How long is short-term treatment? (2) Is it applicable to adolescents? (3) What does time mean to teenagers and adults? (4) Is the time limit perceived as another deprivation? (5) Does the time limit serve as a protection for the adolescent in his struggle for independence, or is it used as a defense maneuver against coming to grips with the problem? (6) What kinds of case situations are appropriate to PSTT? (7) What happens when confrontations are made early in the contact? (8) Is it necessary first to establish a "good working relationship"? (9) How does the worker enable teenagers—especially the younger, inarticulate ones—to focus on a specific problem? (10) Can good service be given when the goal is so limited and many other problems still exist? (11) Does termination present a problem for the worker in letting go and in not being certain that the treatment will be effective?

Reading, discussing, and theorizing can go only so far; sooner or later action must follow, and this action can be very difficult when it involves major changes. Nevertheless, the staff was encouraged to begin trying the PSTT approach. The cases were fully recorded and, in subsequent seminars, reviewed session by session as the treatment was taking place. One of the difficulties was to refrain from simply referring to the content of the case but instead to focus on the differences inherent in the PSTT process. The following condensed case situations and corresponding discussions demonstrate the action of PSTT.

## An adolescent boy's problems

Mrs. B, a 62-year-old black mother of eight, referred her youngest child, 16-year-old David for help. According to the mother, David had displayed no serious problems until the age of 15. The father had died when David was five, and later David suffered a prolonged grief reaction, becoming socially withdrawn, although he was quiet and conforming at home. At the age of 15, he grew rapidly, began to break the close tie to his mother, and became a rebellious adolescent. Since then he had become increasingly aggressive and rebellious at home. He had been in a series of fights at school and his performance deteriorated alarmingly. The mother had gone to juvenile court for help and was referred to Youth Service. David refused to come, but several months later asked that his mother contact the agency.

In the first appointment, the worker was struck by David's high degree of anxiety as manifested by marked head and shoulder tics. David denied any problems; he had come because his mother nagged him. The worker tried to help him understand the differences between Youth Service and juvenile court and between a psychiatrist and a social worker. David relaxed enough to tell that when he had entered high school, he had been taunted by other boys and fights had resulted. Art was his major interest, and he had been removed from class because of his fighting. Could the worker help him get into art class? Also, he needed a job and wanted to get into weight lifting. He went on to tell of living in a bad neighborhood and having to cope with "things you [white worker] never experienced." David thought that one more interview should take care of his problems, but he was willing to take part in five sessions with the major goal of getting into an art class.

In spite of David's obvious, deep-seated problems, the worker chose PSTT, with admission to art class as the major goal because it was a goal David could accept. This frightened boy felt overwhelmed by his environment and was struggling to gain some control over his situation. The activities he desired were attempts at constructive sublimation; the worker saw this as ego strength. The five sessions would allow an opportunity to give specific help regarding the art class and, it was hoped, an experience in mastery and self-respect. There were actually seven interviews over a three-month period. In the first five appointments there were two major themes, the first of which was being admitted into an art program. David saw himself quite powerless in this process and expected the worker to do it all for him.

The worker used this attitude to express understanding of David's feelings about himself and to encourage him to do more for himself. This led to discussion of the establishment, black-white relationships, and power.

The second theme was life in the inner city—the immense danger and the possibility of getting killed at any time. This discussion was motivated partly by bravado and partly by an effort to impress the worker with his knowledge of life, but primarily David conveyed how overwhelmed he felt by the impossibility of doing well and surviving in his environment. The worker recognized the realities but pointed out David's improved and better behavior as an indication that he could manage and succeed. (No effort was made to relate his pessimism to the death of his father.) There was marked decrease in the anxiety symptoms during interviews.

Through the joint efforts of David and the worker, he did enter an art program at a settlement house. With difficulty, arrangements were made with a black school counselor for David to get back into the art program at school. This action necessitated the worker's active intervention; otherwise David would have been lost in the negativism of the inner-city school.

A sixth appointment was agreed upon, pending the school's making final arrangements for David's reentering art class. David arrived for the appointment extremely distraught and angry. The school counselor had "flaked" him off. Despite earlier planning, the counselor said it was not his responsibility, and David should see the art teacher himself. The counselor had acted as if he did not recognize David or had ever heard of him. David was extremely angry; however, he left the office and managed to get through the whole day without getting into trouble in spite of his anger and hurt. The worker gave David a great deal of support for his managing his anger but raised the question about his giving up on himself and not seeing the teacher. The boy insisted that he "didn't have a chance." The worker was aware of the reality factors in this perception and agreed to see the art teacher. A school visit revealed the confusion and lack of concern in the school. Insistence upon a complete check of David's current progress showed marked improvement, and the art teacher was then willing to readmit him.

David was quite relaxed in his last appointment and told of plans to run for the student council. He stated that he was the most articulate boy in his class and that "some things needed to be changed" at school. Almost incidentally, David expressed his satisfaction with art class. He minimized the worker's role, saying he probably could have done it himself but he was "lazy." In his disparagement of the worker, David seemed to be struggling for the worker's recognition of and respect for him as an equal. The worker indicated that in part David needed the help of an adult, but that he had done most of it himself, as his better grades and better control had gained him readmission to art class. David started a discussion of black nationalists, black pride, and so forth. He hoped that someday no one would feel superior to anyone else on the basis of race. He himself was feeling equal to others. David seemed to be feeling much better about himself. He and the worker discussed future contacts. David felt he could go on his own; if he needed the worker, he could always call. The worker fully supported this attitude.

## Treatment techniques

This case shows that the whole treatment in PSTT can take place in the time span approximating the study period of a more traditional, long-term approach. The worker cannot use the beginning sessions primarily for the purpose of evaluation and development of a relationship. The nature of the client-worker relationship differs in PSTT from long-term treatment in that the aim is *not* to build a therapeutically dependent relationship with the resulting transference reactions becoming a focal point of treatment. In PSTT the dependency is not heightened, but rather the relationship takes advantage of the client's potential for independent problem solving. (It is recognized however that in any relationship, transference and counter-transference reactions do occur.) The worker in the David B case used the PSTT relationship to provide a corrective experience—namely, that some adults can be trusted to help in gaining self-mastery. At this time in his development, David could not have tolerated the dependent kind of relationship required for long-term therapy involving personality restructuring; but PSTT did provide an experience in constructive problem solving that he could apply to other areas, such as the student council.

In the very first appointment, the worker must be clear about and accept the problem for which the client is both concretely and preconsciously seeking his help. Starting at the concrete level follows the social work maxim of "starting where the client is"; with David, it was getting into an art class. At a preconscious level, David seemed to be asking for help with conflicts of dependency, which were handled by the worker within the context of the concrete request. At the same time, the worker must assess the problem in relation to the the client's personality, current social situation, and past life experiences. The client and worker mutually must agree on a stated goal to be worked upon within a specific time; the more clearly the goal is delineated, the easier it becomes to evaluate goal-directed behavior. The worker, as the helping person, must then formulate a plan by which the goal may be accomplished and that enables the client to complete the tasks that will solve the problem. In order to remain oriented toward a goal, the worker must closely observe the course of treatment session by session.

The treatment techniques in PSTT are not really new, but they must be used differently from the way they are used in long-term treatment. The all-important sense of timing is crucial to meeting the goal. A major difference lies in the fact that the worker confronts the client early in the contact with behavior patterns that interfere with his problem solving. In long-term treatment, the worker is much less active and attempts to develop the client's self-awareness so that he can make these connections for himself. Consequently, in PSTT, the worker places more emphasis on what Florence Hollis referred to as "procedures of direct influence" and "reflective discussion of the person-situation configuration" and less emphasis on sustaining and encouraging "ventilation" procedures that promote the more dependent relationship necessary for accomplishing the personality-restructuring goals of long-term therapy.[2] Collateral contacts in PSTT must be made quickly so that they can be incorporated into the treatment plan. In the David B case, the worker facilitated planning through contacts at school and at a settlement house.

Termination of the treatment process is in a sense begun in the first interview when the contract is made for a specific number of sessions. The important element of short-term treatment is not so much the length of time but the planned nature of the process. There is no magical set number of sessions, although sometimes it is helpful to connect termination with some significant event, such as the end of a grading period for a school problem.

Many adolescents can present their own plans for the number of sessions; in other cases, the worker must suggest a plan. In the David B case, the time limit was a compromise decision between the client and worker.

After termination, the agency administration must support PSTT with a "revolving door policy" that allows for flexible intake and prompt service as they are needed by clients returning for help with another problem. There are two positions on casework follow-up: some workers think such a contact promotes positive transference to the agency on the part of the clients, lessens their feelings of rejection, and facilitates their returning if further service is needed; others say that the follow-up is an indication of the worker's lack of confidence in his own work and in the client's ability to judge when he needs to return. Both ways have been tried, and the use of follow-up is left to the discretion of the worker.

## A teen-aged girl's difficulties at school

A second case illustrates PSTT with a younger adolescent—a girl whose presenting problem is more vague and whose motivation for help is limited. The case of Martha demonstrates the PSTT process of diagnosis, treatment, and termination. A contract for eight appointments was established with the goal of helping Martha to do better at school and to try to control her laughing, talking, and losing her temper. Follow-up contact with the school indicated that there was considerable improvement, and the goal was reached.

> Martha Ellen, a 14-year-old girl, lived in the inner city with three siblings and her mother. They were supported by public assistance and social security payments. Martha was referred to Youth Service by the assistant principal at a junior high school where Martha had begun the seventh grade a few months earlier. In school, she was disruptive and unable to control talking and giggling; she refused to accept discipline from teachers. She had average ability and performed well academically. Martha and her mother initially agreed to the referral because of fears that juvenile court and placement might otherwise be involved.
>
> PSTT was chosen for this case because neither the girl nor her mother seemed to feel there was a problem they

could not talk about easily, and they showed little interest in counseling. At the worker's suggestion, a contract was made for eight appointments, with the goal of helping Martha to do better at school and to try to control her behavior in school. In the course of treatment, Martha was late for two appointments and missed one; the mother was seen three times.

Martha did not begin to concentrate on the problem until the fifth session, at which time she talked of her inability to control laughter when the boys made comments about the teachers. In the next session, she demonstrated the problem in the interview situation: she came with a friend, Jean, and they were laughing and out of control in the waiting room. In a discussion between the worker and Martha about what made Jean giggle, the elements of sexual excitement and embarrassment became more evident. Martha then wanted to invite Jean to the last two sessions to see if she could help in clarifying the problem.

For the seventh appointment, Martha and Jean came about 15 minutes late and were laughing as they arrived. At first it was difficult for them to overcome their giggling. The worker welcomed Jean and explained that she and Martha were working on the problem of giggling in school. Jean acknowledged that she was familiar with this problem, had some difficulties herself, but that she could usually stop herself, especially after a teacher called her mother. When the worker questioned them about the laughing, both girls readily said that the boys made them laugh by using words that had obvious sexual connotations. The worker tried to elicit the meaning of the words and the girls' feelings about them. Martha claimed she knew but could not explain what they meant because they were too nasty. Eventually Martha was able to say that the words meant "when a man and woman get together."

After several attempts to make the girls talk more freely, the worker was convinced of their inadequate sex information. The worker explained that "getting together" was called intercourse or sex relations, and she suggested that perhaps they knew other names for it. There was an almost breathless silence as the worker described the sex act and pointed out that intercourse was the way to have children, but it was also the way for a man and woman to show their love and appreciation for each other. At first there was absolute silence, but a look of relief on both girls' faces. They were very quiet now, and Martha finally asked, "Is that all?" The worker could not learn more about her thoughts. Both girls then started talking about the movies at school on sex education which hinted that somehow the man and woman got together. Mothers always gave a lot of prohibitions. Martha's mother said to "keep your dress down and don't act all trampy." Jean's mother warned her not to make the mistake of having different children by different men. This raised questions about pregnancies out of wedlock and whether one could have sex relations without being in love. At the end of this session, Martha asked Jean to come back for the next week.

By helping them understand some of the facts, the worker relieved some of the anxiety and enabled Martha to better control the giggling. In the last session, despite Martha's earlier intention to leave at the end of eight sessions, she was ambivalent about termination. However, there was nothing specific she wanted to work on further. By identifying her ambivalence, Martha was then free to terminate with the understanding that she could come back if other problems arose. The focus with the mother was to help her understand Martha's sexual curiosity and preoccupation with growing up and to help the mother give needed social and sex education information appropriate for a 14-year old.

## 'Growing pains' of staff and agency in PSTT

This kind of pioneering presented exciting challenges, but the staff and agency experienced "growing pains" in the actual carrying out of PSTT. Some workers were able to assimilate the PSTT approach into their practice more easily than were others. The ease of assimilation seemed related especially to the following factors: the worker's casework philosophy, his willingness to assume a directive role, his view of the meaning of time, his ability to work well under pressure, and his general adaptability.

Although there are reports of studies that show encouraging results with short-term treatment, the staff and agency experienced some anxiety about whether "experimenting" with adolescent clients and their families was justified. Another big question concerned the values of and attitudes toward the psychoanalytic model of long-term treatment, which is often seen as the foremost type in the "hierarchy of therapies." Was PSTT a second-best sort of treatment or was it really the casework treatment of choice for many clients? It was often difficult for the worker to accept for the focus of treatment the limits of what the client considered to be his problem. Much self-discipline was required to remain focused on the problem as circumscribed by the goal. This difficulty, coupled with the workers' concerns that improvement through PSTT was a "flight into health" rather than a real working through of the problem, made them reluctant to terminate. Thus workers frequently neglected to evaluate the treatment process with clients prior to the final session. Some workers whose practice had always been very goal oriented found it difficult to subject their mode of treatment to a time limit. The support of the total staff and agency administration was of prime importance in helping the individual worker with his own difficulties in learning PSTT.

After several months of experience with PSTT, the full recording had produced material too voluminous for study purposes. A mimeographed form, to be filled in by the worker after each session, was advised to take the place of the usual agency record. This new record form began with a fact sheet that included information about the intake, the PSTT design and rationale, the renegotiations, and the termination. Under the heading of *Presenting Problems* was the problem for which the adolescent and his parents requested help as well as the worker's evaluation of the problem in relation to the client's personality structure, current social situation, and past life experiences. After this, the mutually set goal for the PSTT contract and changes in the goals at renegotiation points were stated. Then the worker outlined his plan for accomplishing the goal. A description of the course of treatment was included next and the content of each treatment session was related to four questions: (1) What use of the time factor was made in this session? (2) What clarification did the worker make in this session of problem, goal, or dynamics; confrontations; or connections? (3) What was the client's reaction to the worker's clarification? (4) What evidence of goal-directed behavior did the client show in this session? Finally, the termination process was reviewed by answering the following questions: What goals were reached? How, in the opinion of the adolescent, the parents, and the worker, was the treatment plan effective or ineffective? The client's and worker's reactions to termination were also recorded. Most of the staff thought that this form of recording helped make the learning of PSTT a more conscious process.

## Conclusion

During the first year of learning PSTT, approximately 10 percent of the case situations at Youth Service were handled by this method. The staff planned to continue the intensive study of PSTT with the goal of using it for at least half of the cases, so that in the future the long-term case might be the exception.

Although many questions still remain unanswered, some of the early fears about PSTT proved to be unfounded. The PSTT approach is helpful with adolescents, who, while they are forming their own identity, are already overly concerned about whether they are normal. Referral to an agency often confirms their worst fears about themselves; the PSTT approach mitigates some of these fears by setting a time limit. This seems to tell the teenager that he is not so badly off, and frees him to work on his problem. The planned time limit forces workers to use their diagnostic acumen in assessing clients and their problems and to formulate appropriate plans for treatment, all within the first session. Workers must make full use of every contact and deal directly and immediately with the material presented by clients. This kind of intensive approach is taxing for workers, but it also defines more realistically what help the agency and worker can offer.

Actual practice has revealed that the appropriateness of a case situation for PSTT and the degree of success in meeting the goal are not determined by the problem or psychiatric diagnosis but rather by (1) the kind of goal for which the client and worker are willing to strive; (2) the positive, intrapsychic, and external factors in the adolescent's and family's life situation which can be utilized in problem solving; and (3) the skill and confidence of the worker. In summary, this was the Youth Service staff's initial learning experience with planned short-term treatment—a practice problem concerning other agencies too—in an attempt to find a new way of delivering services.

# REFERENCES

1. Howard J. Parad and Libbie G. Parad, A Study of Crisis-Oriented Planned Short-Term Treatment: Parts I and II, *Social Casework,* 49:346-55 (June 1968) and 49:418-26 (July 1968).

2. Florence Hollis, The Sustaining Process, Direct Influence, and Ventilation, *Casework: A Psychosocial Therapy* (New York: Random House, 1964), pp. 83-116.

# Preventive Intervention in Infancy and Early Childhood

# 7. TEMPERAMENT AND BEHAVIOR DISORDERS IN CHILDREN

Alexander Thomas, M.D.
Stella Chess, M.D.
Herbert G. Birch, M.D., Ph.D.

In the light of our arguments in the last chapter, it is clearly necessary for the clinician systematically to define and evaluate all etiological possibilities before making a diagnosis and formulating a treatment plan. The need to give as much attention to temperamental factors as to environmental and psychodynamic influences in diagnosis requires special emphasis because of the prevalent tendency to ignore the former and attend exclusively to the latter. A child who stands at the periphery of the group in nursery school may be anxious and insecure, but he may also be expressing his normal temperamental tendency to warm up slowly. An infant with irregular sleep cycles who cries loudly at night may possibly be responding to a hostile, rejecting mother, but he may also be expressing temperamental irregularity. A six-year-old who explodes with anger at his teacher's commands may be aggressive and oppositional, but he may also be showing the frustration reactions typical of a very persistent child when he is asked to terminate an activity in which he is deeply absorbed. A mother's guilt and anxiety may

Reprinted by permission of the New York University Press and the authors from *Temperament and Behavior Disorders in Children,* Chapter 18, pp. 191-203. © 1968 by New York University. Dr. Thomas is Professor of Psychiatry, New York University Medical Center, New York, New York, where Dr. Chess is Professor of Child Psychiatry. Dr. Birch is Professor of Pediatrics, Albert Einstein College of Medicine, New York, New York.

be the result of a deep-seated neurosis, but they may also be the result of her problems and confusion in handling an infant with a temperamental pattern that characterizes a very difficult child.

## OBTAINING DATA ON TEMPERAMENT IN CLINICAL PRACTICE

As indicated in the above examples, an accurate diagnostic judgment requires that data on the child's temperamental characteristics be gathered with the same care and regard for detail that is considered essential for the evaluation of parental attitudes and practices, family relationships, and sociocultural influences. Naturally, the clinician does not have anterospectively gathered behavioral descriptions of a child's developmental course available to him. But neither does he have available such anterospective data on intra- and extrafamilial environmental influences. With all information gathered retrospectively, whether it be on temperament, the attainment of developmental landmarks, the medical history, the patterns of parental functioning, or special environmental events, the clinician must assess the accuracy completeness, and pertinence of the data reported to him. In the author's experience, the collection of behavioral data from which evaluations of temperament can be made has presented no greater difficulties than gathering information on other aspects of the clinical history. Some informants are able to give detailed, factual, and precise descriptions of their children's past and present behavior. Others give vague, general, and subjective reports. In all cases, it is desirable to confirm the accuracy of the data by directly observing the child and, wherever possible, by obtaining information from multiple sources. A number of items in the basic clinical history,[1] such as the course of the child's development and the history of the presenting complaints, will often, in themselves, elicit clues as to significant issues relating to the child's temperament. For example, the parents of a 12-year-old boy reported that he was unable to study or do homework at an academic level appropriate to his intellectual capacity and his grade placement, and that he started many endeavors, such as music lessons or rock collections, but seemed to lose interest in them rapidly. The parents also complained that routines took an inordinate amount of time to be accomplished although the child was cheerful and apparently well-intentioned. He would start on his way to bed, but might be found 15 minutes later puttering with some game that attracted his attention, playing with a brother, or involved in a discussion with his grandmother. The composite of presenting problems in this case suggested that the temperamental quality of distractibility might be an important factor in causing the child's difficulties.

As another example, the parents of a nine-year-old girl reported that she found it difficult to undertake new endeavors and to join new groups of children her own age, and she tended to avoid new situations whenever she could. This presenting complaint suggested the possibility that a temperamentally based tendency to make initial withdrawal reactions to new experiences might be relevant to the reported behavioral difficulty.

Following the taking of a basic clinical history, systematic inquiry can be made into the child's temperamental characteristics during infancy, keeping in mind the necessity to investigate similarly other possible causes for the problem behaviors. The inquiry can be started with the general question, "After you brought the baby home from the hospital and in the first few weeks and months of his life, what was he like?"

First answers to such questions are usually very general ones: "He was wonderful"; "He cried day and night"; "He was a bundle of nerves"; "He was a joy."

The next question is still open-ended: "Would you give me some details that will describe what you mean?"

The replies to this second general question often include useful descriptions of behaviors from which judgments of temperament may be made. Further information requires specific inquiry, which is most economically pursued by taking up areas of behavior relevant to defining each of the temperamental attributes one at a time. The questions asked should be directed at obtaining a number of descriptive behavioral items from which the interviewer can then make an estimate of the child's temperamental characteristics. A list of questions appropriate to each of the nine categories can be suggested at this point.

### Activity Level

How much did your baby move around? Did he move around a lot; was he very quiet, or somewhere in between? If you put him to bed for a nap and it took him ten or fifteen minutes to fall asleep, would you have to go in to rearrange the covers, or would he be lying so quietly that you knew they would be in their proper place and not disarranged? If you were changing his diaper and discovered that you had left the powder just out of reach, could you safely dash over to get it and come right back without worrying that he would flip over the surface and fall? Did you have trouble changing his diaper, pulling his shirt over his head, or putting on any other of his clothing because he wiggled about, or could you count on his lying quietly to be dressed?

### Rhythmicity

How did you arrange the baby's feedings? Could you tell by the time he was six weeks (two months, three months) old about when during the day he would be hungry, sleepy, or wake up? Could you count on this happening about the same time every day, or did the baby vary from day to day? If he varied, how marked was it? About when during the day did he have his bowel movements (time and number), and was this routine variable or predictable?

Parents can generally recall such events. They will say, "He was regular as clockwork"; "I could never figure out when to start a long job because one day he would have a long nap and the next day he wouldn't sleep more than fifteen minutes"; or, "I used to try to take him out for his airing after I cleaned him from his bowel movement, but I never could figure it right because his time changed every day."

## Adaptability

How would you describe the way the child responded to changed circumstances? For example, when he was shifted from a bathinette to a bathtub, if he didn't take to the change immediately, could you count on his getting used to it quickly or did it take a long time? (Parents should be asked to define what they mean by "quickly" and what they mean by "a long time" in terms of days or weeks.) If his first reaction to a new person was a negative one, how long did it take the child to become familiar with the person? If he didn't like a new food the first time it was offered, could you count on the child's getting to like it and most other new foods sooner or later? If so, how long would it take if the new food was offered to him daily or several times a week?

## Approach-Withdrawal

How did the baby behave with new events, such as when he was given his first tub bath, offered new foods, or taken care of by a new person for the first time? Did he fuss, did he do nothing, or did he seem to like it? Were there any changes during his infancy that you remember, such as a shift to a new bed, a visit to a new place, or a permanent move? Describe the child's initial behavior at these times.

## Threshold Level

How would you estimate the baby's sensitivity to noises, to heat and cold, to things he saw and tasted, and to textures of clothing? Did he seem to be very aware of or unresponsive to these things? For example, did you have to tiptoe about when the baby was sleeping lest he be awakened? If he heard a faint noise while awake, would he tend to notice the sound by looking toward it? Did bright lights or bright sunshine make him blink or cry? Did the baby's behavior seem to show that he noticed the difference when a familiar person wore glasses or a new hair style for the first time in his presence? If he didn't like a new food and an old food that he liked very much was put with it on the spoon, would the baby still notice the taste of the new one and reject it? Did you have to be careful about clothing you put on him because some textures were too rough? If so, describe the kinds of things he disliked.

## Intensity of Reaction

How did you know when the baby was hungry? Did he squeak, did he roar, or were his sounds somewhere in between? How could you tell that he didn't like a food? Did he just quietly turn his head away from the spoon or did he start crying loudly? If you held his hand to cut his fingernails and he didn't like it, did he fuss a little or a lot? If he liked something, did he usually smile and coo or did he laugh loudly? In general, would you say he let his pleasure or displeasure be known loudly or softly?

## Quality of Mood

How could you tell when the baby liked something or disliked something? (After a description of the infant's behavior in these respects is obtained, the parents should be asked if he was more often contented or more often discontented, and on what basis they made this judgment.)

## Distractibility

If the child were in the midst of sucking on the bottle or breast, would he stop what he was doing if he heard a sound or if another person came by, or would he continue sucking? If he were hungry and fussing or crying while the bottle was being warmed, could you divert him easily and stop his crying by holding him or giving him a plaything? If he were playing, for example, gazing at his fingers or using a rattle, would other sights and sounds get his attention very quickly or very slowly?

### Persistence and Attention Span

Would you say that the baby usually stuck with something he was doing for a long time or only momentarily? For example, describe the longest time he remained engrossed in an activity all by himself. How old was he and what was he doing? (Examples might be playing with the cradle gym or watching a mobile.) If he reached for something, say a toy in the bathtub, and couldn't get it easily, would he keep after it or give up very quickly?

After completing the inventory of the child's temperamental characteristics in infancy, the next step is to identify those attributes that appear extreme in their manifestations and/or those that seem clearly related to the child's current pattern of deviant behavior. This is followed by an inquiry into the characteristics of these temperamental attributes at succeeding age-stage periods of development. Thus, if the history of the infancy period suggests a pattern of marked distractibility, it would be desirable to gather data on behavior related to distractibility at succeeding age periods and in varied life situations, such as play, school, homework, etc. Similarly, if the presenting complaints indicate that the child currently finds it difficult to undertake new endeavors or to join new groups of age-mates, and if the early temperamental history suggests a characteristic pattern of initial withdrawal coupled with slow adaptation, it would be important to obtain descriptions of the child's patterns of initial responses to situations and demands that arose at different points in his developmental course.

The final step in the assessment of the child's temperament is the evaluation of his current temperamental characteristics. The behavioral information obtained for current functioning is usually more valid than that obtained for behavioral patterns in the past, since the problems of forgetting and retrospective distortion are minimized. The inquiry into current behavior will attempt to cover all temperamental categories, but should concentrate on those which appear most pertinent to the presenting symptoms.

Activity level may be estimated from a child's behavior preferences. Would he rather sit quietly for a long time engrossed in some task, or does he prefer to seek out opportunities for active physical play? How well does he fare in routines that require sitting still for extended periods of time? For example, can he sit through an entire meal without seeking an opportunity to move about? Must a long train or automobile ride be broken up by frequent stops because of his restlessness?

Rhythmicity can be explored through questions about the child's habits and their regularity. For instance, does he get sleepy at regular and predictable times? Does he have any characteristic routines relating to hunger, such as taking a snack immediately after school or during the evening? Are his bowel movements regular?

Adaptability can be identified through a consideration of the way the child reacts to changes in environment. Does he adjust easily and fit quickly into changed family patterns? Is he willing to go along with other children's preferences, or does he always insist on pursuing only his own interests?

Approach/withdrawal, or the youngster's pattern of response to new events or new people, can be explored in many ways. Questions can be directed at the nature of his reaction to new clothing, new neighborhood children, a new school, and a new teacher. What is his attitude when a family excursion is being planned? Will he try new foods or new activities easily or not?

Threshold level is more difficult to explore in an older child than in a young one. However, it is sometimes possible to obtain information on unusual features of threshold, such as hypersensitivity to noise, to visual stimuli, or to rough clothing, or remarkable unresponsiveness to such stimuli.

The intensity of reactions can be ascertained by finding out how the child displays disappointment or pleasure. If something pleasant happens does he tend to be mildly enthusiastic, average in his expression of joy, or ecstatic? When he is unhappy, does he fuss quietly or bellow with rage or distress?

Quality of mood can usually be estimated by parental descriptions of their offspring's overall expressions of mood. Is he predominantly happy and contented, or is he a frequent complainer and more often unhappy than not?

Distractibility, even when not a presenting problem, will declare itself in the parent's descriptions of ordinary routines. Does the child start off to do something and then often get sidetracked by something his brother is doing, by his coin collection, or by any number of several circumstances that catch his eye or his ear? Or, on the contrary, once he is engaged in an activity is he impervious to what is going on around him?

Data on persistence and attention span are usually easier to obtain for the older child than for the infant. The degree of persistence in the face of difficulty can be ascertained with regard to games, puzzles, athletic activities, such as learning to ride a bicycle, and school work. Similarly, after the initial difficulty in mastering these activities has been overcome, the length of the child's attention span for and concentration on these same kinds of activities can be ascertained.

The delineation of the child's temperamental characteristics at different age periods may indicate that changes have occurred over time. There are normal variabilities of temperament, and the fate of any temperamental attribute is dependent upon a host of influences. The issue of stability and instability of temperament is too broad an issue to be considered here and is the main burden of a monograph now in preparation.

Temperamental characteristics may also appear to change because of the influence of the process of socialization in blurring the individual behavioral style evident in new situations and experiences. In other words, routine patternings of response, once they are fabricated as an adaptation to a cultural norm, may serve to minimize individual uniqueness. For example, the first attempt at toilet training will cause one child to scream and struggle violently, another to fuss mildly while he sits on the seat for only a few minutes, and a third child to smile and play while sitting on the seat for many minutes. A year later, when all three children are fully trained, their behavior on the toilet seat may be very similar or show only slight differences as compared to the marked in-

dividuality of response to the initial toileting demand.
Similar blurring of initial differences in behavioral responses as adaptation to the social norm develops may occur with a variety of other experiences, such as entry into
nursery school, the beginning of formal learning,
changes in the family group, new living quarters, etc.
Therefore, when the behavioral history suggests an apparent change in a child's temperament over time, the
data should be scrutinized to determine whether the
change is evident or disappears when the responses to
new situations at the different age periods are compared.

Fragmentary impressions also lead us to speculate
that special factors operating at a specific point in time
may, in some instances, produce significant alterations
of temperamental attributes. Such a factor might be organic, such as an episode of encephalitis, or psychological, such as a series of traumatic environmental events
or a succession of exceptionally favorable life experiences. These speculations require further testing before
they can be uncritically accepted.

In many instances, additional data on temperamental
organization can be obtained by querying teachers or
other adults familiar with the child's behavior. For such
inquiry, the history-taking protocol for the parents can
be utilized if it is appropriately modified to permit a focus
on the areas of the child's functioning with which the
adult is acquainted. Observation of the child's behavior
during a clinical play interview or in the course of psychological testing can also supply useful information on
activity level, approach-withdrawal, intensity of reactions, quality of mood, distractibility, and persistence
and attention span. Temperamental characterizations
that require information on the child's behavior over
time, namely, rhythmicity and adaptibility, cannot be
made from such single observations over a short time
span, and the nature of the clinical observation and testing situations is such that behaviors referable to the sensory threshold characteristic of the child are usually not
observable.

## PARENT GUIDANCE

Once the child's temperamental characteristics have been defined and other significant organismic and environmental influences have been delineated by appropriate clinical and testing techniques, it becomes possible to formulate the dynamics of the child-environment interaction that have led to the behavioral disturbance.

After a pathogenic interaction has been identified, a treatment plan aimed at modifying this process and reducing maladaptation, dissonance, and stress can be formulated for the individual child. Depending upon the identification of the specific areas requiring change, the appropriate treatment procedures may involve shifts in intra- and extrafamilial environmental influences, amelioration of a handicap, such as by perceptual training or remedial education (speech, reading, arithmetic, etc.) psychotherapy, pharmacotherapy, hospitalization, or some combination of therapeutic modalities.

The therapeutic procedure of environmental change through parent guidance merits special discussion at this point because of its usefulness in clinical practice. Parent guidance, as we have used it, involved first the identification of those elements of parental behavior and overtly expressed attitudes that appear to exert a deleterious influence on the child's development. This is followed by the formulation of a program of altered parental functioning which, by modifying the interactive pattern between parent and child, may lead to an amelioration or disappearance of the child's behavioral disturbance. No attempt is made to define or change any hypothetical underlying conflicts, anxieties, or defenses in the parent that may be presumed to be the cause of the noxious behavior or overtly expressed attitudes. The rational of the guidance program is explained to the parents, and special attention is given to the description of the child's temperamental attributes and other pertinent characteristics (superior or subnormal intellectual level, special perceptual or cognitive difficulties, etc.) and to the definition of those parental behaviors which are creating excessive stress for the child. Specific suggestions and advice for changing these behaviors are then offered, with each suggestion illustrated by reference to a number of specific incidents in the child's life. Thus, a discussion with the parents of a difficult child might first define the intrinsic nature of the child's intense negative reactions to the new and his subsequent slow adaptability. The discussion would distinguish these reactions from "willful" defiance or anxiety, then identify those parental behaviors that are aggravating and distorting the child's negative responses and slowness of adaptation to the new, and outline a regime of specific changes in these behaviors that should aid, rather than hinder, the child's adaptive course. Similarly, correction would be made of the parental conception that the low activity level of their child indicates inferior intelligence, deliberate dawdling, or "laziness." The parents would then be advised to eliminate their attempts to force the child to perform at an activity level beyond his capacities.

Even with parents who are eager and able to carry through the program of behavioral change suggested to them, several follow-up discussions may be necessary before they can achieve full understanding and application of changed practices. Reviews of the parents' behavior in a number of specific incidents may also be required before they become adept at identifying the situations in the child's daily life in which they must modify their techniques of management. In other instances, parental misconceptions, confusions, defensiveness, anxiety, or guilt may impede their ability to understand the issues involved in the guidance program, and a greater number of discussions may be necessary to overcome these hindrances to their comprehension and implementation of the advice and suggestions offered. Finally, there are the parents whose own psychopathology is so severe that no substantial change in their behavior is possible through these guidance discussions. In these latter cases, other therapeutic approaches will be necessary, such as direct treatment of the child, psychotherapy for one or both parents, or treatment of both parent and child. Direct treatment of the child may in some cases be advisable concurrent with parent guidance, especially if there is a severe degree of psychopathology in the child.

The therapeutic procedure of parent guidance is based on our conviction that parental functioning with a child may be less than optimal for a number of different reasons. Ignorance, poor advice from professional or other sources, unrealistic goals and values, stereotyped concepts of what is normal or pathological behavior for a child, and difficulty in understanding the best approach to a child with a specific temperamental pattern—any of these factors may be responsible for unfavorable parental functioning and may be amenable to amelioration by parent guidance. Even in those cases where psychiatric disturbance in the parent is the prime cause of noxious parental influence on the child, parent guidance may sometimes result in modifying the unhealthy parental functioning significantly even when no basic change in the parent's personality structure is achieved. This approach to the evaluation and modification of the parent's influence on the child argues that the treatment of a child's behavioral disturbance requires the consideration of direct psychiatric treatment of the parent only if simpler measures have failed and there is substantial evidence that significant psychopathology actually exists in the parent. This formulation stands in some contrast to other current approaches in the field of child psychiatry in which the existence of a behavior problem in a child is considered *ipso facto* evidence of substantial psychopathology in the parent or the nuclear family unit. Typical of this view are statements such as those of Howells, that "it is not possible to separate the child's condition from that of his parents or other adult members of the family"[2] because "the parents of disturbed children are usually themselves also disturbed,"[3] and of Ackerman, that the primary patient, the child, must be viewed "as a symptomatic expression of family pathology," and not just as an "individual in distress."[4] Implicit in these formulations is the concept that effective treatment of a behaviorally disturbed child requires direct psychotherapy of the parents or family to deal with presumed pathology, direct treatment of the child to insulate him from the harmful influences of the parents, or both. Such a treatment program is usually long and expensive, resulting in severe limitations on the number of cases accepted for treatment by practitioners and clinics. Furthermore, the results of treatment procedures based on the equation of child pathology with parent or family pathology have not been impressive enough to justify the burdensome investment of time and money required of the family or community for each case.[5] Our finding that no one-to-one relationship exists between disturbance in the child and psychopathology in the parents suggests that the disappointing therapeutic results may be due, in part at least, to a faulty theoretical premise, which results in treating the wrong patient.

Parent guidance, by contrast, usually requires markedly fewer treatment sessions than does a regime of psychotherapy. As described in Chapter 16, the average number of guidance sessions per case was 2.3 for the successful cases and 2.7 for the failure group. The guidance procedure was considered markedly or moderately successful in approximately 50 per cent of the clinical cases. It may be argued that the special characteristics of the families participating in the longitudinal study and the influence of their long-term contact with the research staff personnel may have made them more amenable to a guidance program. However, the experience of one of the authors (S.C.) in applying a parent guidance approach to private and clinic child patients with a variety of psychiatric problems has been that an approximately equivalent percentage of success has been possible with parents of diverse socio-cultural backgrounds.* The number of sessions required has been greater than with the longitudinal study group, perhaps two to four times as many, but still markedly less than would have been required for any psychotherapeutic procedures.

We are not alone in suggesting that parental functioning can be modified in many cases without elaborate treatment procedures designed to alter basic personality

---

* This experience will be reported in detail in a publication now in preparation (S. Chess and A. Thomas, *Parent Guidance*).

characteristics. Thus, Anna Freud states that she "re-
fuse(s) to believe that mothers need to change their personalities before they can change the handling of their
child."[6] Similar positions are taken by Bibring[7] and Shirley.[8] However, their general assertions of the validity of
parent guidance as a therapeutic technique have not
been translated into systematic and specific procedures
applicable to a wide range of clinical problems. It is perhaps not an unreasonable inference that the development of a useful and comprehensive scheme for parent
guidance may require the systematic consideration of
the parent's practices and attitudes and the child's temperament within an interactionist framework. If such an
approach promises an effective and brief therapeutic
modality for perhaps 50 percent of children with behavior problems, its utilization would appear highly desirable.

## DIRECT TREATMENT
## OF PARENT OR CHILD

In those cases in which parent guidance is unsuccessful or only partially successful, direct psychotherapy of
the parent or child, or both, may be advisable or necessary. Even in such instances, a knowledge of the child's
temperamental characteristics may prove very useful in
the treatment regime. Thus, the therapist's task of delineating and bringing to a mother's awareness a con-
stellation of neurotic attitudes and goals may be expedi-
ted by a comparison of the patient's judgments and expectations of her child with the reality of child's temperament. The finding, for example, that a mother is anxious
or hostile because her daughter warms up slowly to new
social situations may provide the first clue to her neurotic needs for social success. Similarly, a father's refusal
to accept the fact that his high-activity and distractible
son can sit still and do homework only for short periods
may help to clarify his pathological standards of work
achievement. Furthermore, the substitution of healthy
for neurotic attitudes and goals may first be possible for

the parent in relationship to his child because of clear and strong motivation to be a good parent. Making the same change in other areas of the parent's life may then become easier.

For the older-child patient to know his own temperamental characteristics may be important in several ways. The therapeutic effort to develop a positive self-image in the youngster may sometimes require teaching the youngster to appraise his reactive tendencies correctly. This is especially true when certain of his temperamental patterns are different from the average of the group and therefore tend to be considered as abnormal and inferior by the child and his peers. Thus, it may be very valuable for him to learn that if his activity level is low, this does not mean he cannot with sufficient practice become a good ball-player; that if he is "shy" in new social situations because of initial withdrawal tendencies, this does not mean he has to be socially inept; or that if he is easily distracted from tasks, this does not mean he cannot become a reliable worker.

The youngster whose temperamental responses have created unfavorable responses in others or precipitated behavior detrimental to his own best interests can also be taught in the psychotherapeutic situation to direct and guide his behavior to eliminate or minimize such unfavorable consequences. For example, the youngster with intense negative reactions to the new can learn to approach such situations gradually and so minimize the negative reactions that may antagonize others. The high activity child can learn to pace himself with activities requiring him to sit still and give himself breaks for active motor play or exercise. The slow to warm up child can learn to wait patiently until his initial negative response disappears and to explain to others that he is shy at first but will get over it in time.

Naturally, the older the child, the more possible it is to give him such insight into his own characteristics and help him work out routines and approaches that will maximize the positive aspects of his temperamental attributes and minimize their unfavorable consequences.

## PREVENTION OF
## BEHAVIORAL DISTURBANCE

The prevention of behavioral disturbances in childhood covers a vast array of issues, including those genetic, biochemical, temperamental, neurological, perceptual, cognitive, and environmental factors that may influence the course of behavioral development. The child's temperament is only one of the many issues to be considered by professional workers concerned with the prevention of pathology in psychological development, though often an important one. As our findings have demonstrated, the degree to which parents, teachers, pediatricians, and others handle a youngster in a manner appropriate to his temperamental characteristics can significantly influence the course of his psychological development. The oft-repeated motto, "Treat your child as an individual," achieves substance to the extent that the individuality of a child is truly recognized and respected. The other frequently offered prescription of "tender loving care" often has great value in promoting a positive parent-child interaction, but does not obviate the importance of the parent's actual child-care practices being consonant with his child's temperamental qualities.

Finally, the recognition that a child's behavioral disturbance is not necessarily the direct result of maternal pathology should do much to prevent the deep feelings of guilt and inadequacy with which innumerable mothers have been unjustly burdened as a result of being held entirely responsible for their children's problems.[9] Mothers who are told authoritatively that child raising is a "task not easily achieved by the average mother in our culture"[10] are not likely to approach this responsibility with the relaxation and confidence that would be beneficial to both their own and their child's mental health. It is our conviction, however, that the difficulties of child raising can be significantly lightened by advocating an approach of which the average mother *is* capable—the recognition of her child's specific qualities of individuality, and the adoption of those child-care practices that are most appropriate to them.

# REFERENCES

1. Chess, S. *An Introduction to Child Psychiatry* (New York: Grune and Stratton, 1959).

2. Howells, J. G. *Modern Perspectives in Child Psychiatry* (London: Oliver & Boyd, 1965), p. 270.

3. *Ibid.,* p. 279.

4. Ackerman, N. *The Psychodynamics of Family Life* (New York: Basic Books, 1958), p. 107

5. Eisenberg, L. discussion of paper "Who Deserves Child Psychiatry" by A. J. Solnit, *Jour. Amer. Acad. Child Psychiat.,* 5:19 (1966).

6. Freud, A. "The Child Guidance Clinic as a Center of Prophylaxis and Enlightenment," *Recent Developments in Psychoanalytic Child Therapy* (New York: International Universities Press, 1960), p. 37.

7. Bibring, G. L. "Work with Physicians," *Recent Developments in Psychoanalytic Child Therapy* (New York: International Universities Press, 1960).

8. Shirley, H. F. *Pediatric Psychiatry* (Cambridge: Harvard University Press, 1963).

9. Bruch, H. "Parent Education, or the Illusion of Omnipotence," *Am. Jour. Orthopsychiat.,* 24:723 (1954).

10. Mahler, M. "Thoughts About Development and Individuation," *Psychoanalytic Study of the Child,* 18:307 (1963).

# 8. FOUR STUDIES OF CRISIS IN PARENTS OF PREMATURES

Gerald Caplan, M.D., D.P.M.,
Edward A. Mason, M.D., and
David M. Kaplan, M.S.S.W., Ph.D.

The concept of crisis has received increasing attention in mental health investigations because it offers hope for better understanding of the etiology and prevention of mental disorders. This article will review a series of crisis studies to illustrate the theoretical and methodological issues, and problems in crisis research. Some of these studies have been reported elsewhere, but this overview will show how they are interrelated and present their implications for further crisis research.

Our interest in acute crises derives from the assumption that these relatively short periods of psychological disequilibrium, which occur in everyone's life in response

Reprinted from *Community Mental Health Journal*, 1965, **1**, 149–161, by permission of the publisher and the authors. Dr. Caplan is Professor of Psychiatry and Director of the Laboratory of Community Psychiatry, Harvard Medical School, Boston, Massachusetts. Dr. Mason is Assistant Clinical Professor of Psychiatry, Laboratory of Community Psychiatry. Dr. Kaplan is Director of Psychiatric Social Service, Department of Psychiatry, University of Colorado Medical School, Denver, Colorado.

These researches were carried out during the years 1954-1962 at the Family Guidance Center, Harvard School of Public Health, and were supported in large part by the Commonwealth Fund and by the National Institute of Mental Health, grant MH-3442.

We acknowledge the assistance of the following for their part in the Family Guidance Center studies: Dr. Barbara Ayres, Dr. Lenin Baler, Dr. Norman Bell, Miss Mary Foster, Dr. Paul Hare, Dr. Louisa Howe, Miss Charlotte Owens, Mr. Howard Parad, Dr. Thomas Plaut, Dr. Rhona Rapoport, Dr. Harold Stalvey, and Dr. Leonard Weiner.

to developmental transitions or to situational hazards and challenges, are potential turning points which may lead to mental health disorder. Retrospective studies such as by Levy (1945) suggest that sudden changes in vulnerability to mental disorder occur during such periods. We have become interested in studying the grappling with the problem which takes place during the period of disequilibrium; we wish to identify characteristic patterns and correlate these with types of mental health outcome. Our hope is that we may learn to identify persons whose behavior in specific crisis situations predicts a mentally unhealthy outcome. Subsequently, we hope to show that it is possible to intervene at that time and influence these persons to change their behavior so that they achieve a healthier result. The latter hope is related to our conviction that during the upset of a crisis a person usually has an increased desire to be helped and that he is more susceptible to influence then than during periods of relatively stable functioning (Caplan, 1964).

The early work of Lindemann (1944; 1956) on bereavement is a landmark for studies of specific crisis, although attention had been drawn to this subject as early as 1926 (Becker, 1926; Eliot, 1929). Lindemann described various aspects of mourning, indicating that certain of these were associated with a healthy outcome and others with a continuation of dependence on the dead person; among the latter also were a variety of psychosomatic disorders and difficulties in relating to others.

In other significant crisis research, Janis (1958) has described the patterns of reaction of adult patients in a general surgical ward; reports on psychological responses to the stress of severe burns have been made by Hamburg, Hamburg, and deGoza (1953), and on coping behavior of patients with polio by Visotsky, Hamburg, Goss, and Lebovits (1961). Tyhurst (1951) has studied reactions to natural disasters. Hill (1949) and Koos (1946) studied wartime separations and people with "troubles." Silber, Hamburg, Coelho, Murphey, Rosenberg, and Pearlin (1961) have investigated the patterns of behavior of high school students during crises precipitated by the transition from school to college. Murphy (1962) has investigated the variety of coping responses of young children facing the ordinary experiences of life for the first time. Rosenberg and Fuller (1957) have studied the responses of nursing students during the crises related to the succession of stresses which are part of their training. Caplan (1951), Bibring (1961), and others have investigated the range of responses of women during the course of pregnancy.

Some of these studies have been restricted to a description and classification of the way different people behave. Categories of behavior have sometimes been evaluated as desirable or undesirable, adaptive or maladaptive, on the basis of *a priori* value judgments. A few of the studies have attempted to correlate such value judgments with eventual outcome. Several of the studies have tried to elucidate the reasons why different subjects behaved as they did during the crisis and to disentangle pre-existing personality factors from situational influences during the period of the crisis. Rarely has the research attempted to test predictions regarding eventual outcome based upon judgments of current crisis behavior.

In studying these researches, we have been impressed by the following points:

(a) Behavior during a crisis appears to be determined by the interaction of at least four factors, including influences of the situation itself, the pre-existing personality, cultural factors, and the interactions with significant others. Although major emphasis in the past has been on pre-crisis personality, it is no longer possible to consider this factor as the exclusive determinant of crisis behavior. We will discuss this further below.

(b) The varieties of behavior of persons in crisis are classifiable into a relatively small number of patterns.

(c) All crises resemble each other in certain fundamental particulars. Crises are time-limited periods of disequilibrium, or behavioral and subjective upset, which are precipitated by an inescapable demand or burden to which the person is temporarily unable to respond adequately. During this period of tension, the person grapples with the problem and develops novel resources, both by calling upon internal reserves and by making use of the help of others. Those resources are then used to handle the precipitating factor, and the person achieves once more a steady state.

(d) Crises also differ from one another along certain specifiable dimensions: the type of precipitating factors, e.g., whether "developmental" or "accidental" (Caplan, 1964); and the type of challenge or hazard, e.g., death of a loved one, change of occupational role, personal injury, or relocation of domicile. In any subcategory of crises, there appear to be certain regularly occurring psychological and environmental tasks (Caplan, 1961), and different persons accomplish the tasks with a greater or lesser degree of adequacy (Rapoport, 1963).

In line with these considerations, our research on the crisis of prematurity developed along two main related paths: a study of the patterns of the behavior of parents grappling with the problems of a premature birth and a study of the psychological tasks presented by this situation and of the adequacy with which these tasks are accomplished. Each of the studies has consisted of two phased substudies. The first substudy has explored the process of the crisis in order to develop hypotheses on the connection between patterns of grappling or task accomplishment with mental health outcomes. The second substudy represents a preliminary test of these hypotheses on a new sample of parents: data were collected during crisis on the basis of which a prediction of mental health outcome was made, and this was compared with what was actually found by independent observers after the termination of the crisis period.

## PARENTAL REACTIONS TO PREMATURE BIRTH AS AN EXAMPLE OF CRISIS

After preliminary explorations with token cases in several common crisis situations while establishing collaborative relationships with public health workers (Hamovitch, Caplan, Hare, & Owens, 1959), we eventually chose the birth of a premature baby as a suitable example because: (a) it occurred in sufficient numbers (8 per cent of live births) to provide an adequate supply of research subjects; (b) all cases of prematurity in the area were routinely referred by the maternity hospitals to the health department, and each family was visited in its home by a public health nurse before the baby was dischared from the hospital; (c) access to the case was therefore possible relatively early in the crisis; (d) the total list of cases could be sampled; (e) the onset of the crisis was easily definable by the onset of premature labor; (f) the severity of the crisis was likely to be graduated by the danger to the life expectancy of the baby and the degree of unpreparedness of the parents, thus making it feasible to study the same crisis in increasing degrees of severity; and (g) although prematurity occurs more frequently in lower socioeconomic class mothers, a randomly selected sample of study cases would probably include the range of socioeconomic classes and ethnic and social groups found in that area of Boston.

We realized that prematurity had certain obvious disadvantages as a crisis study topic. First, it was usually not a very disrupting crisis as measured by the degree of disequilibrium, and its outcome, whether bad or good, was not likely to be as dramatic as some other crises. Moreover, except in most unusual circumstances, the outcome would be observable in terms of changes in mental health rather than as actual mental disorder, and its value as a focus for crisis research which might lead to the prevention of mental disorder was based on assumptions which would need separate research verification. We felt that we could work out some valid measures of mental health changes based upon our previous studies on disorders in mother-child relationships (Caplan, 1951). We also hoped that our understanding of this crisis would be enriched by our previous studies on normal pregnancy and birth, which would form a baseline of comparable reactions of lesser intensity. The unlikelihood of outcomes in the form of mental disorder did not at this stage seem a serious drawback because our primary interest was focused upon the *process* of the crisis. Any differences in outcome, even if in the middle range of healthiness could become the basis for identifying significantly different patterns of coping and of crisis task accomplishment.

## GENERAL METHOD
## OF DATA COLLECTION

The two exploratory hypothesis-developing studies represent different analyses of the same body of data. This set of study records represents our accumulated data on 86 cases of premature birth in intact families in our study area. There was no systematic selection of the cases. The homes of listed premature births were visited within 7 to 10 days after the birth. Introduced by the public health nurse, we attempted to arouse the motivation of the family to collaborate with us in "a study of how families deal with prematurity, so that we can find out how to improve our public health services" (Mason, 1958a). We used a variety of interviewers in these studies: psychiatrists, psychologists, social workers, mental health nurses, sociologists, and anthropologists. In our early work we sent two interviewers into the home at the same time, one to interview and the other to observe. We occasionally made tape recordings of the interviews for purposes of developing interviewing skills, but the data were chiefly assembled in process records dictated by the interviewer within 4 hours. The mother and the father were seen separately and together, as well as with their children, relatives, and friends when they happened to be present. Some interviews were carried out in our offices, and a few parents were seen there for psychological testing or for specialized psychiatric examinations to elucidate idiosyncratic elements in the case (Parad & Caplan, 1960).

By fitting into the already existing and well-developed nursing service, the interviewers were, at first, thought likely to be able to gain entry to the cases without having to "pay" for their subjects' cooperation by themselves providing help in the crisis. Subsequently, the researchers realized that some flexibility in being helpful did not alter the crisis situation and, in fact, increased the cooperation of the families.

As far as possible, we attempted to see the family members about once a week while the baby was in hospital, and at regular weekly or fortnightly intervals for 2 to 3 months after the baby's discharge from hospital. There was an average of 11 interviews with each family.

Although ideally the relationships between a crisis and its long-term outcome should be investigated, our research never planned to include this. We believed that strategically it would be wise first to demonstrate a correlation with short-term outcome since this would at least be one of the factors determining ultimate mental health outcome. We therefore planned that each case be studied until there appeared to be a stabilization of responses. From our experience in the early cases, this seemed to have occurred by the time the baby had been home for two months. Actually, there may be at least two peaks of upset involved in premature delivery: the more dramatic around the birth and hospital stay, and a briefer upset on the baby's homecoming. Essentially uniform, however, was the expected duration of the crisis, in spite of the variation in degree of upset and patterns of grappling.

Early in the project we tried to obtain data on the response of each individual to the crisis, as well as the interpersonal happenings in the family as a group, in the present crisis as well as in previous hazardous situations. In order to limit the volume of data, we finally decided to focus on the grappling behavior, the time sequence, the associated psychological tasks, and the picture of current and past family functioning. A more orderly collection and recording of data was possible after Interview Guides were developed (Mason, 1958b).

Regretfully, we eventually decided to bow to the inevitability imposed by our current lack of knowledge of the family as an operating social system, to restrict our focus to the reactions of the mother in her crisis struggles, and to study the behavior of other family members only insofar as they affected her and her relationship with her baby. This restriction involved our losing sight of some of the potentially most interesting phenomena of crisis, but we felt that it was all we could handle adequately at that time. However, since the mother usually appeared to be the family member most intensely involved in the crisis of premature birth, apart of course from the baby, our interest in exploring the significance of crisis processes was reasonably well served by concentrating upon her.

For a variety of reasons many of the records, especially those accumulated in the early period of the study, were not satisfactory. There were inevitable gaps in the data as a result of variations in family motivation, interviewer skills, and the types of concurrent situations. Many families found themselves in multiple crises, some of which were unrelated to prematurity. When the time came for the data analysis, it was decided that only records providing consistently full data continuously until the baby had been home from hospital for six to eight weeks would be acceptable. These cases cannot be considered representative of any particular population, but by chance they turned out to be about equally divided among whites and Negroes, and to include families both of low and of middle socioeconomic classes. There was also a representative spread as regards birth weight. Although generalizations may not be possible to a larger population, the cases do illustrate the variety of responses to crisis likely to occur in various subgroups and serve as models for further investigation.

## DEVELOPMENT OF HYPOTHESES ON THE RELATIONSHIP OF GRAPPLING PATTERNS AND MENTAL HEALTH OUTCOME

This study (Caplan, 1960) analyzed the records of ten cases in which two psychiatrist judges could agree on the rating of mental health outcome. A Healthy Outcome was defined as being characterized by unambiguous and positive evidence that all dyadic relationships among family members two months after the baby came home were at least as "healthy" as they had been in the months prior to the premature birth. An Unhealthy Outcome represented a situation in which at least one dyadic relationship was worse after the crisis.

The records were divided into the two contrasting groups and each psychiatrist independently appraised the grappling by parents with their crisis problems. Consensus was obtained in respect to the following three relatively distinct categories of grappling:

*Cognitive Grasp of the Crisis Situation*

In the Healthy Outcome cases, the parents continually surveyed the situation and actively gathered as much information as possible about the baby and the causes and manifestations of prematurity. The assessment of the situation was maintained in consciousness most of the time, and perceptions were reality-based and minimally distorted by irrational fantasies.

In the Unhealthy Outcome cases, there was little active searching for evidence upon which a current assessment of the situation and a judgment about outcome or plans for handling it could be made. Thoughts about danger or burden were suppressed, avoided, or denied, and outcome was considered in terms of a global belief that all would be well or that luck would be bad, both of which appeared dependent more upon inner fantasies than appraisal of external reality.

*Handling Feelings*

In the Healthy Outcome cases, the parents showed a continuous awareness of negative feelings throughout the crisis, and there was free verbal and nonverbal expression of these feelings in interaction with others. Occasionally at peak periods of stress there was a temporary utilization of the defenses of denial, suppression, and avoidance; but anxiety, anger, depression, and frustration were soon readmitted to awareness and a conscious attempt was made to master them, both alone and with the help of others.

In the Unhealthy Outcome cases there was little or no verbal admission of negative feelings, and the parents pretended to be cheerful and denied discomfort. The only negative feeling which was permitted open and continuous expression was blaming others.

*Obtaining Help*

In the Healthy Outcome cases, the parents actively sought help from within the family or the community in relation to the tasks associated with the care of the premature baby, and assistance in dealing with their negative feelings. Emotional assistance included nonspecific support, and specific attention to reassure and share anxieties, relieve guilt, and assuage deprivation. The helping process characteristically included counteracting occasional maladjustive coping patterns.

In the Unhealthy Outcome cases, there was a reluctance or inability to seek help or to accept it when offered. The parents did not help each other in any consistent way, and when they did, they often supported each other in maladaptive grappling, such as urging denial and avoidance of difficulties, stimulating blaming oneself or others for the prematurity, and engaging in bickering as a means of nonspecific tension release.

## Discussion

Based upon the above analysis and in collaboration with other staff efforts, a series of hypotheses was developed linking the contrasting patterns of cognitive and affective handling of the crisis situation, and patterns of obtaining help, to the two extreme types of outcome. At that stage of the research, it was not felt possible to distinguish the relative weight of the various details of the grappling patterns, and the hypotheses had to be couched in global terms. Parents who actively sought information about the premature baby and used this to plan for its future, who expressed negative feelings which were consonant with their perceptions of threat to the baby, and who sought and benefited from the assistance of readily available helping persons, would tend to have a healthier mental health outcome than parents who avoided information, denied feelings, and did not seek or accept help. No causal relationship could be hypothesized between the antecedent grappling patterns and the subsequent outcome rating, and it was felt to be sufficient at the present stage to maintain that a particular grappling pattern was predictive of the likelihood of a healthy or unhealthy mental health outcome. It was recognized that both the grappling pattern and the signs of outcome might be manifestations of the underlying personality of the parents, and might be related because of this rather than because of the dynamics of the crisis and its pattern of resolution. Certainly, aspects of all three categories seemed of an enduring nature related to personality. But the category "Obtaining Help" seemed in addition to include not only interpersonal and cultural elements but also factors related to the social network in which the parents were involved.

## A PREDICTIVE STUDY
## TO TEST HYPOTHESES
## RELATING GRAPPLING PATTERNS
## AND MENTAL HEALTH OUTCOME

The data for this study (Mason, 1963) of 28 randomly selected mothers who were admitted to a lying-in hospital in premature labor consisted of interviews during the first five days following the birth of the baby. Information concerning the mother's cognitive and affective response to the crisis was collected as well as about her relationships with available helping persons, including husband, friends, relatives, and caregiving professionals. Judgments about her maternal qualities were made according to the way she talked about her real and fantasied relationships with babies, and note was made of the nature of her previous experience, if any, with prematurity.

Based upon the data from the interviews and upon the hypotheses of the previous study, a prediction was made in each case of the quality of mother-child relationship to be found six weeks after the baby would be home from the hospital. The prediction took the form of a global rating of the relationship as Good or Poor in regard to the mother's attitudes toward the baby and her effectiveness in taking care of it.

After her discharge, each mother was interviewed in her home by a social worker. Observations of the cognitive and affective response of individual family members to the situation and to the course of events, and of the handling of the practical and psychological tasks were recorded. Particular attention was paid to evidence of the mother's relationship with the new baby.

The social workers who collected this information were not given any details of the earlier interviews and did not know what predictions had been made. The reports for the end of the study period (between six and ten weeks after the baby came home) were rated in regard to the quality of outcome by a clinical psychologist, who was also ignorant of the predictions. The judgment on outcome focused upon the mother-child relationship and was forced into either a "good" or "poor" category, based on the mother's acceptance and care of the child, as well as the latter's progress.

Of the 19 mothers in which both prediction and outcome ratings could be made, 11 were predicted to have a Good outcome and eight were predicted to have a Poor outcome. The outcome ratings agreed in ten of the Good and seven of the Poor predictions.

*Discussion*

This is clearly a rough clinical study involving global judgments both of prediction and outcome categories. There are many overlapping and potentially contaminating factors. However, the findings lend additional support to the implications of the first study that a meaningful categorization of individuals undergoing a hazardous situation can be made along these dimensions. It should be noted that no correlation was observed between outcome and socioeconomic status, cultural group, or pre-

**TABLE 1**
**Hospital Prediction of Early**
**Mother-Child Relationship**

| Prediction | Outcome | |
|---|---|---|
| | *Good* | *Poor* |
| Good | 10 | 1 |
| Poor | 1 | 7 |

$p < .01$ (Fisher Exact Test)

crisis personality. However, no standardized rating of these was attempted. Although the numbers are small, they are statistically significant, and the study does indicate that predictions of the mental health outcome on the basis of behavior *during* the crisis of prematurity are feasible.

## AN EXPLORATORY STUDY TO DETERMINE THE PSYCHOLOGICAL TASKS FACING THE MOTHERS OF PREMATURE BABIES, AND THE RELATIONSHIP OF TASK ACCOMPLISHMENT TO MENTAL HEALTH OUTCOME

This study (Kaplan & Mason, 1960) took the form of a qualitative analysis of the records of cases collected by the research team in its initial explorations. The analysis focused upon the mother's experience of the prematurity crisis, and upon the successive problems with which she was confronted. The researchers isolated four major psychological tasks which appear to be a characteristic of this experience for most mothers, and the adequate accomplishment of which seems to be essential both for successful mastery of the crisis situation and for providing a sound basis for a future healthy mother-child relationship.

The following were postulated as being the four tasks:

(1) The first task confronts the mother at the time of delivery. It is the preparation for a possible loss of the baby, whose life is in jeopardy. This "anticipatory grief" (Lindemann, 1944) involves a withdrawal from the relationship already being established during pregnancy with the expected child. The mother hopes the baby will survive, but simultaneously prepares for its death.

(2) At about the same time the mother must face and acknowledge her feelings of failure due to not delivering a normal full-term baby. The mother struggles with both these tasks until the baby's chances for survival seem secure. According to its weight and physical condition, the baby may continue to remain in hospital for a further

two to ten weeks, and during this period the third and fourth tasks need to be performed.

(3) The third task is the resumption of the process of relating to the baby which previously had been interrupted. The mother has lost the usual opportunity provided by a full-term pregnancy for the development of readiness for the mothering role. Characteristically, there is a point at which the mother really begins to believe that the baby will survive. The event which stimulates activity on her third task may be the baby's gain in weight, a change in feeding pattern, a change in its activity or appearance, or a change in the nurses' manner.

(4) The fourth task faces the mother with the challenge of understanding how a premature baby differs from a normal baby in terms of its special needs and growth patterns. In order to provide the baby with the necessary extra care and protection, the mother must see him as a premature with special needs and characteristics. But it is equally important for her to see that these special needs are temporary and will yield in time to more normal patterns. Her task is to take satisfactory precautions without depriving herself and the child of enjoyable interactions.

In this study no attempt was made to separate the cases into contrasting outcome groups. Instead, the records were inspected in order to identify typical patterns of mothers who apparently accomplished the four tasks and a contrasting group of cases in which the four tasks were not accomplished in whole or in part. In the first group the outcome seemed good, in that the mother developed a healthy relationship to the baby by the time it was two months old. She gave it realistic care in relation to its needs, she took pride and satisfaction in handling it, and she saw the baby as potentially normal.

The cases also included mothers who did not follow the above pattern. Some mothers handled the hazard to the life of the baby and their own maternal failure by denial. Some mothers failed to respond with hope to the indications of the survival and satisfactory development of the infant. In some such cases it appeared that the baby continued to symbolize the mother's failure despite its progress and she continued to perceive it in a fixed distorted way as a case of impending death or abnormality. This perception seriously impeded her sensitivity to the baby's real needs. Other mothers either took insufficient precautions in sheltering the baby from excessive stimulation, prematurely treated it "like a normal infant," or else they continued to coddle and overprotect it after such special care was no longer realistically necessary. They overfed or underfed the baby. There were a variety of signs of tension in the mother-child relationships.

## Discussion

Beyond showing an association between task accomplishment and outcome, this study suggests that certain tasks are specific for certain stages in the crisis and, further, that any interruption in the sequence of these tasks leads to increased difficulty in achieving a healthy outcome. It is important to note that any crisis is usually made up of a number of smaller peaks of upset, sometimes overlapping and sometimes consecutive. Of course, there are frequently chance occurrences and other crises which may be indirectly related and which add to the stress to which the family must adjust. Occasionally in our families, along with the premature delivery, a husband lost his job or the family moved to a new home and this colored the family's crisis behavior. Some writers (Wortis, 1960) believe that the premature delivery is the *result* of another crisis and therefore that such other crises as we found might be caused or at least codetermined by some other common agent. In these studies no attempt was made to determine the "cause" of premature delivery. In regard to psychogenic factors or chronic physical stresses, etc., no pattern of relationship was apparent in examining the data. Although it is true that our sample represented a group more apt to be at a disadvantage both financially and physically, what was important was that *within* such a group distinguishing characteristics about grappling behavior could be identified. Thus, regardless of cultural, socioeconomic, or personality factors, it is believed that there are tasks which are universal.

# A STUDY TO TEST THE HYPOTHESES RELATING TASK ACCOMPLISHMENT TO MENTAL HEALTH OUTCOME

Data on 30 cases of prematurity were collected (Kaplan, 1961) in a form which allowed the prediction of the healthy or unhealthy quality of maternal care on the basis of the mother's handling of the tasks imposed by the crisis of premature delivery. The data collection was carried out by social workers who interviewed the mothers in their homes. Process records of their interviews were kept and observations were made on 11 items which the researcher had derived from the hypotheses on task accomplishment developed in the previous study. The case records were independently coded and rated by other workers so that there would be a minimum of contamination in the composite prediction assessment.

The cases were followed by social workers who were given no information about the mothers' statements or behavior during the period when the babies were in hospital, and were not told the outcome predictions. The outcome data consisted of interview and observation material about maternal behavior. Twelve items were defined to cover the outcome area, and independent judges, who had not seen the earlier parts of the record, coded and rated each of these.

The prediction and outcome categories were then compared in each case in order to test the hypotheses; and a variety of correlations with outcome were also analyzed in order to investigate the relations to outcome of other apparently significant factors, such as birth weight of the babies, parity of the mothers, prior experience with prematurity, visiting patterns while the babies were in hospital, etc.

## Prediction Assessment

The early parts of each record were coded and rated to cover the eleven items assessing the accomplishment of the third and fourth tasks. These included the mother's pattern of visiting the premature nursery, her preoccupation with the infant, her report on her own observations of the infant, the content of her references to the infant which indicated hopes or concerns elicited by changes in his appearance and behavior, her expression of feelings of deprivation in being separated from the infant, her concern with premature traits in the infant, her discussion of actual or potential defects in her infant without medical basis, and her estimate of the infant's care requirements after discharge from hospital. Each item was scored as either present or absent, an appropriate numerical rating was assigned, and these scores were added to form a composite prediction score. The distribution of these total scores made it apparent that three categories of prediction were warranted: Good, Poor, and Very Poor.

**Outcome Assessment**

The records dealing with the behavior and attitudes of the mothers toward their children at the end of the study were rated for items such as evidence of maternal pride, satisfaction in handling and talking about the baby, apprehension about defects in the infant not observed by the doctors, marked indifference to the infant including neglect, overfeeding, and "pushing" to have the infant develop too quickly beyond its premature state.

As with the prediction assessment, the total score of the outcome assessment was obtained by adding together the scores on all the items. The group was then divided into three bands: Good, Poor, and Very Poor outcome.

Table 2 shows the association of these prediction and outcome ratings. Of the 30 cases, 18 were judged to have a Good outcome and of these, 13 were accurately predicted; 10 were rated Poor in outcome, of which 9 had been predicted; and the 2 cases of Very Poor outcome were correctly predicted. The predictions were 80 per cent successful.

One finding among the results of item analysis which is of special interest is the high correlation of the rating of the mothers' visiting pattern with the final overall outcome rating. A good visiting pattern means that the mother visited the baby in hospital at least once a week during the last two weeks of his stay, or that she visited more frequently during this period than in previous weeks. Table 3 indicates that from the visiting pattern

## TABLE 2
### Task Accomplishment as a Prediction of Maternal Care

| Prediction | Outcome | | |
|---|---|---|---|
| | Good | Poor | Very Poor |
| Good | 13 | 1 | 0 |
| Poor | 5 | 9 | 0 |
| Very Poor | 0 | 0 | 2 |

p < .01 (Chi Squared Test)

alone a better prediction of outcome can be made than from all the other prediction items.

This finding means that in our study population the visiting pattern is apparently an excellent index of the whole area of task accomplishment. If it holds up under further study as a simple indicator of outcome it would be most valuable in practice. Unfortunately, any such discrete indicator is subject to considerable overuse or misinterpretation, and might be invalidated by administrative or policy changes in regard to mothers' visiting.

### Discussion

The chief contribution of this study is the further evidence that maternal grappling patterns are predictive of maternal care patterns. Again the hypothesis is supported which suggests that there are certain tasks which pertain to this crisis situation whose accomplishment is correlated with successful outcome.

## TABLE 3
### Visiting Pattern and Outcome

| Visiting Pattern | Outcome | |
|---|---|---|
| | Good | Poor |
| Good | 17 | 2 |
| Poor | 1 | 10 |

p < .02 (Chi Squared Test)

# CONCLUDING DISCUSSION

Our studies have shown that there is some merit to studying the reactions of parents to the premature birth of a baby as an example of a crisis. We did not choose prematurity because we believed that it represented a serious threat to the mental health of the family members and would be likely to be associated with a significantly increased risk of mental illness such as might be found in other crises precipitated by stresses like bereavement or serious physical illness. On the other hand, a study of prematurity has some meaning in its own right from the mental health point of view. Earlier clinical experience had given us the impression that the stress of prematurity might color the behavior and attitudes of a mother to her premature infant through many years of childhood (Prugh, 1953; Spock, 1945). A mother who delivers before term frequently has been observed to urge the baby to eat and grow as if to reassure herself about her ability as a mother. If this emphasis on satisfaction of the mother's own needs outweighs her concern for the needs of the infant, a mother-child relationship may be established which will interfere with healthy personality development in the child (Caplan, 1959; Caplan, 1961).

Although in our four studies we did not conduct follow-up investigations to trace the effects on the children, the not inconsiderable number of mothers whose relationships with their children were rated as "unhealthy" six to eight weeks after the baby's discharge from hospital has confirmed our clinical impression that prematurity may be associated with emotional difficulties. It is, of course, possible that the disturbance of the mother-child relationship which we identified in certain cases was not influenced by the mother's pattern of grappling with the crisis of premature birth, and we will discuss this point later on. But at the very least, our studies do seem to indicate that such disordered relationships can be predicted or identified from the behavior of the mother shortly after the birth of her baby, and it is a plausible assumption that the disorder in mother-child relationships is likely to be of some significance for the future personality development of the premature baby.

Apart from their relevance for the study of factors influencing mental disorder or mental health, our studies of the crisis of prematurity have made some significant contributions to crisis research in general. We have come to believe, particularly in connection with the Family Studies under Rhona Rapoport (1963), that in a study of the processes involved in reacting to a crisis it is meaningful to differentiate both general grappling patterns and also crisis task accomplishment. We have shown that these factors can be defined, that data relating to them can be systematically collected, recorded, and reliably rated, and that some regularity can be found in the association of different patterns of each of these factors and a mental health outcome variable.

In the absence of a clear indication of changes in respect to mental disorder, we have shown that it is possible to define as an outcome variable certain aspects of the interpersonal relationships of persons who have undergone crisis; also we have shown that it is possible to collect data in a consistent manner and report these details in such a way that they can be reliably rated by independent judges and assessments made which will differentiate the outcome in one case from that in another. We have shown that there is a sufficient spread both in the ratings of the antecedent and consequent variables defined in this way so that meaningful associations between the two sets of variables can be documented. Our studies have also shown one approach to the problem of controlling for the investigator's bias in favor of his own hypotheses by using separate sets of workers to collect the data for the antecedent and consequent factors in our equation. In utilizing the services of part-time social workers to collect clinical data by means of structured interviews, we have followed the example of Freeman and Simmons (1963). Our studies have also demonstrated that it is feasible to obtain the cooperation of a high proportion of a randomly selected group of persons in one type of crisis in carrying out research of this type, and we have learned something about the problems of arousing the motivation of research subjects.

In addition to the above, our studies have provided support for our original assumption that it is possible to hypothesize particular patterns of crisis grappling and of accomplishment of crisis tasks which are associated with good and bad outcome. Despite the small size of our samples, our results have supported our assumption that we can make reliable predictions about mental health outcome from a judgment based upon an appraisal both of patterns of grappling and also of task accomplishment. If future studies on the crisis of prematurity with larger samples confirm our findings, we will be in the position of being able to communicate to clinical workers a series of clear-cut behavioral items which they can observe among mothers shortly after premature delivery that will allow them to predict a subgroup likely to have disordered relationships with their children at a crucial period of the latter's development. Whatever other factors are involved in the development of these children, it is plausible to assume that it would be useful to separate out this group for special attention by the doctors, nurses, and social workers who will intervene preventively in order to try to ameliorate the predicted disorder of mother-child relationship or to safeguard the child from its ill effects.

Our studies have not been designed to show a causal relationship between patterns of grappling and task accomplishment and the nature of the mental health outcome; but if such a causative relationship is eventually demonstrated by subsequent studies, our research points the way to a possible rationale for this preventive intervention. Assuming that poor coping and task accomplishment influence the mother in the direction of an unhealthy relationship with her baby, the prevention of a bad outcome might consist of identifying the poor grapplers and influencing them to grapple more adequately and to accomplish their crisis tasks in the appropriate sequence.

Our studies have been inadequate on two counts. The

smallness of our sample has prevented us from differentiating possible differences in crisis grappling and task accomplishment among persons of different socioeconomic classes, educational levels, and cultural backgrounds. Future studies with larger representative samples will reveal whether or not there is one fundamental "good" or "bad" pattern of dealing with crisis or whether there is a variety of patterns of each category which are associated with cultural and social structure differences in a population.

The more significant drawback in our studies has already been mentioned. In this preliminary work, we restricted ourselves to trying to demonstrate an *association* between types of crisis grappling and task accomplishment and varieties of mental health outcome. This association may represent a causal relationship, which would be highly significant for preventive psychiatry, or it may represent two sets of factors each of which is the resultant of an antecedent set of conditions. It may be, for instance, that women with healthy personalities cope adequately with the crisis of prematurity and also develop healthy relationships with their premature babies. Also, it may be that women with unhealthy personalities will manifest undesirable problem solving during the crisis of prematurity and will also have disorders in their relationships with their babies. Not only pre-existing personality factors but also perhaps particular constellations of sociocultural factors which antedate the onset of the crisis may predetermine a mother's behavior during the crisis and even the nature of her relationship to her infant.

The investigation of this problem is particularly difficult. An effective study would demand access to the sample prior to the onset of crisis in order to assess adequately the pre-crisis personality of the mother. In the case of the crisis of prematurity, it is difficult to determine where to draw the base line. The studies of Caplan (1951) and of Bibring (1961) have shown that pregnancy itself leads to significant changes in the manifestations of a woman's personality functioning. Even apart from this difficulty, the only way to study the personalities of women before premature delivery would be to obtain access to a total population of pregnant women with the expectation that a certain proportion of them would deliver prematurely. Since prematurity occurs in only 8 percent of live births, this would be a formidable task (though we might make it a little easier by drawing our sample from the lower socioeconomic class population, in which prematurity is more common). Other examples of crisis might lend themselves more to a design of this type. For instance, the crises associated with certain military stresses such as going into battle for the first time, or predictable crises such as termination of employment in an industry which is in the process of being automated, would present us with a situation in which a researcher might gain access to a population which he can study before, during, and after a crisis.

One research approach does offer some hope of solving the problem of causality. If future researches confirm a consistent contrast in mental health outcome between groups of people who behave differently during crisis in relation to grappling pattern and task accomplishment, it should be possible to isolate a group of poor grapplers who can reliably be predicted to have a poor mental health outcome. If this group is then divided into two, and one subgroup is exposed to preventive intervention so that their grappling is steered in a positive direction while the other subgroup is used as a control, an amelioration in the mental health outcome of the experimental group would favor the hypothesis that the pattern of grappling and task accomplishment was causally related to mental health outcome rather than merely being associated with it because of some antecedent set of factors. We believe that this avenue is well worth exploring.

# REFERENCES

1. Becker, H. A social psychological study of bereavement. Masters Thesis, Northwestern University, 1926.

2. Bibring, G. L., Dwyer, T. F., Huntington, D. S., & Valenstein, A. F. A study of the psychological processes in pregnancy and of the earliest mother–child relationship. *Psychoanal. Stud. Child,* 1961, 16, 9-27.

3. Caplan, G. A public health approach to child psychiatry—an introductory account of an experiment. *Ment. Hyg., N. Y.,* 1951, 35, 235-249. (a)

4. Caplan, G. Mental hygiene work with expectant mothers. *Ment. Hyg., N.Y.,* 1951, 35, 41-50. (b)

5. Caplan, G. *Concepts of mental health and consultation.* Washington: Children's Bureau, 1959.

6. Caplan, G. Patterns of parental response to the crisis of premature birth. *Psychiat.,* 1960, 23, 365-374.

7. Caplan, G. *An approach to community mental health.* New York: Grune and Stratton, 1961.

8. Caplan, G. *Principles of preventive psychiatry,* New York: Basic Books, 1964.

9. Eliot, T. D. The adjustive behavior of bereaved families: A new field for research. *Soc. Forces,* 1929, 8, 543-549.

10. Freeman, H. E., & Simmons, O. G. *The mental patient comes home.* New York: John Wiley, 1963.

11. Hamburg, D. A., Hamburg, B., & deGoza, S. Adaptive problems and mechanisms in severely burned patients. *Psychiat.,* 1953, 16, 1-20.

12. Hamovitch, M. B., Caplan, G., Hare, P., & Owens, C. Establishment and maintenance of a mental health unit—a case history and general principles. *Ment. Hyg., N.Y.,* 1959, 43, 412-421.

13. Hill, R. *Families under stress.* New York: Harper, 1949.

14. Janis, I. L. *Psychological stress.* New York: John Wiley, 1958.

15. Kaplan, D., & Mason, E. A. Maternal reactions to premature birth viewed as an acute emotional disorder. *Amer. J. Orthopsychiat.,* 1960, 30, 539-547.

16. Kaplan, D. Predicting outcome from situational stress on the basis of individual problem-solving patterns. Unpublished Ph.D. Thesis, University of Minnesota, 1961.

17. Koos, E. L. *Families in trouble,* New York: Kings Crown Press, 1946.

18. Levy, D. M. Psychic trauma of operations in children. *Amer. J. Dis. Children,* 1945, 69, 7-25.

19. Lindemann, E. Symptomatology and management of acute grief. *Amer. J. Psychiat.,* 1944, 101, 141-148.

20. Lindemann, E. The meaning of crisis in individuals and family living. *Teachers Coll. Rec.,* 1956, 57, 310-315.

21. Mason, E. A. Family study method. In *Family Guidance Center Report to the Commonwealth Fund,* 1958, Chapter 3. (a)

22. Mason, E. A. Interview guides. In *Family Guidance Center Report to the Commonwealth Fund,* 1958, Appendix 3. (b)

23. Mason, E. A. A method of predicting crisis outcome for mothers of premature babies. *Publ. Hlth. Rep.,* 1963, 78, 1031-1035.

24. Murphy, L. B. et al. *The widening world of childhood—paths toward mastery.* New York: Basic Books, 1962.

25. Parad, H. J., & Caplan, G. A framework for studying families in crisis. *Soc. Wk.,* 1960, 5, 3-15.

26. Prugh, D. Emotional problems of the premature infant's parents. *Nurs. Outlook,* 1953, 1, 461-464.

27. Rapoport, R. Normal crises, family structure and mental health. *Fam. Process,* 1963, 2, 68-80.

28. Rosenberg, P. P., & Fuller, M. L. Dynamic analyses of the student nurse. *Group Psychother.,* 1957, 10, 22-37.

29. Silber, E., Hamburg, D. A., Coelho, G. V., Murphey, E. B., Rosenberg, M., & Pearlin, L. I. Adaptive behavior in competent adolescents. *Arch. gen. Psychiat.,* 1961, 5, 354-365.

30. Spock, B. Avoiding behavior problems. *J. Pediatrics,* 1945, 27, 363-382.

31. Tyhurst, J. S. Individual reactions to community disaster. *Amer. J. Psychiat.,* 1951, 107, 764-769.

32. Visotsky, H. M., Hamburg, D. A., Goss, M. E., & Lebovits, B. Z. Coping behavior under extreme stress. *Arch. gen. Psychiat.,* 1961, 5, 423-448.

33. Wortis, H. Discussion. *Amer. J. Orthopsychiat.,* 1960, 30, 547-552.

# 9. BRIEF INTERVENTION AS A PREVENTIVE FORCE IN DISORDERS OF EARLY CHILDHOOD*

Bernice Augenbraun, M.A.
Helen L. Reid, M.S.W.
David B. Friedman, M.D.

Many pediatricians conceive of themselves as having three tasks: to treat children when they are ill; to keep children mentally and physically healthy, and to promote satisfying and growth-enhancing parent-child relationships. The busy pediatrician is hard pressed to meet all these tasks adequately. By training and often by temperament and inclination he is best able to cope with the first two. Over a period of time, through experience in practice, or with the help of special postgraduate training programs, most pediatricians develop skills in dealing with parent-child relationships. But many pediatricians also complain that lack of time in their busy offices and inadequate training in this field makes it difficult for them to cope adequately with emotional problems in

Reprinted from the *American Journal of Orthopsychiatry,* 1967, **37,** 697-702, by permission of the publisher and the authors. Copyright, the American Orthopsychiatric Association, Inc. Bernice Augenbraun is Chief Psychiatric Social Worker in the Department of Child Psychiatry, Cedars-Sinai Medical Center, Los Angeles, California, where Helen Reid is Casework Specialist. David Friedman is Professor of Pediatrics, University of Southern California, School of Medicine, Los Angeles.

* Presented at the 1966 annual meeting of the American Orthopsychiatric Association, San Francisco, California.

children and their families, even when these problems produce recognizable physical or behavioral symptoms.

Pediatricians have made a number of attempts to solve this dilemma. Some offer advice and reassurance and refer those families who need more help to outside specialized psychiatric personnel. Although this is obviously necessary in some instances, referral to an outside service presents its own set of complexities and often is unsuccessful. Others, most often those with special training, have set aside time in their offices and tried to meet families' needs through counselling procedures before resorting to referral. Still others, particularly those working in pediatric groups, have tried adding psychologists, social workers and public health nurses to their regular office staff.[1,2]

The work described in this paper represents a fusion of two ideas. The first is that psychotherapeutic consultation as a readily accessible part of pediatrics practice is in accord with the goals of such practice, is the least complex way of making specialized service available to families and can provide the pediatrician with an understanding of family interaction more useful for his purposes than the usual dynamic formulations of psychiatric consultations. The second idea is that some of the newer techniques of family interviewing can provide for rapid identification of family problems, alleviation of children's symptoms or for more successful referral, should this be the final recommendation. The authors offered a maximum of three family interviews to families in which there was a preschool child who had symptoms with no organic basis and which did not respond to the usual kinds of pediatric intervention. The service was offered continuously for one year. The mode of referral was simply a firm suggestion from the pediatrician to the parents that they make an appointment with the consulting therapist to discuss the problem. The limitation of service to three interviews with a follow-up interview six to nine months later was made clear from the beginning. Thus the stage was set for immediate problem solving rather than long-term exploration. All symptomatology was acceptable, and the families actually seen included children with behavior problems, sleep and feeding disturbances, excessive crying, recurrent upper respiratory infections and gastrointestinal disturbances.

## FAMILY INTERVIEWING

Several years of experience with the technique of family interviewing with the preschool child as the identified patient, has revealed numerous possibilities for the use of this technique for alleviation of pathological interaction in the family with the goal of freeing normal developmental processes within the young child.* Family interviews can help to bring to awareness the impact on the family of the behavior of individual family members, parents and child alike. This awareness may lead to behavioral change or serve as a rational preparation for referral. By interpreting to the parents the child's many ways of communicating the therapist can demonstrate to parents that his behavior is meaningful. The impact of perental behavior on the child can be explored immediately and dealt with, as can the reciprocal effects of the child's behavior on the parents and their relationship to each other. The individual psychodynamic origins of their behavior can be explored to some extent, particularly as a diagnostic tool in determining depth of pathology. Also, the therapist can demonstrate appropriate ways of parenting.

Family interviews typically involve meetings with the child, both parents, and the therapist in a room in which the child is free to move about and make use of a variety of play material. This affords a setting which allows for suitable modes of expression for both parents and child in interaction with each other and the therapist. In this instance the interviews were held in the pediatrician's office to emphasize them as part of pediatrics service.

The parents are encouraged to talk about family problems as they see them and about their feelings about

---

* The authors are indebted for training and consultation to Saul L. Brown, Chief, Department of Child Psychiatry, Cedars-Sinai Medical Center, Los Angeles, California.

themselves, each other, and their children. The child is
similarly encouraged, but preschool children, whose
ability to use words is limited, often demonstrate their affect through the use of toys and in behavioral interaction
with adults. The therapist has an opportunity to observe
and understand the meaning of interaction between the
individual family members and to assess within this context the degree of individual pathology.

Continuing efforts in the use of family interviewing
with the preschool children present have been reported
in previous papers.[3,4] Experience with long-term treatment with families led to certain observations. Often the
symptomatology in the child seems to disappear rapidly
as the family interviews bring to the fore the disturbed interaction between the parents. Even when such interaction continues, focusing the problem between the
adults serves to free the child sufficiently so that normal
growth processes can reassert themselves. This observation led us to wonder about the use of family interviews
as a technique for rapid alleviation of the kind of symptomatology in young children that is traditionally first
brought to the attention of the pediatrician.

## THE TECHNIQUES EMPLOYED

The goal of brief intervention makes certain demands
on therapist and family alike. The therapist must make a
rapid identification of the factors in family interaction
that are contributing to the maintenance of the child's
symptom. He must be able to delineate this clearly to the
entire family, including the child, through confrontation
of actual behavior as seen in the family interview and
through interpretation of the ramifications of such behavior in symptom production. He must be able to explore sufficiently the affective origins of the behavior in
order to provide the family with a rational and compre-
hensible framework for understanding the roots and effects of their behavior. Finally, he must be able to demonstrate more appropriate behavior in a way that is sufficiently syntonic to the personalities involved that it can
be learned and adapted by family members. For many

families the development of conscious awareness of explicit behavior and insight into implicit conflicts and motivation will provide an ability to control behavior which enables them to learn more effective modes of interaction. Families which include adults with adequate ego strength for the rapid integration of insight and whose symptom-producing behavior is not rooted in profound unconscious conflicts, are, of course, most responsive to techniqes of brief intervention.

> The Morris family came for consultation with their two-year-old daughter, Lynn, because of Lynn's recurrent bouts of severe diarrhea associated with uncontrollable temper tantrums. They were a pleasant appearing couple in their late twenties, married three years, and demonstrating mutuality and affection. Lynn was bright, charming, and pretty with much curiosity about her surroundings. The diarrhea occurred first at the age of two months along with an upper respiratory infection and recurred periodically accompanying infection. Since age 18 months, however, the diarrhea had been associated with temper tantrums rather than physical illness, and it impeded toilet training. All other development was normal.
> In the first interview the parents described Lynn's tantrums as the result of her insistence on having her own way and her violent reaction to any thwarting. The mother was quite aware of her guilt over frustrating Lynn and her wish to submit rather than endure Lynn's screams or provoke the physical symptoms of diarrhea. The father had similar difficulty in limiting the child. The effects of their behavior was clarified by an episode in the interview. The therapist had removed from Lynn a favored toy monkey to test the child's response to a firm limit. Lynn accepted the move without much protest and turned to something else. The parents were quite astonished at the absence of a tantrum, and later in the session after the toy had been returned to Lynn, the mother attempted to repeat the move. She was extremely hesitant but was able to forestall Lynn's beginning tears with the offer of a substitute toy. The father protested on the unnecessary and unjust nature of the frustration and became very identified with what he perceived as the "hurt" and "deprived" child. While on the one hand, he urged the mother to limit Lynn, on the other, he became angry at her for doing so. Lynn immediately became seductive with the father, clearly appealing to him for rescue. This episode became an effective starting point for exploration of the parents' feelings, for interpretation of Lynn's behavioral response, and for demonstration of Lynn's capacity to understand their interaction and use it for her own manipulative purposes. The child's need for firm and unambivalent control and her positive response

to this was demonstrated through the therapist's direct interventions with her.

In the second interview Lynn began to play with the light switch and continued despite the adults' expressed irritation. The father, although seated closest to the child, did not intervene. When the therapist questioned this, the father was able to amplify his feeling about limit-setting as somehow hurtful and punitive. This feeling was much intensified by the child's bouts with illness and diarrhea. The mother, in turn, could explore her own feelings about being cast into the role of villain by the father's attitude. This in turn led to a discussion of children's needs and allowed the parents to begin to conceptualize the role of limit-setting as constructive to a child's growth and safety. This result was further underscored by Lynn's positive response to the therapist's firmness. In the third interview the parents reported considerable ongoing discussion between them about their attitudes toward Lynn and, in effect, a working through of their previous ambivalence. In subsequent follow-ups, temper outbursts were reported as minimal and the diarrhea had disappeared.

In other families the child's symptom may represent his use as an object of displacement for serious but covert marital disturbance.

The Robbins family was seen because of repeated complaints from the mother of intractable and defiant behavior on the part of their boy, Billy, two and a half years old. Billy was an active, handsome little boy, whose use of speech was fairly mature and who demonstrated a great deal of exuberance and curiosity in the course of the sessions. The first family meeting revealed the reality of the mother's complaints. Billy was very difficult for her to control and seemed to disregard whatever she said to him. At the same time he freely came to her for warmth and affection and seemed quite trusting of her to provide this. He was equally free in turning to his father for affection but also obeyed his father quickly and without resistance. The discrepancy between the boy's behavior with his mother and his father was used as a starting point for the mother's description of the difficulty she had with Billy at home. Some effort was made to explore Mrs. Robbins' mode of dealing with Billy in order to discover in her behavior cues to Billy to disobey. These were not apparent. Mr. Robbins was very critical of her complaints about Billy and felt she exaggerated the problem. He felt that Billy was not at all difficult and that this was a reflection of his wife's weakness. The quality of his criticism of her seemed very depreciating and afforded the first opportunity for wondering whether Billy did not pick up his father's depreciation of and contempt for the mother's authority. The father denied this at first but, then (partly in anger at the therapist) began to

talk in a very depreciating way about all women. Mrs. Robbins, in turn, accused her husband of expecting her to act
as a subservient maid-servant to him. Mr. Robbins agreed
in an amused way and further derided his wife for not
working and felt that maintenance of the household and a
young child was hardly sufficient effort on her part to
"earn her keep."

This theme was further elaborated in the next interview
as both parents felt freer to talk about their marital difficulties. The specific interaction that affected Billy became
quite clear. Whenever Billy started to do something for
which his mother said no, he would glance at his father
who, with a wink and a laugh, indicated his permission for
the activity. When mother then attempted to step in and
limit or punish Billy, father would intervene with a remark
about letting the boy do what he wanted, or praising the
boy for his aggressiveness. This interaction was pointed
out again and again to the parents. The mother picked up
on it immediately and saw it as a model for all areas of interaction with her husband. He tended to deny it at first
but then began to admit these feelings within himself and
his strong conviction that Billy ought to be allowed to do
pretty much as he pleased, or at least, should not be subject
to a woman's control. Billy was involved in these discussions with direct statements about his looking at his father
for permission and his feeling that daddy would let him do
things mother did not want him to do. Billy made no verbal
response to this but remained very concentrated on the
therapist. Shortly after these remarks were made, he began
to study his mother very closely and became obviously
more accessible to her discipline.

By the third interview both parents agreed that they had
made more effort to cooperate with each other in Billy's
control and the mother felt he was now quite manageable.
The marital problem, however, had burst forth and the
mother was even contemplating divorce. This led to a discussion of referral for help with the marital problem.

The problem in the Robbins family obviously could not
be resolved through brief intervention. But the delineation of the marital problem and its specific impact on
Billy's behavior, as well as the focusing of the adults'
energies on the problem between them, freed Billy as an
object of displacement. The way was opened for meaningful referral based on the parents' own recognition of the
source of the problem.

In still other families, where symptoms spring from
profound personality disturbances in the parents, referral is not feasible because there is too little accessibility
to brief intervention techniques and too great a resis-

144    Children and Their Parents in Brief Therapy

tance to awareness of disturbance. In these instances,
however, family interviews may provide diagnostic
material which permits therapist and pediatrician to
develop modes of intervention for the pediatrician to employ during his ongoing contact with the family in order
to minimize damage to the child.

Most of the families seen responded positively to the interviews and viewed them as a helpful measure. At the
least, they experienced a lessening of anxiety, and the
pediatrician noted a sharp decrease of anxious demanding calls from parents. In some instances, as noted, the
child's symptoms disappeared during the interviews,
and a year later the children remained symptom-free. In
a few cases, notably a youngster with a traumatic neurosis and several with severe personality disorders, successful psychiatric referral was carried out.

## CONCLUSION

Psychotherapeutic consultation as a regular part of
pediatrics practice can be an effective aid in meeting the
pediatrician's goal of maximum health of the child.
When employed in this way, it becomes an acceptable
pediatric service and does not involve the complex over-
tones of direct referral. The use of family interviews as
the modality for consultation opens exciting possibilities
for rapid and effective intervention in childrens' symptomatology before this becomes fixed in the pattern of
family life.

Family interviewing techniques, employed in the way
described here, actually may lead to alleviation of symptoms in the child through the development of insight in
family members and integration of more appropriate
ways of parenting. In families where the child's symptoms are a manifestation of more profound problems,
the frank exploration of difficulties and demonstration
of their effect in the interview situation itself can lead to
a more meaningful understanding of the existence of
problems and a readiness to accept referral for help. At
the very least, consultation through family interviews
can provide diagnostic understanding which will allow

the pediatrician to plan meaningfully for his ongoing role with the child and family.

Brief intervention through family interviewing can be applied to any setting which allows for early discovery of children's problems, not only in pediatrics practice but in nursery school and well-baby clinics as well. This method deserves experimentation and testing as a mental health tool in such large-scale programs for the preschool child as Project Head Start.

# REFERENCES

1. Townsend, E. H. 1964. The social worker in pediatric practice: An experiment. *Amer. J. Diseas. Children.* 107:77-83.

2. Wiskingrad, L., J. T. Shulruff, and Alice Sklansky. 1963. Role of a social worker in a private practice of pediatrics. *Pediatrics.* 32:(1).

3. Tasem, Marjorie, Bernice Augenbraun, and S. L. Brown, 1965. Therapeutic efforts in family interviews with both parents and preschool child. *J. Acad. Child Psychiat.* 4 (No. 2).

4. Augenbraun, Bernice, and Marjorie Tasem. Differential Techniques in Family Interviewing with Both Parents and Pre-School Child. In press. *J. Acad. Child Psychiat.*

# Problems Related To School

# 10. A MODEL FOR INTE-GRATING SPECIAL EDUCA-TIONAL AND COMMUNITY MENTAL HEALTH SERVICES*

## Daniel Kelleher, Ph.D.

In viewing the rapid growth of both special education and community mental health programs, one is struck by the need for models of intervention that allow for an integration of their approaches. Such a structure would allow each problem to be seen in the particular way that leads to its most effective solution. For example, one should not have to choose between explaining that a child has reading problems because of a "psycho-dynamic equating of forbidden hostility with intellectual curiosity," or because of poor teaching methods in the first grade. Both statements are "true," but one might better ask, "As this child comes to us today, what are all the different levels and perspectives of explanation that can be applied to his problem, and what course of action does each view or explanation suggest? Then, given these explanations and these potential action choices, and given the current resource potentials of the child,

Reprinted from *The Journal of Special Education*, 1968, **2**, 263-272, by permission of the publisher and the author. Dr. Kelleher is Professor and Director, Urban Studies Program, University of Puget Sound, Tacoma, Washington.

* The work reflected in this paper was done while Dr. Kelleher was director of the Communications Project, Child Study and Treatment Center, Western State Hospital, Tacoma, Washington. The editorial assistance of Dr. Dana Hanford of the Olympic Center for Mental Health and Mental Retardation, Bremerton, Washington, is gratefully acknowledged.

family and community, what are the most feasible and strategic points of attack on the problem?"

To effectively address oneself to such questions, one needs to have all pertinent factors before him, arranged in such a way that the therapist, the client, and others concerned are able to choose between the various alternatives. Services tied to a single approach tend to exclude many potential clients as being "inappropriate"—thus increasing their alienation from community and school.

This paper presents a structural model that attempts to move toward this goal. The model was derived from experiences in a pilot project concerned with children, families, therapists, schools and other social agencies (Kelleher, 1967). The program, in brief, attempted to integrate the efforts of parents, therapists, teachers, and child care counselors to intervene in the behavior patterns of seriously disturbed children. The aim was to allow each of these persons to enhance this unique contribution to the child's life, to allow overlap with other people interacting with the child, and to avoid competition and blaming (Kelleher & Lytle, 1964).

To achieve this, the model needed three characteristics: (1) It should depict the many persons involved as having parallel and overlapping roles; (2) It should use language that would be useful to all of them; and (3) it should describe the situation in ways that would lead directly to action by the appropriate combination of these people.

## Description of model

The model presented here results from a mixing together of several viewpoints: communication theory (Watzlawick, 1964), family theory (Satir, 1964), reinforcement theory (Skinner, 1961), psycho-dynamic theory, existential theory (May, Angel, & Ellenberger, 1958), cognitive theory (Bruner, 1960), ecological psychological theory (Hanford, 1966), and "game playing" theory (Berne, 1964; Haley, 1963). It views the child's behavior as the outcome of the interplay of forces of the "child-in-a-system." A child can be said to have a total life space which can be broken down into sub-systems. Each system is organized around a particular function, i.e., learning to read, playing football, dealing with mother, etc. Each is located in a certain geographical place and is populated by certain people.

The child and the system exert reciprocal influence on one another. Part of the reality of each of them lies in their separateness and part lies in their relatedness. Crying will occur when there is a crying child in a situation where crying is a viable option. The behavior can be altered by shifting the attributes on either side of the equation. But the most carefully planned settings will never eliminate crying completely, and some people would not cry regardless of how inviting the setting. Any comprehensive program needs to incorporate methods that will produce change on either or both sides of the equation.

Since humans are social beings, a child's behavioral pathology usually occurs in his relationships to other people. Therefore, it has proven useful to depict the interaction of a child with his system as: (1) a child (2) with another person (3) in a setting. Figure 1 diagrams the interplay of forces that produce behavior. To start with, there are the attributes and assumptions of the child, the adult, and the setting, e.g., a child's loneliness, a parent's need to dominate, or the quiet of a church.

As two people begin to relate to each other, these assumptions become translated into concrete rules that will govern the behavior of each person. These rules will develop from the interplay between each person's inner assumptions and the assumptions and attributes he perceives in the setting. For example, a dominating parent going into a silence-demanding church with her child will adopt the rule that it is her job to keep the child quiet.

## FIGURE 1
## Schematic Diagram of Systems Analysis Model

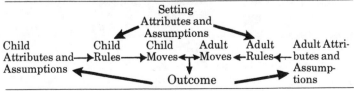

The child's rule, derived from loneliness, is that one does what one is told, to avoid further loneliness. The interplay of these two rules produces "shushing" by the parent and silence by the child. The outcome of this modifies the original assumptions and attributes of the system.

When a child's life is marked by stereotyped patterns of interaction with unsatisfactory or inefficient outcomes that block growth in important areas, he is likely to appear to be "emotionally disturbed." In assessing the child's problems and planning treatment, it has proven useful to outline these interaction patterns, rather than simply to diagnose the child's "condition." Classical diagnostic procedures fail to take into account that the child's condition and his setting are interdependent. Whether or not the classical labels are "correct," they often fail to lead to useful programs of action.

Figure 2 is a detailed analysis of a stereotyped interaction system. It is one that is quite common among children having academic problems in school; it could be labeled "dumb defiance."

In actual practice, we seldom need to outline all the components of an interactional system, and in this case we will leave out the personal assumptions and attributes of the teacher. Her behavior will be seen wholly in terms of the institutional attributes and assumptions that influence her in the classroom. The hypothetical situation shown on the chart could be described in the following narrative.

The child encounters the teacher after having been raised by a controlling and rejecting mother. This particular child has reacted to this circumstance by feeling helpless and deprived. He builds up great anger toward his parent and seeks revenge for the wrongs he feels were inflicted upon him. In his family, there is a rule that anger and defiance are never openly expressed. Therefore, the child is in a bind: he has unmet dependency needs which create anger and the need for revenge, but open expressions of his feelings would cause the parent to act even less loving toward him. This forces him to find a way of relating to parents (and later on, to others) that will allow him to gratify his dependency needs, feel in

## FIGURE 2
## Analysis of "Dumb Defiance"

### Setting Attributes and Assumptions

Teaching involves teachers educating children. It is the child's job to absorb and make use of what the teacher teaches.

Children must not make demands that interfere with the rights of other children in the classroom.

| Child's Attributes and Assumptions | Child's Rules | Child's Moves | Teacher's Moves | Teacher's Rules |
|---|---|---|---|---|
| Deprivation → Feeling helpless ........... Anger against parent | Let authority move first. | 1. Sits passively. | 2. Gives assignment. | Teachers assign work. |
| Revenge ............. People control other people ... | Cannot defy or control openly. | 3. Says he can't understand. | 4. Gives explanation. | Teacher's job to explain |
| Unmet dependency needs ...... | " " | 5. Does problem wrong. | 6. Gives help. | Children need much help to learn. |
| Anger or defiance against parent ......... Parents withdraw completely . | " " | 7. Dawdles at work. | 8. Assigns homework in anger. | It is unfair to spend too much time with one child. |
| ∴ Anger cannot be expressed openly ............. | Do what you are told. | 9. Takes work home. | | |

**Reinforcement Situation**

Moves 2, 4, 6, 8 reinforce child's assumption that he can control the teacher's behavior.

Move 9 reinforces assumption that teacher can control child's behavior.

Move 6 reinforces doing problems wrong as a way of getting dependency needs met.

Move 8 reinforces child's idea that he is stupid and helpless.

Move 7 reinforces dawdling as a way of getting back at people.

charge of things, and get angry revenge. Furthermore, the tactics he chooses must include disguise, for he must appear not to be doing any of these things.

When he meets the teacher in the classroom, the child plays out the interaction according to the "rules." He has learned that in order to be in charge of the relationship with an authority figure, it is best to let the authority make the first move. Therefore, the child first waits for the teacher to assign work. The teacher makes the expected complementary move and assumes the responsibility for defining the task. The child then responds passively by saying he doesn't understand. The teacher accepts the child's definition of himself as helpless, and makes active moves to explain and teach. The child then does the work (compliance), but does it wrong (defiance). The teacher continues to assume that it is her job to see that the child learns; she gives further help. The child continues by working on the problems assigned but taking too long a time to do them. The teacher responds by becoming disgusted and, in an angry tone of voice, assigns the child homework so that he can catch up.

The pattern, as a whole, appears to have unsatisfactory outcomes for both teacher and child, so one would wonder why it is repeated. However, a look at the circumstances surrounding each move will show a reinforcement pattern that maintains the system. In the first place, the teacher responds to every passive move on the child's part with an active move. This reinforces the child's assumption that people control other people. This reinforcement occurs even if the teacher herself is not really operating according to the assumption. That is, if the child's passive move is intended to elicit an active move by the teacher, then an active move by her—for whatever reason—will reinforce the child's view that he can control her. This system is particularly successful in the classroom, where direction and control generally come from the teacher, since the rules of the school dictate that the teacher be in charge of the class. Thus, even very good teachers, who truly accept learning as a reciprocal process, will get caught in this game because of the basic nature and institutionalized pattern of the school setting.

At Move 6, where the teacher gives help, the child's dependency needs are met and thus his move of doing the problem wrong is reinforced. At Move 8, several behaviors and expectations are reinforced. When the teacher becomes disgusted and angry, the child's need for revenge has been met. (Also, he will get revenge on his parents when he goes home and engages them in a struggle about doing the homework.) In addition, the teacher's anger and the child's inability to do the work have reinforced the child's view of himself as stupid and helpless. This, in turn, strengthens his need for gaining control and revenge, thus setting the stage for a repetition of the cycle the next day.

### Intervention techniques

In a systems approach, the goal is to modify the interaction in any way that will increase the likelihood of a more effective outcome. The outcome may be changed by varying any part of the system. One need not necessarily find the "real" or "underlying" cause of the problem. It is true that in order to increase the probability of effective long-range outcomes in a variety of situations, we must be able to change some of the assumptions, attributes, and rules that the individual brings to new situations. But these personal qualities will change as the outcomes of his activity change. The feelings of worthlessness of the child in the example above will be modified only when his interactions with people repeatedly have a positive outcome. Thus, any method that results in changed outcomes will change the individual's "dynamics," whether or not the method works directly with them. Even classical individual dynamic therapy can be seen as a method providing repeated experiences with new outcomes (Hobbs, 1961; Jackson & Haley, 1963).

Therapists are traditionally detached from the situations they attempt to treat. They act as diagnosticians, observers, interpreters, clarifiers, commentators, models, or blank screens—all concepts that imply being "outside" the situation and operating on it as a detached expert. However, the most obvious way to change a system is to inject into it additional people who are determined to operate according to assumptions that run contrary to those which control the system. In the examples of intervention to be outlined below, staff members are more often active participants in a system than expert manipulators of it.

In the project mentioned above (Kelleher, 1967), we used several different types of people with different backgrounds and levels of training. With the possible exception of the child care counselor, the categories of personnel are familiar to the reader. In brief, they are professionally untrained staff chosen from the ranks of hospital attendants. Their role evolved over the years along with the development of the systems analysis model. They became experts in direct intervention in ward, classroom, and home, who clarified ambiguities in communication, expectations, and behavioral consequences. They tended to have a more "personal" realtionship with the children than did the rest of the staff and, to some extent, to act as "models" for the children. But their primary role was to analyze the structure of a setting and intervene personally to change the interaction and the outcome for the child.

The question arose: Could the staff be "participants in the problem" and still maintain their role as "experts in solving problems?" Since in an historical sense, the staff have not participated in producing the problem, they are necessarily put in the position of seeing themselves as "healthy" and the patients as "sick," as long as they adopt a "historical" view of the cause of the problem. Even such stances as "We all have had problems," or "We meet the client at his own level" are not free of an air of condescension.

But if one adopts a primarily existential stance of "this-person-a-parent-here-with-me-the-expert-now," he sees himself, an imperfect expert in solving problems, face to face with a parent, an imperfect expert in parenting. Neither one knows at that moment where the ultimate solution will lie. Both are confused. From that moment on, both are a part of "the problem" if the problem is seen as the question of how to move toward more effective patterns of interaction. Their future interactions will be a groping together to arrive at a negotiated common ground of action and understanding. Thus, each can maintain his unique, expert role while at the same time conceding his confusion about the problem and promising his responsible participation in its solution.

If we look at a child-in-a-system, we can be impressed either by its stability or by its instability. At times it seems that the introduction of small changes (e.g., growth of the child, new people, or new expectations) can cause a realignment of forces that produces wholly new outcomes for the child. Crisis intervention operates on the principle that small interventions cause large changes (Hanford, 1965). At other times, the system seems to act in very powerful ways to prevent changes in the components, and to force new components to fit the old system or be rejected—thus maintaining the same outcome for the child. When more is learned about the formal operation of general feedback systems of this type, we may be able to predict with more precision whether a particular intervention is apt to change the system or be absorbed by it. We now depend upon the human "computer" for decisions about appropriate points of intervention.

# SOME THERAPEUTIC APPROACHES

## Family therapy

One can change the child-teacher system outlined above in a number of ways. One might work with the child outside the classroom with a view to changing his assumptions inside it. Conjoint family therapy (Satir, 1964) could be undertaken, with the goal of clarifying family messages about the giving and receiving of dependency, thus making the family more responsive to the child's legitimate requests for attention. In working at this, one would probably find it necessary to re-structure the relationship between mother and father around showing affection. Or one might choose to focus on the family "rule" that any open defiance leads to withdrawal of affection. If the child learned to show open defiance, he might experiment with it in the classroom. This would test the teacher's assumptions about whether or not a child can be forced to learn.

The Project staff found that a therapist meeting with a family once a week, pointing out their ineffective patterns of interaction, sometimes had little impact on their system. Often, families with extensive, ingrained, destructive interaction patterns would entice the therapist into joining the system, or the therapist would rationalize a reason for terminating therapy. In order to avoid this, the staff adopted the practice of using multiple therapists, who were encouraged to enter into the systems in very involved and often biased ways, thus creating a high impact over a short period of time.

At times, staff teams would go into the child's home for several hours or several days. This on-the-spot intervention in an on-going family routine seemed to have a powerful impact in many cases. Usually, careful follow-through in subsequent family sessions or visits to the home were necessary to make certain that gains were consolidated. In one case, a staff team went to a family's home at 7 a.m. to work on the routine of getting the son ready for school, as this difficulty was a prototype for the family's basic problem.

From time to time it was apparent that a child or parent would benefit from a change in subjective internal states, and that the changes sought would best occur in the context of a "human" or "therapeutic" relationship with another person. Historically, such an experience has been provided by either individual or group therapy based on dynamic, intrapsychic conceptions of personality change. Subjective experiences that transform internal dynamics cannot be forced or prescribed. They "happen" when two or more people leave themselves open for such an experience. But the situation and context that will maximize the probability of such a "happening" can be planned (Gordon, 1961).

The staff sometimes planned a one-to-one relationship between a child and a staff member, designed to change the child's basic attributes or assumptions. As we were able to specify more concretely what such a relationship should accomplish, it became apparent that a person with extensive training in individual therapy was not always necessary. Rather, the child care counselors could meet with the child on a scheduled basis to: provide an atmosphere where no demands were made, and the child was valued for himself alone; discuss the child's history in order to desensitize internal turmoil around past relationships; establish trust, provide practice in talking openly and directly with another person; and provide a neutral person against whom the child could throw all his distortions about life.

Some of the recent developments in T-groups (Bradford, Gibb, & Benne, 1964) and in marathon and encounter groups such as those at Esalen Institute, Big Sur, California, offer possibilities for providing a structure within which a person can experience a highly subjective relationship that modifies some of his most basic assumptions. If such an experience can be discussed in a family planning session afterwards, the person can be helped to translate the internal subjective changes into behavioral interactions with others.

One of the more powerful methods for producing change within an individual is chemical intervention. Rarely, however, is the giving of drugs viewed as involving social, as well as chemical, intervention. Hummel & Lubach (1966) point out the need to take into account the setting in which drugs are used, in planning for and assessing their effects.

## Teacher therapy

A second way to operate on the child-teacher system mentioned above would be to work with the teacher. It seemed to the Project staff that more attention needs to be paid to direct re-structuring of the teacher or school side of the behavioral equation. All too often, problems at school are interpreted as arising from historical problems at home, and the whole burden for change is placed on the family. We found that the most effective point of intervention was usually the point of origin of the complaint. If a teacher is dissatisfied with the way she and a child are interacting in the classroom, the place to start is the classroom (Ellis, *et. al.,* in press). Moving on to family problems is a later step—used only when classroom intervention is insufficient. (The reverse is true when there is an original or simultaneous complaint from the family.)

Thus, the Project staff usually attempted to deal directly with the setting in which the teacher worked. For example, in the situation described above, the traditional structure of the classroom, in which the teacher "teaches to" the child, allows this sequence to continue to its unsatisfactory end. If the child were transferred to a Montessori or learner-controlled classroom system, the usual sequence would immediately be broken up because the child would be responsible for making choices about learning and consequences would ensue directly from his attack on the material, rather than through his skill in manipulating the teacher.

Also, many teachers have a sterile, wishy-washy idea about the need for kindness and permissiveness with children who are defined as disturbed. Much of the fault for this seems to lie with mental health professionals who, historically, have advanced the notion that children with problems should be protected from stress, pressure, high expectations, or anything that might produce guilt or anxiety. In the experience of the staff, the most common problem in public schools is not the rigid, authoritarian teacher who suppresses the children's freedom and creativity, but rather the teacher who is hesitant, confused, and inconsistent about standards of behavior and expectations for learning.

It is true that a child will learn only when he wants to. Learning is the mutual responsibility of the teacher and the learner. If either one does not share control, learning does not occur. In fact, the child-teacher interaction described above is pathological to the extent that it operates on the false assumption that control of any relationship can be one-sided. This does not mean that the best way for a teacher to encourage a child to assume his responsibility is to abdicate hers. We found that a teacher could make loud, clear statements that she was here to expedite learning and that if the child intended to maintain the relationship he would have to participate in the learning process. Such statements were not perceived by the child as threats, but rather as opening up the possibility for him to engage, through his own choice, in a productive relationship with the teacher. (In a very few cases, after being presented over a period of time with clear choices about learning, a child would let the staff know that under the circumstances as they were for him at that time, he chose not to learn. Since the staff was not interested in simply outsmarting the children or using subtle blackmail under the guise of giving a choice, we accepted the child's decision and planned a program for him that was not based on academic learning. It is to be hoped that the social system will be flexible enough that these children can later change their minds.)

The introduction of reinforcement (operant conditioning) methods into the classroom also proved useful in modifying the teacher-setting variable (Holland &Skinner, 1961). Besides their usefulness in building skills, operant methods, in many instances, induced the teacher to pay more attention to what she and the children were doing in the classroom. Often teachers resort to wholistic statements about children such as, "He's *always* dawdling." Introducing objective behavioral observations (Flanders, 1960; Naumann & Parson, 1966) and reinforcement programs encouraged the teachers to look at the details and sequences of the teacher-child interaction. Further, a well-thought-out reinforcement program often operated as a "communications system" for the child, in which the giving of the reinforcement was, in part, a "cue" about the teacher's or parents' expectations.

In the case above, it would be useful to program the child's schoolwork carefully and work out a reinforcement system in which the parents would dispense the rewards after receiving a report from the teacher. This kind of approach gets at the child's assumptions about dependency and helplessness, besides putting the teacher-child interaction on a cooperative rather than competitive basis. Also, the process of working out the details of the program between school and parents offers an opportunity for communication and the clarification of expectations between the two parties.

Another example of establishing a clear setting expectation occurred with a child who had a long history of wild temper tantrums who was placed in a regular classroom. A child care counselor was assigned to sit there with him for two weeks. The goal was to establish in the child's mind that idea that the school had all resources necessary to handle his behavior, and also to allow the teacher and principal to evolve a philosophy and plan for handling the child when the counselor was no longer there. About a year later, a brief meeting between the counselor and a new teacher established the fact that the child could be held responsible for his behavior, even though he had been known to have an "emotional disturbance."

A third way to operate on a child-teacher interaction system is simply to prescribe different moves on the part of the teacher. This method, in which straightforward directions and advice are given to teacher, parent, or therapist, was successful in a surprising number of cases—contrary to traditional reservations about advice-giving. For example, at Move 6 in Figure 2, instead of giving help when the child did the problem wrong, the teacher could move away and indicate that when he was ready to ask for help, she would give it; this would reinforce asking for help directly and responsibly rather than indirectly and helplessly.

Or at Move 8, where the teacher angrily gave homework, a staff person could tell the child that he would be given plenty of time, and that he himself would sit with the child until he was able to get the answers right or say that he did not want to do the problems at all. This person would then stay with the child for as long a time (night and day) as he needed to make up his mind. The staff person would avoid vindictive lectures; he would simply indicate that he was going to remain until they "got things worked out."

This method strikes at the heart of this particular interactional system. The child is angry and defiant, but is ex-

# 11. A PROGRAM FOR EARLY INTERVENTION IN SCHOOL PHOBIA*

Samuel Waldfogel, Ph.D.,
Ellen Tessman, Ph.D.,
and Pauline B. Hahn, Ph.D.

During the past five years we have been conducting a clinical investigation into the causes and treatment of school phobia. From the beginning, a distinct relationship between prompt therapeutic intervention and remission of the acute symptom was noted (7). When treatment was initiated shortly after the symptom appeared, school attendance in most cases was resumed after a few weeks. By contrast, when treatment was delayed for a semester or more after the onset of the phobia, it persisted for months and even years after psychotherapy was begun. The relationship between the speed of intervention and the course of the symptom is shown in Table 1. The 26 cases included in this table were all seen at the Judge Baker Guidance Center during the first two years of the study, both the child and his parents being treated in accordance with established child guidance practices.

Reprinted from the *American Journal of Orthopsychiatry,* 1959, **29**, 324-332, by permission of the publisher and the authors. Copyright, the American Orthopsychiatric Association, Inc. Dr. Waldfogel was Director of Research, Judge Baker Guidance Center, Boston, Massachusetts. Dr. Tessman (now Dr. Berger) and Dr. Hahn are Senior Staff Psychologists at the Judge Baker Guidance Center.

* This work has been conducted with the partial support of the U. S. Public Health Service. During the initial period of the study (1953-55) support was received through Mental Health Grant MH661, and subsequently through Mental Health Grant M826.

### TABLE 1.
### Relationship Between Timing of Treatment
### and Symptomatic Improvement

| Treatment Begun | Treatment Required Before Regular Attendance | | | Total |
|---|---|---|---|---|
| | Up to 3 wks. | 3 wks. to 3 mos. | Over 3 mos. | |
| During same semester as onset of symptom | 15 | 5 | 1 | 21 |
| One or more semesters following onset of symptom | 0 | 0 | 5 | 5 |
| Total | 15 | 5 | 6 | 26 |

It can be seen that the majority of children treated during the same semester in which the symptom appeared had returned to school within three months. In the five cases where treatment was delayed none had returned to school by three months. The majority required between six months and a year of psychotherapy before regular school attendance was established, and in one case the phobia persists after four years of therapy.

It was further noted among this group of 26 cases that the severity of the personality disturbance accompanying the acute symptom varied considerably so that some children required much more treatment than others. In addition it appeared that the most seriously disturbed children and families were found in the group that was already beyond the fourth or fifth grade. With these children, interestingly enough, signs of trouble had almost always appeared earlier in their school careers, but had been neglected only to erupt in a more virulent form later on.

On the basis of these observations it was decided to undertake an exploratory program of early case finding for preventive purposes. The operation of this program has already been described (6). Briefly, the aims of the program were: (a) to identify cases of school phobia at their earliest manifestation; (b) to differentiate them on the basis of the severity of the underlying personality disturbance; (c) to develop methods of "emergency" treatment within the school for children in whom the problem appeared to be a focal one; (d) to refer to the clinic for intensive treatment those in whom the symptom appeared to represent a more widespread and serious personality disturbance. It was hoped that preventive methods could be evolved that would effect significant economy in therapeutic time in some instances, and prevent a chronic emotional disability from developing in others.

In order to implement this program the cooperation of the Newton Public Schools was secured, and a field unit of the Judge Baker Guidance Center was installed in their Division of Counseling Service.[1] The elementary school principals were invited to participate in the program and were instructed in the signs of incipient school phobia. They were requested to refer a child for evaluation as soon as these signs appeared. It was hoped thereby that intervention might begin before the child had definitely withdrawn from school.

The therapist tried to visit the school as soon after referral as possible, in order to get firsthand information from the principal and teacher regarding the child's previous school adjustment and his current status. If the child was still managing to attend school, it was then arranged for the therapist to meet the child. With the very youngest children, interviews could be held in a quiet corner of the classroom. With the older children it was the practice to retire to a nearby room for privacy. At this point an interview with the mother was scheduled in order to obtain a developmental history and to determine the degree of her neurotic involvement with the child. In the cases (the minority) in which the child was not attending school, arrangements were made to see both mother and child at the Division of Counseling Services. In a few instances, when it seemed indicated, an inter-

[1] The field unit consisted of the three authors, who, because of time limitations, were able to devote only between a half day and a day per week to the study. In this connection the authors wish to express their gratitude to Dr. Edward Landy, Director of the Division of Counseling Services, whose interest and support were instrumental in assuring the success of the project.

view was held with the father as a part of the process of evaluation.

The decision as to whether to proceed with limited intervention in the school or to refer the case to the clinic for more extended treatment was made after the first few contacts. It was based on a clinical evaluation of the relationship between mother and child and an assessment of their respective strengths. The decision was a tentative one and could be revised if the clinical picture changed. The evaluation was made with the aid of a number of diagnostic criteria which were derived from the recognition that school phobia has its dynamic origin in the hostile dependent relationship between mother and child. The specific dynamics of this relationship have been discussed elsewhere in detail (2, 3, 4, 6) and will not be repeated here. However, the criteria for determining choice of treatment will be described briefly.

1. *The degree of emotional separation of mother and child.*   This was judged by their past history as well as by their reactions to the immediate crisis. An attempt was made to evaluate the degree to which they were dependent on each other for gratification as well as the extent to which they utilized the symptom for secondary gain. The outlook was more promising when the child was actually struggling against his fear, and when the mother continued to exert pressure on him to conform to the demands of the school despite his discomfort.

2. *The degree to which the mother repressed her hostility toward the child.*   A favorable prognosis was associated with the mother's ability to face and express hostile feelings without overwhelming guilt. By contrast, some mothers resigned themselves without protest to every imposition foisted upon them by the child's problems and demands. Others reacted with more fury, but simultaneously denied their anger.

3. *Initial response to therapeutic intervention.*   Immediate reactions to the arrival of the therapist varied. It was regarded as a hopeful sign when the mother and

child could use the support offered by the therapist to permit them to function more effectively in dealing with the acute problem. In cases where there was less inherent strength, the therapist became the object of their frustrated dependency longings. He was perceived as someone who ought to rescue them magically from their plight, and his introduction into the picture precipitated a collapse of what little remaining will they had to fight their regressive wishes.

4. *Reaction to reality stress.* A valuable prognostic criterion in some cases was the response to reality crises that arose fortuitously. For example, in one instance the maternal grandmother died within a few weeks after the initial contact. In other instances either the child or some member of the family became ill, sometimes requiring hospitalization. Since events which threaten loss or separation often precipitate the acute symptom, the child's ability to weather these storms was regarded as a favorable sign.

In the cases where it was decided to limit therapeutic intervention, all interviews with the child were conducted in the school. Usually no more than ten half-hour interviews were required. At the beginning an attempt was made to see the child every week, but after the acute crisis subsided the interval between interviews was increased to allow for a gradual tapering off. The mother was usually seen less frequently than the child, but she was encouraged to telephone the therapist whenever a problem arose.

The specific therapeutic practices employed were based on a dynamic *theory of crisis* and evolved gradually as the study proceeded. Our theoretical position was influenced by the concept of the "corrective emotional experience" advanced some years ago by Alexander and French (1), as well as by recent developments in social psychiatry initiated by Erich Lindemann and his associates (5). The fundamental postulates of our viewpoint are twofold: 1) An emotional crisis reactivates unresolved conflicts that underlie the personality disturbance, thereby making them more visible and accessible to therapeutic intervention. 2) During a time of crisis emotional experiences are intensified and have a greater and more permanent impact than ordinarily. The second proposition has two important corollaries. (a) The experience of failure to resolve the crisis satisfactorily is potentially traumatic and may lead to regression, increased vulnerability and ego constriction. (b) The experience of mastery, by contrast, has a therapeutic impact, counteracting earlier failures and freeing the ego for further growth and development.

In accordance with our over-all plan of treatment, every effort is made to keep the child in school despite the fact that this often causes him and his mother considerable distress, and they would prefer to escape this responsibility. During the acute phase, their anxiety around separation as well as their resentment at their dependence on each other stands out in bold relief, and skillful handling will permit the therapist to capitalize on this situation to help them gain insight and achieve greater autonomy. It is most important for him to recognize that under these circumstances their angry and dependent feelings will be transferred to him, especially since he is perceived as imposing difficult demands. He must be prepared to support these feelings and yet stand firmly behind the demands of reality. It is our impression that in so doing, he not only enhances his therapeutic effectiveness, but also decreases the likelihood of any serious regression.

In addition to offering support the therapist provides an opportunity for the cathartic expression of such feelings as rage, fear, and guilt at a time of acute distress. Beyond that he is able to clarify and interpret conflicts at levels not too far removed from conscious awareness. Finally, he is in a position to encourage greater maturity and autonomy in both mother and child.

There are a number of therapeutic advantages in operating directly in the school. To begin with, the therapist can offer direct support to the child in the feared situation. In addition he can help the principal and the teacher by relieving them of their sense of helpless bewilderment and guilt. By modifying their feelings toward the child he is able to work with them toward altering whatever reality factors exist to aggravate the child's fears. Sometimes adjustments need to be made, such as reducing the pressure of work and allowing the child to attend only part of the day. On rare occasions, the child must be transferred to another class. This is necessary when the teacher and child (or his mother) have become particularly threatening to each other, and requires the utmost delicacy in handling. The therapist who is present in the school is in a much better position to assess the situation as it develops, and plan his strategy accordingly.

The actual operation of these principles is demonstrated concretely in the case presentation that follows. This case is fairly typical of those that were seen on a limited basis, and the favorable therapeutic outcome is not in any way exceptional.

Sue, who was five and one-half years-old at the time of referral, was in her second semester in kindergarten. Before starting she had looked forward to going to school, entered without any difficulty, and seemed to be enjoying it a great deal. However, on one occasion during the first semester she became sick to her stomach for no apparent reason and had to be sent home. At Christmas time the parents left town for a few days, and when they returned Sue became ill with a virus infection. When it was time for her to return to school she became panicky, complained of stomach-aches, vomited, and wept because she didn't want to go back to school. Her mother, however, put pressure on her to go to school, and though there were increased absences Sue continued to attend. The problem persisted until finally after about two months the case was referred to the field unit for help.

According to the mother (Mrs. M), Sue had changed quite suddenly from a happy, buoyant, independent child to a fearful, clinging little girl for no apparent reason. It developed, however, that the phobia had appeared just a few weeks before Mrs. M. was scheduled to have an ear operation. This operation was especially significant since it was necessitated by a condition that had developed during mother's pregnancy with Sue. There was a progressive loss of hearing in both ears which, if left untreated, might have led to total deafness. A year before, one ear had been successfully operated on; but she had tried to conceal the operation from the children by telling them that she was going on a trip for two days. Apparently, Sue's own illness, the impending operation, and the absence of the parents at this critical time had combined to precipitate the acute symptoms.

Although Sue had been experiencing acute anxiety attacks every morning before going to school, when first seen by the therapist, she appeared as a charming and vivacious little girl who quickly established a very comfortable relationship. She was small for her age, and this reinforced the general impression of immaturity which she gave. A slight impediment in speech added to her somewhat infantile quality.

Sue was seen 14 times over approximately four months. The interviews centered around three general areas: her concern about mother, her conflict about whether to "grow up or be a baby," and some of her fantasies around oedipal conflicts. In relation to her mother Sue verbalized her fear that something might happen to her. She was afraid that her mother might get into an accident, be run over by a car, and then have to go to the hospital. She recalled mother's hospitalization the previous year. Her fantasy was that mother had to go to the hospital because she had cut herself on a vase, which had been broken by a bad little boy. He had tried to conceal the damage by putting the broken parts together, and mother, not knowing this, picked it up and cut herself. There were other similar fantasies, which expressed Sue's guilt about her hostility. The therapist explained that hostile feelings were not necessarily equated with badness, and this seemed to be effective in relieving some of her guilt. Following this she felt free to express openly her wish to be a baby again, both verbally and by exaggerated infantile behavior. At the same time she proudly displayed all her mature accomplishments, such as writing her name, and looked forward eagerly to going into the first grade. The therapist accepted and indulged her regressive impulses and simultaneously supported her strivings toward greater autonomy and maturity.

As therapy proceeded, more and more time was spent in fantasy and doll play centering about the family romance. She vacillated between her desire to re-establish a close union with mother and her wish to displace mother as the object of father's affection. At this time she developed a very intense relationship with a little girl in her class, which was accompanied by open displays of affection and fantasies that they were twins, had the same name, and would marry each other. It appeared that she was attempting to resolve some of her oedipal conflicts and bisexual strivings through this friendship, which in many ways was characteristic of latency.

Sue's mother was also seen during this period but only about half as frequently. Mrs. M could not recall very much about Sue's early development, but did stress her independence and how quickly she seemed to have grown up. She responded with anger to Sue's sudden regressive behavior—the baby talk, excessive demands, etc.—and at the same time wondered guiltily if she had babied her enough as an infant. Her conflicting feelings resulted in her inability to deal successfully with the mounting demands that Sue was making on her. During the early interviews she focused on these day-by-day problems and was helped to see that her incapacitation was largely a result of her guilt.

Subsequently she expressed a good deal of anxiety about her pending ear operation. At the same time she reported that loud sounds were painful to the ear that had already been operated on, and she found this very frightening. The noise that disturbed her more than any other was Sue's high-pitched shrieking when she quarreled with her older sister. The resentment that stemmed from Mrs. M's fear that Sue's hostile outbursts would damage her again were patently related to her anxiety that some calamity might befall Sue if she went to school when she was upset. As Mrs. M was able to express these concerns and her guilt over her hostile impulses was relieved, she could perceive her own part in the disturbed relationship more objectively, and her anxiety diminished.

At this point Sue's symptoms began to subside. Mrs. M arranged for her own operation, which she had postponed while Sue was at the height of her phobia. Moreover, she was able to discuss this with the children and prepared them adequately. Nevertheless, there was a mild recurrence of some of Sue's phobic symptoms at the time of the operation. The school year drew to a close shortly thereafter, and the interviews were discontinued with the understanding that if further help was needed in the fall, mother would get in touch with the therapist. This was not necessary, and when a follow-up study was done in the winter, it was reported that Sue had been completely symptom-free all that year. She appeared to be enjoying school very much, was doing superior work, and was described by her teacher as an exuberant and charming little girl.

A total of 36 children with symptoms of school phobia were referred to the Judge Baker field unit during its two years of operation in the Newton school system. The distribution of cases according to sex and grade is given in Table 2. Though the frequency of girls, in this group, is somewhat larger than that of boys, the difference does not appear large enough to alter our previous impression that the incidence of school phobia is approximately the same for the two sexes. The present grade distribution confirms our previous findings that school phobia is a disorder which occurs primarily in the elementary school grades. The frequency tends to be highest from kindergarten to the fourth grade, and then decreases; only five of the 36 cases were found in the fifth and sixth grades.

## TABLE 2.
## Sex and Grade Distribution
## of the School Referrals

| Sex | Grades | | | | Total |
|---|---|---|---|---|---|
| | Kdgn. | 1-2 | 3-4 | 5-6 | |
| Boys | 3 | 7 | 3 | 1 | 14 |
| Girls | 6 | 5 | 7 | 4 | 22 |
| Total | 9 | 12 | 10 | 5 | 36 |

To obtain some indication of our therapeutic effectiveness a follow-up study was conducted during the next year. For the children treated in the school the follow-up was done from six to 18 months after the termination of contact with the child. In the case of the four children who were referred to the clinic for intensive treatment, three were still in treatment at the time of the follow-up.

The follow-up evaluation was based on information received from each child's teacher or principal, or both, who were interviewed personally. We were interested in obtaining a description of the child's general functioning in school and the status of his symptom since termination of the contact. In regard to the symptomatic picture we inquired about regularity of school attendance, manifestations of anxiety in the classroom, and whether the parents had reported any indications of reluctance to attend. In addition we were interested in obtaining an evaluation of the child's school functioning in regard to academic performance and class adjustment to determine if there had been any displacement of the symptom into another area of functioning.

The distribution of the 36 cases according to the type of intervention and their status at the time of follow-up is presented in Table 3. Of the 36 children, 16 were seen for brief therapy in the school and four were referred to the clinic for intensive treatment. In five of the remaining 16 children, symptomatic remission had occurred by the time the child was contacted. Since the situation in these cases had become stabilized before contact was established, it was decided to intervene only in the event of an

## TABLE 3.
## Results of Follow-Up of School Referrals

| | Total | Symptom | | | Academic Performance | | | Classroom Adjustment | | |
|---|---|---|---|---|---|---|---|---|---|---|
| | | Absent | Recurring | Persisting | Superior | Satisfactory | Unsatisfactory | Good | Minor Problems | Poor |
| Therapy in school | 16 | 14 | 2 | 0 | 7 | 9 | 0 | 6 | 10 | 0 |
| Therapy in clinic | 4 | 4 | 0 | 0 | 1 | 3 | 0 | 2 | 2 | 0 |
| Spontaneous recovery | 5 | 4 | 1 | 0 | 2 | 3 | 0 | 0 | 5 | 0 |
| No therapy | 11 | 3 | 5 | 3 | 3 | 6 | 2 | 1 | 6 | 4 |

173

exacerbation of the acute symptoms. In the remaining 11 cases in which there was no therapeutic intervention, either the parents were uncooperative, or therapeutic time was not available.

Of the 16 children who had brief therapy in school, 14 were symptom-free and had been symptom-free since the termination of contact. Two had recurring symptoms; i.e., there had been brief symptomatic flare-ups since termination. However, in neither of these children did the symptoms persist. Academic performance was either superior or satisfactory for this group, and no severe problems in classroom adjustment were reported. The four children treated in the clinic showed a similar pattern.

The same pattern was also found among the five cases of spontaneous recovery. In only one of these was there any recurrence of the phobic symptoms, and none had any serious learning or behavior problems.

The remaining 11 cases in which there was no thera-peutic intervention differ from the above groups. Only three children were symptom-free; five had recurring symptoms and three had persisting symptoms. Correspondingly, a greater number of severe school problems were reported.

While the difference in the rate of recovery in the treated and untreated groups is impressive, it must be remembered that the numbers in both groups are small, and—even more important—the cases were not randomly selected. There is reason to believe that some bias has entered into the composition of the groups. For example, seven of the afore-mentioned 11 untreated cases were uncooperative, and it is our impression that there is a relationship between unwillingness to accept treatment and the severity of the problem. This would imply that the 20 children in the treated group were on the whole less disturbed. If this was in fact the case, a relatively larger number of spontaneous recoveries might have been anticipated in this group than in the un-treated group had there been no intervention. How large this number would have been, one can only surmise. However, it was our definite impression, based on our clinical experience, that without help, many of these cases would have developed into severe chronic problems. To establish this conclusively would have required a more carefully controlled investigation than it was possible for us to conduct.

We feel certain that many of the cases referred would have been neglected had it not been for our active program of case finding. While 36 cases may not seem like a large figure over a two-year period, it must be remembered that we were operating in a small school system, and that the over-all incidence of school phobia is small. Actually, the number turned out to be much larger than had been anticipated on the basis of the previous experience of Newton's Division of Counseling Services. Apparently their experience had been mainly with the most severe, protracted cases.

The success of this pilot program has implications that go beyond the problem of school phobia. It is well known that other emotional disturbances often find their central expression in the school, appearing as behavior difficulties, learning problems, and the like. This gives the school tremendous potential—which has hardly been tapped—for the early detection and prevention of emotional disorders, and places it in a strategic position in any comprehensive program of mental health.

## REFERENCES

1. Alexander, F., & French, T. M., *Psychoanalytic Therapy.* New York: Ronald Press, 1946.

2. Eisenberg, L. School Phobia: A Study in the Communication of Anxiety. *Am. J. Psychiatry,* 114: 712-718, 1958.

3. Estes, H. R., Haylett, C. H. & Johnson, A. M. Separation Anxiety. *Am. J. Psychotherapy,* 10: 682-695, 1956.

4. Johnson, A. M., Falstein, E. I., Szurek, S. A. & Svendsen, M., School Phobia. *Am. J. Orthopsychiatry,* 11: 702-711, 1941.

5. Lindemann, E. *The Meaning of Crisis in Individual and Family Living. Teach. Coll. Rec.,* 57: 310-315, 1956.

6. Waldfogel, S., Coolidge, J. C. & Hahn, P. B. *The Development, Meaning and Management of School Phobia: Workshop. Am. J. Orthopsychiatry,* 27: 754-780, 1957.

7. Waldfogel, S., Hahn, P. B. & Landy, E. *School Phobia: Causes and Management. School Counselor,* 3: 19-25, 1955.

# 12. SCHOOL PHOBIA: RAPID TREATMENT OF FIFTY CASES*

## Wallace A. Kennedy, Ph.D.

School phobia, a dramatic and puzzling emotional crisis, has attracted considerable attention for a number of years. Phobias in general are the subjects of widely differing theories of dynamics and treatment. The controversy regarding the treatment of children's phobias dates from the earliest case studies presented by Freud (1909), continues through the laboratory demonstrations of Watson and Jones (Jones, 1924) to the more recent experimental treatment of Wolpe (1954). There have been five broad reviews since the earliest paper presented by Johnson et al. in 1941: Klein (1945), Waldfogel, Coolidge, and Hahn (1957), Kahn (1958), Glaser (1959), and Sperling (1961). These reviews in the main support the contention that the major weight of evidence thus far leans toward the psychoanalytic interpretation of phobias, while the work of Wolpe is more consistent with the approach presented herein.

The psychoanalytic theory stresses the role of the

Reprinted from *Journal of Abnormal Psychology,* 1965, **70,** 285-289, by permission of the publisher and the author. Dr. Kennedy is Professor of Psychology and Director of Clinical Training, Florida State University, Tallahassee, Florida.

* The research reported herein was supported through the Human Development Clinic of Florida State University, Tallahassee, Florida.

mother in the development of school phobia. A close symbiotic relationship, which displays itself in an overdependency, is present between the mother and child. Stemming from an unsatisfactory relationship with her own mother, the mother finds it difficult to cope with her own emotional needs. The father often is in a competing role with the mother, and seems to try to outdo her in little tasks around the home: in trying to strengthen his own image, he depreciates that of the mother. He too overidentifies with the child. Thus, the emotional climate of his family prevents the child from ever finding out whether or not he, of his own volition, can solve problems. Possessive, domineering parents tend to make the child's growth toward independence difficult. His guilt regarding his own impulses is transformed into depression: the anxiety can reach extreme proportions.

On the other hand, Wolpe sees the phobia as a learned reaction, which he treats through direct symptom attack with what he calls reciprocal inhibition, or desensitization.

Interest in the school phobia problem, which occurs at the rate of 17 cases per thousand school-age children per year, has been greatly intensified in the past few years. An extremely significant advance was made by Coolidge and the Judge Baker group in 1957, when they presented evidence that there were not one, but two types of school phobia, which, although sharing a common group of symptoms, differed widely in others. These are referred to as Type 1 School Phobia, or the neurotic crisis and Type 2 School Phobia, or the way-of-life phobia. The common symptoms are: *(a)* Morbid fears associated with school attendance; a vague dread of disaster; *(b)* Frequent somatic complaints: headaches, nausea, drowsiness; *(c)* Symbiotic relationship with mother, fear of separation; anxiety about many things: darkness, crowds, noises; *(d)* Conflict between parents and the school administration.

At the Human Development Clinic of Florida State University, ten differential symptoms between Type 1 and

## Ten Differential School Phobia Symptoms

| Type 1 | Type 2 |
|---|---|
| 1. The present illness is the first episode. | 1. Second, third, or fourth episode. |
| 2. Monday onset, following an illness the previous Thursday or Friday. | 2. Monday onset following minor illness not a prevalent antecedent. |
| 3. An acute onset. | 3. Incipient onset. |
| 4. Lower grades most prevalent. | 4. Upper grades most prevalent. |
| 5. Expressed concern about death. | 5. Death theme not present. |
| 6. Mother's physical health in question: actually ill or child thinks so. | 6. Health of mother not an issue. |
| 7. Good communication between parents. | 7. Poor communication between parents. |
| 8. Mother and father well adjusted in most areas. | 8. Mother shows neurotic behavior; father, a character disorder. |
| 9. Father competitive with mother in household management. | 9. Father shows little interest in household or children. |
| 10. Parents achieve understanding of dynamics easily. | 10. Parents very difficult to work with. |

Type 2 School Phobia have been determined. A differential diagnosis can be made logically and empirically on the basis of any 7 of the 10.

## PROBLEM

In the Fall of 1957 the Clinic embarked upon an experimental procedure for the treatment of Type 1 School Phobia—a procedure similar to that of Rodriguez, and Eisenberg (1959) with one major exception: whereas Rodriguez made no distinction between types of school phobia and treated in the same manner all cases which came to the clinic, the 50 cases reported herein were selected on the basis of the criteria mentioned above. The Florida State University Human Development Clinic, as a teaching and research clinic, does not generally see deeply disturbed children, but refers them to other agencies.

In the eight-year period covered by the report, there have been six cases which would meet the criteria of Type 2 School Phobia. These six cases were treated by supportive therapy for the children and parents. None of the six Type 2 cases had more than three of the ten Type 1 criteria, and the results were completely dissimilar to those reported for the 50 Type 1 cases. All of the Type 2 cases were chronic in

## TABLE 1
### Year of Treatment and Sex
### of 50 Type-One School Phobia Cases

| Year | | Male | Female | Total |
|------|---|------|--------|-------|
| 1957 | | 1 | 0 | 1 |
| 1958 | | 1 | 1 | 2 |
| 1959 | | 4 | 2 | 6 |
| 1960 | | 4 | 8 | 12 |
| 1961 | | 6 | 3 | 9 |
| 1962 | | 5 | 4 | 9 |
| 1963 | | 4 | 5 | 9 |
| 1964 | | 0 | 2 | 2 |
| | Total | 25 | 25 | 50 |

nature. All had family histories of one or more parents seriously disturbed. Two of the cases were diagnosed as having schizophrenia; two were diagnosed as having character disorders with the school phobia being a minor aspect of the case. One of the six was hospitalized; one was sent to a training school. Of the four remaining, two were able to go to college, although their records were poor and their symptoms continued. These six cases were in treatment for an average of ten months. In no circumstances was a school phobia case changed from Type 1 to Type 2, or vice versa.

This experimental procedure with Type 1 School Phobia was begun with considerable caution, with only one case in 1957 and two the following spring. The treatment involved the application of broad learning theory concepts by blocking the escape of the child and preventing secondary gains from occurring. In addition, the child was reinforced for going to school without complaint. This rapid treatment procedure has now been followed with 50 cases.

## Subject Population

Subjects for the 50 cases over an eight-year period were school-age children, all suffering from the first evidence of a phobic attack, from the geographical area served by the Human Development Clinic of Florida State University. The subject distribution by year and sex is illustrated in Table 1, by symptom and sex in Table 2, by age and sex in Table 3, and by grade and sex in Table 4.

The fathers' mean age for the male subjects was 36; the mothers', 35. For the female subjects the fathers' mean age was 38; the mothers', 36. The boys' mean age was nine; that of the girls', ten. There was no definite pattern in birth order of the subjects, or in number of siblings.

## TABLE 2
## Symptom Checklist and Sex
## of 50 Type-One
## School Phobia Cases

| Symptom | Male | Female | Total |
|---|---|---|---|
| 1. First attack | 25 | 25 | 50 |
| 2. Monday onset—Thursday illness | 24 | 25 | 49 |
| 3. Acute onset | 25 | 23 | 48 |
| 4. Lower grades | 22 | 18 | 40 |
| 5. Death theme | 22 | 22 | 44 |
| 6. Mother's health an issue | 23 | 21 | 44 |
| 7. Good parental marital harmony | 24 | 23 | 47 |
| 8. Good parental mental health | 23 | 24 | 47 |
| 9. Father helper in the house | 21 | 21 | 42 |
| 10. Parents achieve insight quickly | 24 | 25 | 49 |

## TABLE 3
## Age and Sex
## of 50 Type-One
## School Phobia Cases

| Age | Male | Female | Total |
|---|---|---|---|
| 4 | 0 | 1 | 1 |
| 5 | 3 | 1 | 4 |
| 6 | 2 | 3 | 5 |
| 7 | 3 | 2 | 5 |
| 8 | 3 | 1 | 4 |
| 9 | 3 | 5 | 8 |
| 10 | 4 | 3 | 7 |
| 11 | 1 | 2 | 3 |
| 12 | 3 | 0 | 3 |
| 13 | 2 | 4 | 6 |
| 14 | 1 | 2 | 3 |
| 15 | 0 | 0 | 0 |
| 16 | 0 | 1 | 1 |
| Total | 25 | 25 | 50 |

## Method and Results

During the course of the past eight years, 50 cases of Type 1 School Phobia have been treated. Five of these cases might be considered semicontrols because they were untreated Type 1 cases of some duration, or they were Type 1 cases unsuccessfully treated elsewhere before they were seen at the clinic. One of these semicontrol cases had been out of school for one year, and the other four had been out for over three months.

All 50 of the cases responded to the treatment program with a complete remission of the school phobia symptoms, and follow-up study indicates no evidence of any outbreaks of substitute symptoms or recurrence of the phobia.

In the follow-up schedule the parents were phoned in about two weeks, and again in six weeks, to see if the progress had continued. They were then phoned on a yearly basis, except in 1961, when follow-up interviews were conducted reaching 19 of the 21 cases completed at that time. During the course of the eight years, six families were lost because of moving with no forwarding address. Of these lost cases, none had been followed less than two years, two were followed three years, and one for four years.

# RAPID TREATMENT PROCEDURE

The rapid treatment program for Type 1 school phobia involves six essential components: good professional public relations, avoidance of emphasis on somatic complaints, forced school attendance, structured interview with parents, brief interview with child, and follow-up.

## Good Professional Public Relations

It is necessary to establish good communication with schools, physicians, and parent groups, such that the cases are likely referred on the second or third day of the phobic attack. This groundwork involves the typical mental health consultation and case-by-case follow-up with the referring source.

## Avoidance of Emphasis on Somatic Complaints

If phobic qualities predominate, that is, if the child conforms to seven of the differential symptoms of Type 1 School Phobia, emphasis on somatic complaints should be avoided. For instance, the child's somatic complaints should be handled matter-of-factly, with an appointment to see the pediatrician after school hours. Abdominal pains will probably require the pediatrician to make a prompt physical examination, but this can probably be done on the way to school.

**TABLE 4**
**Grade and Sex**
**of 50 Type-One**
**School Phobia Cases**

| Grade | Male | Female | Total |
|---|---|---|---|
| Nursery School | 0 | 2 | 2 |
| Kindergarten | 4 | 0 | 4 |
| First | 4 | 4 | 8 |
| Second | 0 | 1 | 1 |
| Third | 6 | 4 | 10 |
| Fourth | 3 | 4 | 7 |
| Fifth | 2 | 2 | 4 |
| Sixth | 3 | 1 | 4 |
| Seventh | 2 | 2 | 4 |
| Eighth | 0 | 2 | 2 |
| Ninth | 1 | 2 | 3 |
| Tenth | 0 | 1 | 1 |
| Total | 25 | 25 | 50 |

## Forced School Attendance

It is essential to be able to require the child to go to school and to be willing to use any force necessary. In all of the present cases, simply convincing the parents of this necessity and having them come to a firm decision, has generally been enough. The ability to be decisive when necessary has been essential.

Have the father take the child to school. These fathers are not unkind, and they can show authority when necessary.

Have the principal or attendance officer take an active part in keeping the child in the room.

Allow the mother to stand in the hall, if she must, or to visit the school during the morning, but not to stay.

## Structured Interview with the Parents

Stressing the following points, conduct with the parents a structured interview designed to give them sufficient confidence to carry out the therapeutic program even in the face of considerable resistance from the child.

*Lead the interview.*   The confidence of the parents is

greatly increased by the interviewer's verifying the history rather than taking it. Correctly anticipating seven out of ten variables within a family structure is well calculated to induce full cooperation.

*Be optimistic.* Stressing the transient nature, the dependable sequence of a difficult Monday, a somewhat better Tuesday, and a symptom-free Wednesday, tends to lighten the depression of the parents regarding their child's unwillingness to go to school.

*Emphasize success.* Type 1 cases always recover. Ninety percent of the Type 1 phobics stay at school most of the first day. Along with optimism comes a slight mobilization of hostility which helps the parents to follow the plan.

*Present the formula.* Simply but directly, with repetition for emphasis, outline a plan for the parents to follow, assuming that it is the end of the school week by the time of the referral and that the interview with the parents is conducted on Thursday or Friday.

## Parent Formula

Do not discuss in any way, school attendance over the weekend. There is nothing a phobic child does better than talk about going to school. Don't discuss going to school. Don't discuss phobic symptoms. Simply tell the child Sunday evening, "Well, son, tomorrow you go back to school."

On Monday morning get the child up, dressed, and ready for school. Give the child a light breakfast to reduce the nausea problem. Have the father take the child matter-of-factly off to school. Don't ask him how he feels, or why he is afraid to go to school, or why he doesn't like school. Simply take him to school, turn him over to the school authorities, and go home.

If the child therapist has not seen the child the previous week, he may see him after school on the first day.

On Monday evening, compliment the child on going to school and staying there, no matter how resistant he has been, no matter how many times he has vomited, cried, or started to leave. If he has been at school for 30 minutes on Monday, progress is being made. Tell the child Monday evening that Tuesday will be much better, and make no further mention of the symptom.

Tuesday can be expected to be a repetition of Monday, but with everything toned down considerably. On Tuesday evening, encourage and compliment the child strongly for doing so much better.

Wednesday should be virtually symptom free. Wednesday evening, with considerable fanfare, give a party for the child in honor of his having overcome his problem.

## Brief Interview with the Child

The child himself should be seen only briefly by the child therapist and only after school hours. The content of the interview should be stories which stress the advantage of going on in the face of fear: how student pilots need to get back into the air quickly after an accident, and how important it is to get right back on the horse after a fall. In addition the therapist can describe real or imaginary events in his own childhood when he was frightened for awhile but everything turned out all right: all to stress to the child the transitory nature of the phobia.

## Follow-Up

Follow-up by phone, being chatty and encouraging and not oversolicitous. In the long-range follow-up, chat with the parents about further school phobia symptoms, incidence of other phobias, school attendance records, academic progress, and the occurrence of other emotional problems in the child.

# DISCUSSION

Two legitimate concerns have been expressed regarding preliminary reports at local meetings. The first is a concern about the claim of complete remission for all 50 cases—a claim inconsistent with the usual child guidance clinic success rate—and the consequent belief that the criterion for success is simply too narrow. Only self-report data and reports from school administrations are available regarding the symptom-free nature of these children once this phobic episode has passed. It is true that no diagnostic evaluation has been undertaken with any of these children during follow-up. It must be remembered, however, that the definition of symptom remission is restricted to those obvious symptoms which might conceivably lead the parents or school officials to re-refer the children to the clinic. In this regard, these 50 children in the Type 1 School Phobia group are symptom free.

Because of the nature of the Human Development Clinic and the nature of this project, careful selection has been exercised in accepting cases, as mentioned above. Due to the relationship between the schools and the clinic, and the clear definition of cases suitable for the project, there is reason to believe that the majority of Type 1 School Phobia cases in the five-county area the clinic serves have come to our attention, whereas the local county mental health clinic has received a high percentage of the Type 2 cases. The success of the Type 2 cases of school phobia accepted by the Human Development Clinic for teaching purposes has not been remarkable.

The second concern is that perhaps what is called Type 1 School Phobia is not really a severe phobic attack at all, but borders on malingering of a transient nature which would spontaneously remit in a few days anyway. In fact, because of the apparent sound mental health of the family as a group, its middle-class values which stress school, and the family's good premorbid history, including the academic record of the child, there is little reason to doubt that the majority of the cases would eventually return to school whatever treatment was undertaken. However, our five semicontrol cases and evidence seen from other clinics of Type 1 cases that have been out of school for prolonged periods suggest that this method of treatment may accelerate or facilitate the remission. Recommendation for the use of this technique is restricted, then, to those cases showing Type 1 symptoms which, in spite of their possible transient nature, present a rather serious problem to teachers, parents, and counselors.

# REFERENCES

1. Coolidge, J. C., Hahn, P. B., & Peck, A. L. School phobia: Neurotic crisis or way of life. *American Journal of Orthopsychiatry,* 1957, **27,** 296-306.

2. Eisenberg, L.: School phobia: a study in the communication of anxiety, *American Journal of Psychiatry,* 1958, **114,** 712.

3. Freud, S. *Analysis of a phobia in a five-year-old boy.* (Std. Ed.), New York: W. W. Norton, 1909.

4. Glaser, K. Problems in school attendance: School phobia and related conditions. *Pediatrics,* 1959, **55,** 758. (Abstract)

5. Johnson, A. M., et al. School phobia: A study of five cases. *American Journal of Orthopsychiatry,* 1941, **11,** 702. (Abstract)

6. Jones, M. C. A laboratory study of fear: The case of Peter. *Journal of Genetic Psychology,* 1924, **31,** 308-315.

7. Kahn, J. H. School refusal—some clinical and cultural aspects. *Medical Officer,* 1958, **100,** 337. (Abstract)

8. Klein, E. The reluctance to go to school. *Psychoanalytic Study of the Child,* 1945, **1,** 263. (Abstract)

9. Rodriguez, A., Rodriguez, M., & Eisenberg, L. The outcome of school phobia: A follow-up study based on 41 cases. *American Journal of Psychiatry,* 1959, **116,** 540-544.

10. Sperling, M. Analytic first aid in school phobias. *Psychoanalytic Quarterly,* 1961, **30,** 504. (Abstract)

11. Waldfogel, S., Coolidge, J. C., & Hahn, P. B. Development, meaning and management of school phobia. *American Journal of Orthopsychiatry,* 1957, **27,** 754. (Abstract)

12. Wolpe, J. Reciprocal inhibition as the main basis of psychotherapeutic effects. *A.M.A. Archive of Neurology and Psychiatry,* 1954, **72,** 204-226.

# 13. A PROJECT TO TEACH LEARNING SKILLS TO DISTURBED, DELINQUENT CHILDREN

Salvador Minuchin, M.D., Pamela Chamberlain
and Paul Graubard, Ed.D.

This paper will describe a pilot project conducted at the Floyd Patterson House, a community residential treatment center for juvenile delinquents. The project was designed to explore certain hunches and experiences of the authors after extensive work with multi-problem lower-class families.

It has been our experience that the psychological disturbance of the children in such families almost always is accompanied by lack of achievement in school and academic subjects, despite individual intelligence tests showing that some children are of normal or superior intelligence. It was felt that an exploration of the learning style of the disturbed delinquent not only would help us discover ways of teaching the disturbed child, but also might bring to light evidence about ways of teaching his psychologically healthier but equally non-achieving siblings and peers.

Reprinted from the *American Journal of Orthopsychiatry,* 1967, **37,** 558-567, by permission of the publisher and the authors. Copyright, the American Orthopsychiatric Association, Inc. Dr. Minuchin is Director of the Philadelphia Child Guidance Clinic and Professor of Child Psychiatry and Pediatrics at the University of Pennsylvania, Philadelphia. Pamela Chamberlain is a remedial educator and volunteer coordinator, Floyd Patterson House, Wiltwyck School for Boys, New York, New York. Dr. Graubard is Assistant Professor of Education, Department of Special Education, Ferkauf Graduate School of Education, Yeshiva University, New York, New York.

The authors of this paper also were interested in exploring the feasibility of a model of interdisciplinary collaboration between clinician and educator. In this project the clinician, whose background and orientation included work in social psychiatry and family therapy, developed a profile of the cognitive-affective style of the children of disorganized low socio-economic families. This profile was developed in such a way that it helped the educators in the project develop an intervention or repairing curriculum which made it feasible to teach these children.* This paper will, therefore, be organized in two sections. The first section will present an overview of (1) socialization processes in the disorganized low socio-economic family as gathered through the psychiatrist's tools and (2) some of the assumptions about the influence of these processes on the learning style of the child and his encounters with school. The second part will describe the intervention curriculum and the pilot project which was developed to explore ways of enabling these children to learn.

## Socialization Processes in the Disorganized Low Socioeconomic Family†

We will (1) summarize certain family interactions that contribute to disturbances in focal attention of the child and (2) delineate characteristics of the communication patterns in the child.

1. Parents' responses to children's behavior are global and erratic and, therefore, deficient in conveying rules which can be internalized. The parental emphasis is on the control and inhibition of behavior rather than on guiding and developing responses. The unpredictability of parental controlling signals handicaps the child's development of rules. Since the child cannot determine what part of his behavior is inappropriate, he learns to

*For a review of the literature, see the December, 1965 issue of the *Review of Educational Research,* Vol. 35,5.

†This section has been elaborated further in a paper entitled *Psychoanalytic Therapies and the Low Socio-Economic Population,* by S. Minuchin, M.D.

search out the limits of permissible behavior through in-
spection of the parents' mood responses. He learns that
the rules of behavior are directly related to the power or
pain of an authoritarian figure.

Lacking norms to regulate behavior, and caught in experiences which hinge on immediate interpersonal control, the children need continuous parental participation
to organize interpersonal transactions. Because of the
undifferentiated qualities of the parent-child style of contact, these transactions are generally ineffective and perpetuate a situation in which an overtaxed mother responds erratically to a confused child. The child then
behaves in ways which will reorganize his "known"
environment: controlling contact by the mother. Thus,
the child learns to search the immediate reaction of
others for clues to the solution of conflict situations, and
remains relatively unexercised in the use of focal attention for observing himself as causal in a situation, or in
learning how to differentiate specific characteristics of a
situation.

2. In the disorganized low socio-economic family there
is a deficit of communication of information through
words and the attendant rules which regulate the commu-
nicational flow. In the overcrowded and overburdened
living conditions of these large families the adults pay
little attention to the requests and needs of individual
children. The children in turn accept the fact that their
words by themselves will not be heard. In the development of the necessary techniques for making their needs
known, the children discover that intensity of action or
sound is more effective than the power or cogency of an
argument.

Transactions involving power operations occupy a
large part of family interaction, and the ranking of each
other can occur around an infinite variety of subjects.
The attempt is made to resolve conflict by a series of escalated threats and counterthreats. The conflict itself is
unresolved and will appear and re-appear in other con-
texts.

Diffuse affect is communicated through kinetic modi-
fiers such as pitch and intensity of voice tone, grimaces

and body movements. In the resolution of conflict it often seems that it is unnecessary to hear the content of what is being transacted. Specific subject matter rarely is carried to a conclusion. It is unusual for more than two family members to participate in an interaction around a specific point. A topic usually is interrupted by a disconnected intervention of another family member. Since interactions usually revolve around issues of interpersonal accommodation, the "subject matter" can shift abruptly without changing the nature of the interpersonal conflict that is being negotiated.

The end result is a style of communication in which people do not expect to be heard and, therefore, assert themselves by yelling. There is a lack of training in elaboration of questions to gather information or garner the nuances of degree. There is also lack of training in developing themes to their logical conclusion, and there is no closure on conflicts. This communication style can be entirely adequate for the transactions of gross power and nurturing relationships, but it is insufficient to deal with chronic and subtle conflicts requiring the search for, ordering of, and sharing of different or new information.

There is an interaction effect (1) between the style of control exercised by the parents, which consists primarily of immediate but erratic reactions and, (2) the characteristics of the comunication process in the family. Consequently, the child is trained to pay attention to the person with whom he is dealing rather than to the verbal content of the message.[1] Because the child is trained to focus on the hierarchical organization of the social relationships in the family, he is less free to take in the more autonomous aspects of the transaction or the specific content. Numerous observations of both classroom and clinical sessions bear out this conclusion: in this population it is the prevailing practice to allow the constant defining of interrelatedness of people to out-weigh the meaning of the content of all but the most dramatic content messages.

Being trained in this communication and control system prepares the child to clash with the demands of the school because the style violates certain school-held assumptions about the characteristics of learners. School emphasis is on the recruitment of focal attention to the service of abstract content and on the use of this content for symbolic exploration of the world.* These expectations violate the child's orientation and methodology of processing data. The child copes with the cognitive anxiety aroused by school demands by eliciting from the teacher that which is most familiar to the child in relating to people—proximal control. Thus, much of the "acting out" or disruptive behavior in the classroom is an attempt to repair relations with an important figure, and recreate a "familiar environment." The teacher usually perceives such behavior as an aggressive act and responds with removal of the child from the school.

We suggest, therefore, that the child's difficulty in school behavior and learning is related to: (1) difficulty in focusing attention; (2) communications style that handicaps the child in the enlistment and ordering of new information, and (3) the child's search for a solution to conflicts in interaction with teacher.

Within this context an intervention curriculum was designed to initiate children into the methods of learning in schools. The goal was to instruct them in the communications system used in school and to train them in observation of others as well as in self-observation.

### Subjects

The subjects were six children in residential treatment at the Floyd Patterson House, a unit of the Wiltwyck School for Boys. All of the children had been remanded to the treatment center for aggressive and dissocial behavior. They belonged to the lowest social class, as defined by Warner,[2] and it had been impossible to contain them either at home, at school or in the community. All

*Dr. Alan B. Wilson, during the discussion of this paper, reminded us that public schools in general do not encourage and reward attention to abstract content, and the exploration, ordering, and conceptualization of the world, but on the contrary, many schools with culturally deprived children encourage "mechanical reasoning" and docility.

but one had been in residential treatment for at least a year. The children comprised one full special class for emotionally disturbed children which was run by the Board of Education and housed in a regular public school. The children carried various psychiatric diagnoses, but no child was diagnosed as psychotic or organically impaired.

## Procedure

Class sessions were conducted at the residential center during school hours by a remedial educator. The children were told that they were going to receive remedial lessons at the center during school time and that they were required to attend. The goals of the program were made explicit. In fact, the keynote of the entire project was explicitness, and every step of the curriculum process was spelled out.

The children were told that they were going to be taught a curriculum which would help them do well in school even if the teacher did not like them.*

The children also were told that if they could master the communications curriculum, they could probably leave the special education class and begin learning in regular public school classes because of what they would bring to the situation.

A room with a one-way mirror and an observation booth with sound equipment were used. A procedure was initiated in which the children assumed alternate roles as participants and observers. Two children rotated in the role of observers behind the one-way mirror. The family therapist and educational director trained the children in the process of rating the other children's ability to respond to the teaching, and in specifically enumerating behaviors which enhanced or interfered with learning.

*Teachers liking them, or not liking them, was the primary way that children saw things happen in school. They got a good mark on a spelling test because the teacher liked them, or they were suspended because the teacher did not like them.

The emphasis in judging was on performance in relation to learning, rather than on conforming or being well behaved. At the end of each session, the "judges" would tell the children their rating and the specific reasons for each point lost or earned. A small monetary reward was given for each point by the educational director. The "judges" were also rated and given points and a monetary reward by the educational director and therapist.

## Curriculum

The 10 sessions focused specifically on communication and unraveling the process and mysteries of the classroom to the children. Lessons were sequentially built around the following skills: listening, the implications of noise, staying on a topic, taking turns and sharing in communication, telling a simple story, building up a longer story, asking relative and cogent questions, categorizing and classifying information, and role playing.

Each session was structured in the form of games.* It was felt that the use of games where the processes could be labelled by the teacher was the most efficacious way of teaching skills. The selection of games was made from activities designed for teaching listening skills to kindergarten or primary-age children. The teacher felt that the children functioned at approximately a five-year developmental level in terms of communication skill—even though their chronological age averaged 10 and their mental age was only slightly lower.

The teacher relied on her knowledge of the daily life of the children in school and the treatment center to introduce familiar elements in the stories and games. It seemed much simpler to involve them in focusing atten-

---

*Many of the games were adapted from or suggested by *Listening Aids Through the Grades* by David and Mary Russell, and *The Preliminary Perceptual Training Handbook* published by the Union Free School District in the Town of Hempstead, Uniondale, New York. The teacher kept as her own reference point the section on *Education of the Senses* in the *Montessori Method* by Maria Montessori.

tion on a story in which the names were familiar, for example, than on a story about a fictional character.

The first topic introduced was *listening,* and the first game played was Simon Says, a game the children already enjoyed and felt safe with. It was spelled out that winners in this game were people who knew how to listen and pay attention.

In the game that followed, the children listened to messages read over the telephone and then attempted to repeat them exactly. The difference between guessing and careful listening then was made explicit, and the results were contrasted.

The strength of the children is reading faces and expressions was discussed. It was explained that in the games played in these sessions it would be more useful to listen to the words than to try to feel out the speaker, since winning would depend on skill at the former exercise.

Number games also were played. The children had to listen to a series of digits and report a certain one. There was discussion around what it is like to wait to respond, to hold directions in mind, to concentrate, and other experiences common to classroom learning.

Since the children were making too much noise at the outset of these sessions, *noise* was a natural topic for the next lesson. A game was designed in which a child would tell a story and the others would begin, one at a time, to make such sounds as knee-thumping, seat-tapping, key-jangling, and the sorts of extraneous noises the children introduced during classroom discussions. One of the children increased the volume of his voice until he silenced the noisemakers and could finish his story, although at considerable expense to his vocal cords. Another child helplessly repeated the same words until he felt himself defeated, and joined in the noisemaking. Dialogue was developed on the effect on the speaker and the listener when such noise was going on, and this was related to its implications for classroom learning.

Since children had difficulty starting one at a time to make their noises and stopping them on cue, the next topic which evolved in the group was *taking turns.* Simple, well known nursery rhymes were divided up, with each child taking his part in turn. Discussion centered on the difficulties of listening for one's own part, talking in turn, waiting for the other person to speak. Again, it was seen that the familiarity of the material was reassuring to the children and disposed them to thinking they could win the games.

In a later session, an unfamiliar story, made up by the teacher, was told and all the children participated. They had to listen for their own parts, decide when to come in, and let the others know when they were finished speaking.

At this point, it was possible to initiate discussion of the *logic in stories and then in conversations*. In a later session, the children cued each other in on "getting off the topic."

After the first five sessions, the mechanics began to become incorporated and the sessions turned to conceptual skills. Moreover, as the children began to experience hearing and being heard, *judging and being judged in positive terms,* and winning money and praise for explicit achievements, they seemed to join the teacher in wanting to understand the games and to win them.

This response was noticeable in the reduction of noise level in the room, in the questions about process from the children, and in their beginning attempts to regulate their own behavior in the direction of school expectations. At the same time, the children began to anticipate verbally what they would win or how they had lost. Outside the classroom they talked about what they would do with their winnings.

In the sixth and seventh sessions, the teacher engaged the children in games which involved skills such as *categorizing.* From a start with "I Spy," involving objects in the room, the children were able to move to variations of 20 Questions. The latter involved asking questions so they could order their universe.

The children became actively involved in problems about which questions helped another person to guess the answer, and why some questions were irrelevant. They displayed growth in framing especially good questions and recognizing what made them useful. Excitement in the group was high as success grew.

After the children had had some experience in concentration on formal aspects of communication, the teacher turned to *role playing* to help them discover how attention to these skills could assist them in the classroom. She and the children took turns playing out situations in which a child "won" in an interaction with a teacher because of attention to the words being said, by asking good questions instead of blowing up, or by waiting his turn, etc.

Although they were later able to analyze what they had done, the children in the heat of role playing would be so overcome with indignation that they could not prevent themselves from flaring up and attacking the speaker.

They took the roles they felt they played with adults and authority figures. Although playing those parts involved much farce, there was also empathy by now with what the adult was experiencing. A child playing the part of a guidance counselor said to another child, "I'm willing to listen to you, and I expect you to let me finish."

It was obvious that the role playing brought the usefulness of the tools they were learning to a level where children could reach out and label their own actions accurately. In the final summarizing session, the adults and the children played roles in situations demanding various skills which had been the focus of the project, with children alternating in back of the mirror as judges.

Both the "judges" and the children in the group were quick to pick up and label "mistakes" purposefully incurred by the adults as getting off the topic or "asking irrelevant questions." More impressive, children within the group displayed an ability to help each other in these areas. Their increased self-awareness and their pleasure in their mastery of new skills caused the project to end on a note where adults and children were engaged in mutual pleasurable recall of the learning that had occurred.

## Observation

Beyond the one-way mirror, the two rotating "judges"

were trained in the process of rating the performances of their peers. The rating was done on a continuum from 0 to 5. At first, children seemed only to feel that they were being judges when they were giving out zeros, an interesting commentary on their previous experience of being judged. After the lesson, the "judges" came into the classroom and reported the rating of each child in the group. They needed to describe the reason for each evaluation. In this way the "judges" were being trained for differentiated observation and reporting. After the first lessons, the children accepted the peer evaluation with very little questioning.

From early notions of, "Give me all five, or I'll mess you up afterward," or "I'm going to give both of them 0's because I lost last week," the children moved to statements such as, "Really, you don't give points because you like somebody, but for good listening."

As they began to get the idea of judging performance rather than behavior, they also began to differentiate in their ratings between 0 and 5, giving a 3 for a response that was "good, but not so good," or a 4 for a point that was "almost right, but not quite." At the same time, they began to say, "When you were cursing (banging your seat down on the floor, etc.) you weren't listening to the teacher," instead of, "I gave you a 0 because you messed up."

The alternating in the "judging" functions seemed to have significant effects on the behavior and in the process of self-observation in the children. They were conscious of being observed and therefore observed their own behavior. A child stopped himself in the beginning of a fight, looked at the mirror, and put his hands in his pockets; children would apologize to the one-way mirror, etc.*

## The Teacher

In this project the teacher and the children were

*We have elaborated elsewhere that we consider this process of self-observation and self-control due to increased awareness of an observing other as an intermediate step in the development of introspection in the acting-out child.

working within an explicit mutuality of goals. The children were trying to move to a regular classroom and to learn how to learn; the teachers were attempting to teach the children a program that would facilitate their own goals.

The teacher introduced familiar topics, was explicit in her expectation, geared the introduction of new themes to the children's level of readiness, shifted from abstract to concrete demands depending on their level of cognitive anxiety, focused continuously on the learning task, and deemphasized her role as a controller, or as a provider or rewarder. The rewards given were for performance, and the teacher reminded the children that the "judges" were their peers and, by implication, themselves. In general, the teacher's self-expectation was to present herself to the children as a benign and highly differentiated adult related to them through the complementation of their task.

In the beginning the program focused the children's attention on discrete elements of communication, listening, taking turns, labelling, etc. But to the extent that the mechanical aspect of communication was mastered, the teacher introduced the idea of the *relationship* of the discrete pieces of information. She taught "how to ask questions that will give you the best information for the solution to your problem." In role playing the relationship between personal behavior and interpersonal outcome was underscored.

## Results and Discussion

The results of this pilot project are based on clinical observations of the children's behavior in and out of the sessions, and verbal reports by the counselors. We decided to rely on observations of the process to gather information for a more systematic study. We are well aware, that the conclusions of this paper are quite limited, but we hope to extend our research in an area that appears quite promising. Within this scope, we shall discuss our observations.

*Attention.* There was a marked increase in the children's ability to maintain focal attention for increased lengths of time. In the beginning, children were disruptive and unable to pay attention. From the fifth session on, however, the disruptive behavior and the noise diminished, and the concentration on achievement became central. The increased ability for differentiated attention was clearly seen in the behavior of the "judges." From initial emphasis on rating only "all or nothing" patterns (5 or 0), they were later focusing on gradients of behavior and after the session were able to remember the why's of their rating, organize their data and report on the behavior of their peers and also of the teacher.

In the sessions the division line between attention and disruptive behavior was very frequently criss-crossed by the children. When the teacher made an assumption that the children had greater ability than they had, or she moved too quickly for them, the structure they had been able to maintain broke down and their old maladaptive functioning reappeared.

Hyperactivity and diffuse disorganized behavior seemed to accompany lack of explicitness in the teacher's expectation about goals and the means of attaining them. We think that the children coped with situations of cognitive anxiety by an adaptation that has been proved successful at home: search for the controlling interpersonal contact with the teacher.

*Style of Communication and Cognition.* From initial reliance on speed of response and intensity of sound and activity, the children moved to increased use of verbal responses within the context of "the rules of the game." They listened, took turns, and searched for the best questions. In their search for the right words, they slowed their tempo considerably.*

In the last sessions, when children were playing 20 Questions and later role playing, their language was not only improved in the "mechanics" of dialogue, but they

*This self-editing process seems similar to Bernstein's description of the "hesitation phenomena" in middle-class children.

were using a more differentiated and conceptual style. This was very evident in the 20 Questions game in which the child needs to organize and shrink the universe to find the correct answer. Their ability to improve very rapidly in this game in one session from "random and very concrete questions" to categories and system "questions" would seem to indicate the *availability* in these children of a more conceptual style of thinking and reporting that is generally not used in the classroom or in their daily life, This untapped capacity is *available* under certain conditions and not in others. As a matter of fact, at the end of each period when the rules were over and the "judges" became peers, the children's self-monitoring evaporated and their diffuse hyperactive "bumping" on things and each other reappeared. The seesawing from a "restricted" to an "elaborated" cognitive-communicational style according to the conditions of the field raises interesting theoretical considerations. It suggests (1) that between the ages of 10 and 12 the cognitive-communicational style of these children could be reversible, (2) that educational remedial intervention with this population could be carried successfully with children much older than four years and (3) that we should study changes over a period of time before assuming that they are integrated in the child's new way of learning.

Children's learning in the project was manifested in their life at the institution and in the classroom. For example, one child observing two adults talking at the dining-room table said to them: "I like to see the way you are talking." This same child in a family therapy session "rated" the members of his own family for performance in the therapeutic task and told them the reasons for his rating.

A rather withdrawn and silent boy told his remedial teacher, "I could tell you the names of the things on this table and we could play a game with them." He then invited her to play a 20 Questions game.

Children were heard by the counselors *planning* strategies of how to win the money in the session and what they would do with it. In informal talks with peers and in group therapy children would monitor each other: "You are talking out of the subject," "Do not interrupt, he is talking," etc. They would even correct the counselor for "not hearing" or "talking out of turn."

*The General Considerations.* The intervention curriculum and teaching methodology appeared to be quite effective in changing the learning behavior of the children during the length of the project. This change was achieved by focusing not on behavior, but on cognitive growth. We think that with these children, as in the general field of learning disabilities, the underlying correlates of the disability must be remediated before successful teaching of the skill *per se* can be accomplished.

In our population, but also perhaps in the group of disadvantaged children, they must master a curriculum which develops an ability to (1) focus attention and (2) use communication rules in ways that facilitate gathering and ordering of information. These tasks must be learned before they can master meaningful academic skill.

While the teacher emphasized in the beginning discrete skill in listening and simple learning labelling, the children moved very quickly (10 lessons) to complex and formal operations: categorizing and role playing. The proper balance of concrete and abstract ingredients seem necessary in the curriculum for development of the capacity to move ahead in learning. It was surprising to the authors that so much change in the children could be achieved in such a short time. We attribute this phenomenon to the favorable effect on this program of the therapeutic milieu in Patterson House.

It seemed natural that most of the children regressed to previous patterns of contact and communication when the conditions of the field changed. We couldn't expect internalization of new behavior patterns in five weeks. But we finished the project with an optimistic sense that the road is worthwhile.

## REFERENCES

1. Bernstein, B. **1961**. Social structure, language and learning. *Educational Research,* 3 (June).
2. Warner, L., *et al.* **1960**. *Social Class in America.* Harper Torchbooks, New York.

# Group and Family
# Approaches

# 14. BRIEF GROUP THERAPY IN A CHILD GUIDANCE CLINIC

Norman Epstein, Ph.D.

The Children's Psychiatric Center of Eatontown, New Jersey, is a child guidance clinic serving Monmouth County, which has a population of over 400,000. Although the agency offers both brief and long-term treatment, the basic unit of service is the brief therapy program, which has evolved from an experiment into the predominant treatment modality. Parents are seen either individually or in groups for a period of six weeks, during which time children are usually seen individually by the person performing the therapy (to be referred to hereafter as the therapist), who is free to decide on the number of sessions that will be held in any one week. All the helping professions are involved. The therapist may be a social worker, a psychologist, or a psychiatrist. An integral aspect of the program has been the development of a brief group therapy service for parents and the beginning of brief groups for adolescents. The model utilized is that of private practice, with the practitioner assuming responsibility for the total case.

It is not felt or claimed that brief group therapy is the treatment of choice for all applicants. A long-term treatment program is maintained for those who do not seem to benefit from the brief program. During the fifth and sixth group sessions, the therapist will talk to each group

Reprinted with permission of the author and the National Association of Social Workers, from *Social Work,* 1970, **15,** 33-38. Dr. Epstein is Director of Social Work and Group Therapy, Children's Psychiatric Center, Eatontown, New Jersey.

member to determine what each feels he has achieved
and what has yet to be accomplished. For some members
it is obvious that ongoing treatment will be necessary.
The key to determining this is the chronicity of the
problems. Some families need constant support through
an interpretation of reality. Families that require
intervention on the basis of family engineering also are
obviously unsuited for brief therapy, as are cases involving brain damage, chronic delinquency, alcoholism, and
multiple problems.

## PHILOSOPHICAL ORIENTATION

In order to place the brief group therapy program in a
meaningful perspective, a description of the philosophical orientation of the agency is necessary. Therapy is
viewed as a means of enhancing and developing competence in parent and child. For the parent, this means
a realistic appraisal of his expectations of himself and
his child. For the child, treatment often involves direct
confrontation in an attempt to highlight and present
vividly the futile behavior pattern that leads to school
failure and turmoil at home.

Erosion of the dividing line between school and home
has swelled the waiting lists of child guidance clinics.
Parents often need help with and armament against
becoming substitute teachers in their rush to convince
school officials that they are competent. As parents are
called on to monitor homework and their children's
grades, a precious area of childhood privacy has been
rapaciously invaded. A common area in which the
parent seeks help is coming to meaningful grips with his
expectations of the child's academic performance. Sharing this common grief in the group often provides relief
from feelings of uniqueness and helplessness. A usual
therapeutic intervention is to help parents accept the fact
that children do homework in a variety of ways.
Techniques for helping the parents of the child who does
not do his homework have also been evolved and they
may range from complete nonintervention to a system of
deprivations imposed on the child. The crucial concern is
appropriately matching parental behavior to the child.

Therapy may include offering advice and suggestions and basic education in daily living. A crucial component is education to improve competence in parent-child relationships. The concept of education is utilized in its broadest sense, that is, training to cope with the difficulties that arise in the daily lives of parent and child.

The success of the brief therapy program rests on the agency's confrontation with the questionable assumptions that are often incubated and perpetuated in child guidance clinics. An immediate consequence of these assumptions has been the long waiting lists that deny service at the moment of need. Child guidance myths have often resulted in a lack of clarity of focus with innumerable areas of the patient's life subjected to the process of therapy, while the basic parent-child relationship is often neglected in the pursuit of seemingly more interesting psychodynamics.

The Children's Psychiatric Center does not ritualistically attempt to trace parent-child conflicts to the parents' marital difficulties, and it has been the staff's experience that even when these conflicts do exist, successful treatment of parent and child is not invariably dependent on resolution of the conflict. It has become increasingly clear that parents are capable of assuming meaningful responsibility in their parental roles despite marital difficulties. It has also been the author's experience that few marital conflicts are ever resolved in child guidance clinics and that the attempt to resolve them may result in long-term therapy with eventual loss of focus on the original complaints. Marriages that have achieved a tenuous balance may even be endangered.

Another area of therapeutic endeavor that has eventuated in the spending of innumerable costly hours and much energy with questionable returns has been the attempt to resolve infantile conflicts. This investment of energy has often been predicated on the belief that the problems of children and parents evolve from their respective unresolved infantile conflicts. This questionable assumption, unsupported by any known hard core research, has been accompanied by the mystical correlate that meaningful resolution of behavior is dependent on insight into the conflictual antecedents. The implication is that neither parent nor child is capable of accepting responsibility for his behavior and changing this behavior without insight and the working through of the unconscious conflicts.

The therapist does not focus on transference and countertransference. Treatment is geared to helping people live more comfortably; working out problems through resolution of a countertransference relationship is alien to this endeavor. The parent does tend to view the group leader as an expert in child-rearing, but his role is primarily to lead parents on a search for solutions.

Experience leads us to question whether symptom removal necessarily leads to symptom substitution. The agency's follow-up program does not support any such formulation that is central to the more traditional analytical conceptualizations. The development of a brief therapy program is dependent on giving up the questionable formulations concerning intrapsychic dynamics that are at best speculative and often irrelevant to the problems of daily life. Parents and children are not perceived as victims of unrelenting needs that are compelling them toward maladaptive behavior. A crucial premise of therapy is that perhaps one of the most difficult life tasks is that of parenthood, for which society provides no meaningful formalized educational experience. Parents often function with respect to their children out of a lack of knowledge of what to do in situations that are open to several alternate responses.

Child guidance clinics are often inundated with requests for help from parents who face a number of common problems in relation to child-rearing tasks. The majority of children for whom help is sought are first-borns. It is around the first child that parental inexperience in child-rearing develops into concerns and anxieties, including legitimate uncertainty in relation to the number of alternative courses of action that might be pursued in the daily confrontations with the child. Perhaps a crucial difference between the parent who seeks professional help and one who does not is that the former is often quite impatient with and subdued by his lack of certainty and is the victim of a fantasy that magical answers exist to remove all frictions, fears, and anxieties from the parent-child relationship.

It is here that the folklore of child guidance clinics has contributed to parental confusion. A generation of parents have been brainwashed into believing that one must never be uncertain in the raising of one's children. They are ready to find hidden dynamic meanings in all behavior and as a result feel constrained from reacting to their children more spontaneously.

A cornerstone of the brief therapy program is examination of the myth that common sense and the giving of advice are therapeutically useless. Therapists have been trained to distrust the process of advice-giving and to equate it with lack of respect for the patient's ego-functioning capacities. This tends to overlook the obvious, namely, that *a priori* assumptions based on questionable beliefs about intrapsychic dynamics deprive parents of a chance to test out their ability to incorporate and utilize sound principles of child-rearing.

Before the effectiveness of advice-giving and basic education is dismissed, the therapist is encouraged to offer them to see whether this makes any difference. Another crucial aspect of the program is the growing conviction that the task is not to change human beings but rather to recognize that there are various levels of competence and functioning. Human behavior has a range of expression that need not become the object of therapeutic attack for the purposes of eradicating a mythical pathology. The concept of pathology, borrowed from physical medicine, appears to be irrelevant in the discussion and description of human social behavior.

## OPERATION OF THE PROGRAM

Prior to the beginning of treatment all parents are asked to complete and return by mail a printed questionnaire designed to elicit pertinent factual information concerning the development of the child, including birth and medical history. An extensive list of problems is provided and the parents are instructed to underline behavioral descriptions that are the focus of their concern. Factual material pertinent to the parents' occupations, age, and marriage, as well as a history of previous treatment, is elicited on another form. The more formalized intake procedure, which is felt to be rather burdensome and of dubious value, has been dispensed with. Focus is on identification of the family's problematic behavior pattern and on working toward helping both parties achieve greater mastery over the relationship.

If at all possible parents are seen as couples, which necessitates evening meetings. The nonresident parent may also be invited to participate in the group. Groups have been formed for parents who share the experience of divorce or separation.

The setting up of parents' groups is the responsibility of the therapist. Experience has taught that to put the parents of a 15-year-old in the same group with the parents of a seven-year-old is to court difficulties. The parents of the 15-year-old quickly develop a feeling of *deja vu* while listening to the parents of the younger child. The therapist will strive for homogeneity not only in terms of the age of the children, but also in presenting problems. Parents with children who appear to manifest chronic, markedly deviant behavior will not knowingly be included in a group with parents facing less severe difficulties.

The group meets for a total of six weekly sessions, a number based on national statistics indicating that the average number of appointments kept in agencies is five. The withdrawal rate during brief therapy is low, and time is utilized as a crucial treatment dimension. The therapist and group members are quite conscious of the time factor, which acts as a stimulus.

## PATTERN OF THE SESSIONS

Although the style of different therapists varies, a common pattern has emerged. The first session is utilized to elicit from the parents information about and concrete examples of what they feel is the difficult behavior. They are encouraged to relate and describe the difficulties they are experiencing with the child at home, at school, and in the community. Focus on group dynamics is useless. The time dimension of the group does not permit exploration of group dynamics, nor are they especially relevant to the group's purposes.

By the middle of the second session, or perhaps by the third session, the therapist will have begun to highlight with each individual parent and couple what he sees the difficulty to be, and will attempt to involve them in a discussion of his views. Concomitant with this, he will bring to the group a host of observations that include clarification, redefinition, advice-giving, and—perhaps of greatest importance—helping the parents evaluate their expectations of themselves and the child. The area of unrealistic expectations is usually the crucial one for parents and children and provides the most fruitful area for exploration. The parent who has a self-expectation of excessive competence usually has a similar expectation of his child. These expectations can more appropriately be traced to cultural demands that are imperfectly absorbed and applied than to unconscious conflicts.

The role of the therapist is by necessity an active one. Although the silent member of a group may be receiving vicarious benefits, verbal participation will be actively encouraged. The therapist needs to be aware that when the group does become active in discussion, much time may be spent in irrelevant communications and the dissemination of inaccurate observations and information. It is for this reason that the encouragement of group interaction has important limitations. The therapist is a counselor and teacher whose goal is to enlist the parents' strengths in an effort to develop strategies to cope with their difficulties. As in all therapeutic endeavors, the artistry of intervention cannot be reduced to a firmly outlined plan of action.

A crucial component in the group's success rests on the fact that while the parents are meeting, the child is being seen on an individual basis. This affords a means of checking the parents' perceptions and bringing to them the therapist's own evaluation of the child. As staff members have moved away from compulsively seeking unconscious pathology to explain behavior, they have become more available to help the child understand how a specific type of behavior can irritate adults. The child may be given new strategies that will make him more successful in coping with an adult's expectations.

A common experience is that parents are more prone to find pathology in the child's behavior than the therapist. The therapist's evaluation often comes as a relief to the parent who has anticipated that he will seek out and confirm the existence of a host of pathologies. A major undertaking is to help the parents become more accepting of a wide range of behaviors without reacting to their children as pathological specimens.

By the fourth group session the parent is being openly encouraged and educated to deal with the child through using different strategies. What may work for one child may be totally useless and inadequate with another. The parents are encouraged to bring to the group their experiences with different coping methods. They are taught to cope with the child in the same way that the child is taught to cope with both his parents and the school in such a manner that his behavior reduces the existing level of tension. Group members are encouraged to devise and openly discuss alternate possibilities of response to the child. Mutual criticism and evaluation are integral ingredients of the process.

An integral aspect of the program is the therapist's availability for follow-up. Parent and child are assured of the therapist's readiness to be available for review and consultation. This knowledge often serves as an important reassurance. As a result, parents and children are willing to experiment with new approaches to situations without continuing in long-term treatment.

## ONLY CHILDREN AND FIRSTBORNS

The Children's Psychiatric Center recently experimented with two specific groups: parents of only children and those for whom the child in treatment was the firstborn. Experiences with these groups have tended to confirm and highlight the meaningfulness of the center's approach. In the process of setting up the groups, parents were told that with the oldest child in the family or with an only child the parent constantly experiences the pangs of first-time parenthood. Staff were careful not to imply that parents were experiencing difficulty because their children were disturbed or victims of parental pathology. The accepted attitude was that to be a parent for the first time is usually strewn with difficulties since all experiences with the child are novel.

The parents openly discussed with one another how many of the things they were experiencing they had never experienced before and how as a result they were confused about what was appropriate. It was found that parents who had never experienced living with an adolescent were most frightened by their observations of the youngster's behavior. Reassurance was often a meaningful therapeutic technique.

Several months later a follow-up session was held with the first of these groups. All the parents claimed a vast improvement in their living situation and spoke of feeling far more relaxed in dealing with their children. The tensions and irritations that had brought them to seek help were almost completely nonexistent. Of course, as in the daily life of all people, there were new tensions and anxieties, but the parents were far more accepting of these as the normal course of events. There had been a major and dramatic shift in attitude toward the child, which is the objective the center is attempting to achieve.

## ADOLESCENTS' GROUPS

An interesting development of the program has been groups for adolescents. These groups have been mixed, composed of both boys and girls, and the presence of the girls appears to act to tone down the usual "horsing around" in which boys are prone to engage. Since the center's experience with brief adolescent groups is rather new, the results are still being examined.

It is often a commonplace to hear adolescents in treatment complain: "When the hell do we get out of here? When does it all end?" A major leverage point in the present program is the fact that the group will meet for six weeks only. The reaction has been surprising. They seem to feel "if it meets for only six weeks, then we can take anything." During this six-week period the adolescents are pushed, cajoled, and exhorted to examine the usual adolescent hangups with parents, school, and community. Taking the six-week time factor as a crucial dimension of therapy, they seem to sense that it is worthwhile to get right down to business.

Adolescents are not treated as carriers of emotional problems. It has been found that reinterpretation of adults' motives and questioning the adolescents' perceptions is a valuable technique. As is true with all adolescent groups, the therapist's ease in working with the adolescent is generally a crucial factor; his readiness to confront without flinching will often determine the success or failure of the venture.

The adolescent group is given an opportunity to meet with the parent group in order to facilitate communication. Both groups are prepared for this confrontation and basic ground rules are devised to assure that the meeting will not degenerate into open conflict.

## RESULTS

The brief group therapy program has been crucial in extending the center's services to a large county population. It has dramatically shortened the waiting lists such that the usual waiting period for service is eight weeks instead of six to ten months. The long-term treatment list is extremely small, and the concept of long-term treatment is undergoing evaluation. Does long-term mean interviews extended over a two- or three-year period? Is it not possible for it also to include seeing a patient for three to four months to work on a difficulty that may not have been resolved in the brief therapy program?

Perhaps the greatest benefit in the training of new staff members has been the movement away from the compulsive seeking of pathology. Staff have become more accepting of a wide range of behavior without concomitantly offering endless therapeutic intervention.

The brief therapy program has demanded an intense involvement between the center and community resources on behalf of the child. Consultation with school personnel and community center staffs is a crucial factor in environmental manipulation on behalf of the child. The therapeutic task is not confined to office interviews, but is part of a broader effort to increase and facilitate social adaptation.

## CONCLUSION

The majority of children and parents do not need to continue beyond the brief therapy program. The diminution of anxiety and a more realistic level of mutual expectation as well as the learning of basic coping techniques have resulted in the improvement of functioning as reported in follow-up research questionnaires. The brief group therapy program has constituted not only a meaningful learning experience for parents and children, but also for therapists, who have developed a deeper appreciation and compassion for a multitude of human adaptive styles. The need to reevaluate glib assumptions of pathology has resulted in a program that addresses itself to bolstering the coping abilities of parent and child as well as making dramatic reductions in waiting lists for service.

# 15. THE LAGUNA BEACH EXPERIMENT AS A COMMUNITY APPROACH TO FAMILY COUNSELLING FOR DRUG ABUSE PROBLEMS IN YOUTH

Louis A. Gottschalk, Gilbert C. Morrison,
Robert B. Drury and Allen C. Barnes

In February 1968, the Superintendent of the Laguna Beach School District, in collaboration with the Assistance League of Laguna Beach, and the South Community Hospital of Laguna Beach, contacted the Department of Psychiatry and Human Behavior, College of Medicine, University of California, Irvine, asking for professional help in dealing with the growing drug-abuse problem among children at the elementary school, junior high school, and high school levels of the Laguna Beach School District. After several joint meetings, it was decided to launch an experimental evening clinic for children, with their parents, involved in one way or another with the drug abuse problem.

Reprinted from *Comprehensive Psychiatry,* 1970, **11**, 226-234, by permission of the publisher and the authors. Dr. Gottschalk is Professor and Chairman, Department of Psychiatry and Human Behavior, College of Medicine, University of California, Irvine, California, where Dr. Morrison is Assistant Professor, Dr. Drury is Associate Clinical Professor, and Dr. Barnes is Clinical Instructor.

We acknowledge the assistance of the following people in making this study possible: William L. Ullom (Superintendent of Public Schools, Laguna Beach, Calif.); Roberta M. Harnetiaux (District Nurse, Laguna Beach Schools); Robert D. Hollister (Director of Pupil Services, Laguna Beach Schools); and The Assistance League of Laguna Beach.

A preliminary meeting with the Superintendent of the Laguna Beach Public Schools, a number of school principals and counselors, as well as with interested lay people and practicing physicians in the community, was held in which junior high and high school students, who were either officers in the school government or were honor students, participated voluntarily as resource-people to provide some ideas of the severity of the problem and why some students were prone to use psycho-active drugs. It was a stimulating meeting in which the students spoke freely and expressed some of their own personal viewpoints about the drug-abuse situation. Some of their ideas were as follows.

One student said that if students had more opportunity to be self-determining in the courses they took and in the nature of their course work, they would be much less likely to feel frustrated or resentful and, hence, less likely to use "pot" or "acid." This student, a senior honor student, generalized from his own experience in his wish toward independence and in his current satisfaction that he was being given considerable self-determination in his academic life. He reasoned that since this arrangement gave him satisfaction and afforded him decreased resentment toward the adult generation, such an approach would be of ameliorative value to all students.

"There was nothing to do in Laguna Beach; it was boring living there. Yes, there were beautiful beaches and interesting things occurring on the main street, Pacific Coast Highway, but there was a shortage of recreational activities and facilities for young people."

"The hippies looked interesting, the way they dressed, and I didn't feel like I was anybody when I first went to junior high. If felt insignificant and unimportant, so I got my mother to let me wear some clothes like the hippies and for a few days felt as if I was someone, and then suddenly I realized with those clothes on, I wasn't myself, and I had to find myself some other way. I know the hippies use a lot of drugs, and I guess I would have had to if I had continued to feel that I was like them."

"The older generation doesn't tell the truth about many of these drugs. They say that marijuana, even one puff of it, is bad for you and will do bad things to you. Students have taken one or two puffs and nothing has happened to them, and the students figure that you can't trust what the older generation says about these drugs. You have to find out for yourself."

## THE INITIAL PLAN

Two of us (L.A.G. and R.B.D.) from the Department of Psychiatry and Human Behavior, University of California, Irvine, became initial participant-observer therapists in an Evening Clinic held in the space-facilities of the Assistance League of Laguna Beach, California.

One very large sitting room was available, a smaller room which could be divided with a folding wall into two rooms, and a kitchen. These were the principal space-facilities utilizable. The front of this building contained a variety of clothes which the Assistance League gets donated to them and resells in order to help them carry out their good works. The school superintendent made available to the clinic a school nurse, who was to function as a liaison between the schools and the evening clinic. The school nurse was commissioned to help find cases, and she was instructed to invite any students or parents who wanted to talk with volunteer psychiatrists at the clinic about hallucinogenic drugs or any other kinds of drugs being used in some unsanctioned manner. The clinic's initial goals were merely two-fold: to try to provide sound medical opinion about any of the drugs that might be used, their pharmacological effects and their undesirable or desirable side-effects; and to try to reduce the generation gap.

The general plan to achieve these goals was rather simple. The psychiatrists wore name tags to identify themselves and provided nametags for all participants. From 7:30 to about 7:45 or 8:00 p.m., everyone met in the main room, seated themselves in chairs made available for this purpose, while people walked in and introduced themselves. It was understood that parents could come in by themselves if their children would not come with them. It was also understood that children could come by themselves, although it was made clear that there was a preference for the parents to accompany their children, if possible. After everyone was introduced, one of the psychiatrists made a short announcement that the clinic had as its purpose to answer questions about drug use and drug abuse and to provide help on any personal or family problems that might be contributing to the unwise use of pharmacological agents. The group was advised that some group members might like to keep confidential their participation in this clinic, and, hence all participants were advised to maintain confidence about attendance at this clinic. On the other hand, there was no need to feel ashamed about such attendance and all were encouraged to feel free to tell other people about the clinic if it was of avail to them. The whole group was told that the younger people in the group would be allowed to talk freely about drugs or other related matters in a group of their own in the next room and that after they had had a session of about 45 minutes, the group and the adult group would come together, have some soda, coffee, and cookies, and meet together for another 15-30 minutes.

It was made clear to the total group at this time that each separate group (youths and parents) should maintain confidentiality and retain group secrets, unless any one participant in either group wanted to express his own personal views about any relevant matter in front of the whole group.

The two psychiatrist-therapists rotated, on different evenings, meeting with the adult or youth group, but both psychiatrists were always present when the whole group (youths and adults) met together. It was made clear to all that they could attend once or many times, depending upon their own needs. Other psychiatrists occasionally dropped in to participate in the short-term therapeutic program during the first year of operation of the clinic.

During the second year of operation of the Laguna Beach Clinc, two other psychiatrists (G.C.M. and A.C.B.) assumed the leadership of the therapeutic program of the clinic. The treatment they followed had essentially the

same short-term goals as during the first year of operation of the clinic. Further experimentation was tried on
the format of the treatment, including limiting the attendance each clinic session to groups of six families
seen for eight consecutive weekly sessions.

## CHARACTERISTICS OF THE
## CENTER'S CLIENTS

Although it is difficult to characterize in simple terms
the youth and their families that have participated in
the Drug Abuse Clinic because of their wide disparity,
some findings have occurred with such frequency and
relevance that they can be noted. The youth and their
families demonstrate more internal turmoil, marital discord, emotional distance, and behavior symptomatic of
psychiatric disorder than most families in the community. There are more broken homes with one parent or
step-parent, significant differences between parents of a
family in their concepts of child-rearing practices, and
children who have moved from their homes to other
homes in the community and have separate living arrangements. Many signs of maladjustment, in addition
to drug use, are reported by the teenage drug users. For
example, poor school work in children with high intellectual ability, frequent truancy, occasional running
away, and overt alienation from parents are described.
Not infrequently the teenagers volunteer that feelings
of alienation from peer groups and strong feelings of
self-consciousness and inadequacy have led them to
seek out or respond favorably to drug pushers and users.

Other characteristics of the youth coming to our Drug
Abuse Clinic are interesting. In general, they come from
upper middle-class homes with comfortable affluence.
They are of average to above average intelligence. They
are often quite open and articulate in their complaints
about their parents, homes, schools, and society. They
tend to relate to the present with little regard for the future, and they view the use of drugs as potentiating their
awareness of themselves and the here and now. They
insist on their right to do as they please, whatever the

consequences, as long as it does not directly affect others. They aggressively disparage adults' criticism of their drug use by stressing their parents' use of alcohol, cigarettes, stimulants, such as coffee, and the many drugs that the parents use from over-the-counter or medical prescription sources.[3,5] The observed interaction between the teenagers and their parents demonstrates the disrupted communication, manifested by veiled and open threats with few areas of common agreement or understanding. The parents' almost panic-like reactions to the knowledge that their children using drugs is potentiated by the youths' discoveries that they have found areas where their parents can neither control nor coerce them. Katz[4] has described similar characteristics among youth in Wyoming, where he set up peer-oriented therapy to rehabilitate drug-users. Frank and his colleagues[2] at UCLA also encounter similar personality patterns among drug-users and have focussed their efforts on an innovative preventive program—DARE.

Some incidental observations that are of relevance in understanding this estrangement is the youths' conviction that their parents neither understand nor appreciate their situation. They place a mystical trust in the supplier of their drugs and repeat with almost the fervor of a mass conversion the types of personal and group experiences gained from the drugs. Their subjective experience from the pills they take may contrast markedly with the known effects of the drug. Illustrative is the authoritative boasting of a couple of lads that they both had a great "trip" after each swallowed one birth control pill pilfered from a mother's supply. When involved in group activities in which drugs are used, these youths rarely stay with one drug; they will often take whatever is offered by peers at the gathering. Barber[1] has discussed in detail the education and communication processes among lay child and adult drug users.

An interesting contrast to medical professional experience with many students and private patients who experiment with marijuana or try its effects at a gathering or party, this group has used a wide variety of substances, in various combinations and sometimes for a

long period of time. Drugs have included LSD, mesca-
line, marijuana, cough syrups, glue, a wide variety of
tranquilizers, sedatives, hypnotics, psychomotor stimulants, and even heroin and cocaine.

The parents seem to have little concept of the extent
that their children have used drugs, and little knowledge
of when and where they have used them. They frequently
state that they understand that occasionally their children use marijuana, and they are uncertain why the
school has referred them to the clinic. At the same time,
their children, in an adjoining room, are discussing extensive use of drugs and many parties in which drugs
were used. They pull pills or marijuana from their purses
or pockets to demonstrate their current drug or supply.

## SUMMARY OF FINDINGS
## ON QUESTIONNAIRE

No formal record keeping whatsoever was carried out.
To help evaluate the effectiveness of this clinic in the
spring of 1969, questionnaires were submitted to 29
family members before and after an eight-week period of
attendance. The respondents were asked to comment as
to whether the clinic had met the needs which had
brought them to the Center, whether they would want to
continue attending subsequent group treatment sessions, and whether they would recommend the Center to
others. A review of the questionnaires revealed a rather
consistent quality in the responses of the parents and
youths (Table 1). The parent's response was strongly favorable with 82 per cent reporting that the clinic had met
their needs, that they would recommend it to others, and
that they wished to continue themselves. The youths
were somewhat less satisfied than their parents; however, 58 per cent reported that their experience at the Center was useful and that they wished to continue in subsequent groups. Interestingly, 92 per cent of the youths
said that they would recommend the clinic to other
families, but 34 per cent did not consider the experience
useful to themselves.

The parents' questionnaires reported perplexity with

the problem, surprise that there was difficulty, occasionally the feeling that the school was forcing them to do something for which they had little choice, and occasionally specific requests for help. All expressed feeling that there was a problem in communicating with their children, but the difficulty was often attributed to "the generation gap," typical teenage problems, and the feeling that someone outside the family had led their child astray.

A common finding from both the questionnaires and the comments of the parents and children was the attribution of family difficulties to the school. It was our impression that this was a displacement, that is, putting blame elsewhere. It was not possible, however, to move effectively to individual and family problems without first giving people the opportunity to voice vaguely veiled or open anger at the school. Both the parents and children felt some of the course work was irrelevant, that the teachers varied widely in their interests, and that arbitrary decisions were made for which neither the students nor the parents were given the opportunity to share responsibility. Many of these feelings were initial "transference" reactions to coming to our Drug Abuse Clinic, and it was only after this possibility was explored that the parents were able to talk about having desired help with family problems for a period of time, sometimes for several years, but of having found only limited professional resources. The discussion group then moved to a discussion of drugs with almost an immediate polarization. The parent-group expressed the perspective of drugs as dangerous, addicting, and leading on a hopeless road to total destruction (with this view it is possible to have some understanding of the extent and need for the use of denial and displacement). The young people viewed the drugs as "mind-expanding" bringing on beautiful experiences, and leading to brilliant self-understanding, and offering broad solutions to life problems (a not uncommon desire of adolescents facing the threats and realities of the stress of the world).

The youths' questionnaires were remarkably similar in

content in that they typically stated that they had no problems, were forced either by parents, school or court to attend, and that all life difficulties were related to "the system." Such an obvious denial of internalized problems in personality adjustment was not maintained by many of the youths, once a rapport was established in group discussions.

It is worth noting that the majority of the group felt that the limited number of group sessions was insufficient, that they would continue attending the clinic if it were possible, and that the group experience had proven to be good for communication within the family, one of our initial goals.

## TYPICAL STEPS IN GROUP PROCESSES

The steps followed by the groups (youth and adult) seem to be similar. Initial anger at the court, the school, and "the system" was openly expressed and often was the first common topic found by members of the group. The second theme usually had to do with the completely opposite polarity between the young people and their parents as far as the effect of the drugs was concerned. The groups usually touched base with the therapist with respect to the issue of trust and confidentiality, and then they rapidly moved on to beginning expressions of anger between the parents and their children. The initial evidences of an opening of channels of communication between generations were comments by children to their parents and vice versa that were caromed off of another child's parents, with one parent coming to the aid of the other, and the finally the parents and children talking directly to each other in a way that other members of the group could comment, modify, or correct the exchanges.

## VALUE, LIMITATIONS, AND FEASIBILITY OF DRUG ABUSE CENTERS FOR YOUTHS

Our Laguna Beach Drug Abuse Center for Youth has served as a problem-clarification and communication-

## TABLE 1
## Self-report Responses
## of Two Family Groups
## Attending Drug Abuse Center

| | Did the Clinic Meet Your Needs? | | Would You Recommend the Clinic to Others? | | Would You Want to Continue Coming to the Clinic? | |
|---|---|---|---|---|---|---|
| | Parents | Youths | Parents | Youths | Parents | Youths |
| Favorable | 14 ( 82%) | 7 ( 58%) | 17 (100%) | 11 ( 92%) | 15 ( 88%) | 7 ( 58%) |
| Neutral | 2 ( 12%) | 1 ( 8%) | 0 | 1 ( 8%) | 2 ( 12%) | 3 ( 25%) |
| Unfavorable | 1 ( 6%) | 4 ( 34%) | 0 | 0 | 0 | 2 ( 17%) |
| Total | 17 (100%) | 12 (100%) | 17 (100%) | 12 (100%) | 17 (100%) | 12 (100%) |

facilitating occasion between children and parents and has not functioned primarily for the purpose of individual problem solving. We are attempting to encourage both the young people and their parents to view and discuss their similar and different views about the usual problems of adolescence and parenthood. We also aim to provide informal scientific information about drugs, their pharmacology, their uses, and adverse side-effects, and dangers.

The importance of the Assistance League in facilitating our task-orientation cannot be overlooked. Of major value has been its willingness to provide a separate and neutral meeting ground, distinct from the School system, with clear sanction for discussing school problems in a setting not identified with the school. This has provided an opportunity for the school "to have an out" when parents ask where they can go for help with their problems (when related to school, the family, or situations such as drug misuse). The "neutral" ground of our clinic's geographic location might be contrasted with the large general hospital or university clinic where our society teaches people to go when they have serious and seemingly unsolvable problems or crises or with the store-front clinics which are now provided because of a neighborhood's limited knowledge of other professional resources or insufficient funds to make use of private or more formal types of community facilities.

We believe that with our Laguna Beach Clinic we are providing services to relatively "closed" family styles with rather fixed defensive patterns that more often have characterological rather than more obvious evidence of psychopathologic processes. One extreme, however, was the family with a frankly psychotic daughter who was seen in our clinic between her hospitalizations. The other extreme was the family who said "our boy just went astray," whereas his view was the he "should have known enough not to hide (his) marijuana in his sock!"

An important consideration for developing a clinic such as ours in other school districts would be the ability of school and community officials to attract qualified local mental health professionals in order to staff and operate such an informal clinic. We emphasize the importance of the informality of our clinic or Center. We have done no record keeping, letter-writing, or maintenance of continuing files, not that we do not believe these are useful, but because we have a low budget. This is in marked contrast to other clinics, private and public with which we are involved, where there is quickly generated enormous demands for clerical staff, responses to referral sources, and feedback to supporting community groups—all of these requiring considerable money and organization.

Other programs could be handled in a way similar to ours with the school functioning as a referring source without expecting individual response as to whether a family follows through or regarding the degree of their participation. In our program this has been effectively handled with the intial interest of the school nurse and continued this year with a school counselor who was successful in functioning in both capacities (school counselor and group participant). This latter person, that is, a representative of the school, must have a clear understanding with the school that he acts in the capacity of referral while maintaining the confidentiality of the family. This specific capacity must be recognized by school officials, the school representative in the position, and by parents so that this topic can be dealt with when it comes up in a recurring fashion in the group meetings. Such programs need: 1. the liaison professional with the school who functions as both a referral person and a professional within the group; 2. community professionals who have an interest in the school and the community as their home; 3. school officials who are willing to make a referral of a child, with behavioral, emotional, or scholastic difficulties. There is no doubt in our minds that the results of such a Family Counselling Center are well beyond the expectations for such minimal intervention.

## REFERENCES

1. Barber, B. *Drugs and Society*. New York, Russell Sage Foundation, 1967, pp. 68-75.

2. Frank, I. Psychedelic drug abuse among our youth. *In* Feldman, R., and Buck, D. P. (Eds.) *Drug Addiction and Drug Abuse.* Boulder, Colo. Western Interstate Commission for Higher Education, 1969, pp. 39-49.

3. Gottschalk, L. A. The mild addictions to tobacco, alcohol, and the pills. *Med. Dig.* 14:39-54, 1968.

4. Katz, C. Drug program at Evanston State Hospital. *In* Feldman, R. and Buck, D. P. (Eds.) *Drug Addiction and Drug Abuse.* Boulder Colo. Western Interstate Commission for Higher Education, 1969, pp. 3-11.

5. Manheimer, D. I., Mellinger, G. D., and Balter, M. B. Psychotherapeutic drugs: Youth among adults in California. *Calif. Med.* 109: 445-451, 1968.

# 16. CRISIS INTERVENTION WITH A MULTI-PROBLEM FAMILY: A CASE STUDY

Paul Argles, M.S.W.
and
Marion Mackenzie, M.B., M.R.C. Psych.

## INTRODUCTION

The importance of periods of emotional crisis for both individuals and groups, including family groups, has received increasing attention during recent years. Caplan (1961) defined "Crisis" as a state of emotional upheaval that is "provoked when a person faces an obstacle to important life goals that is for a time insurmountable through utilization of customary methods of problem solving. A period of disorganization ensues, a period of upset; during this many abortive attempts at solution are made."

The history of many psychiatric patients suggests that significant changes in personality development appear to have taken place during a period of crisis, and further examination has shown that during such periods the individual seems to have solved his problems in a maladaptive way and has emerged less mentally healthy than he had been before the crisis. "The progression towards mental illness can be accelerated during successive crises where solutions are maladaptive; however, since each crisis also has a potential for healthy adjust-

Reprinted from *Journal of Child Psychology and Psychiatry,* 1970, **11**, 187-195, by permission of the publisher and the authors. Mr. Argles is Senior Psychiatric Social Worker and Dr. Mackenzie is Consultant Psychiatrist at the Department for Children and Parents, The Tavistock Clinic, London.

ment this progression may be halted and reversed by a successful coping experience" (Caplan 1963).

The direction of personality development in both individuals and family units is therefore influenced by the kind of adjustment that is made in any particular crisis.

The concept of crisis is considered by some to be significant throughout life. Personality development is perceived as proceeding in a succession of phases with transitional periods between one phase and the next, which are characterized by cognitive and affective upset (Erikson 1951, 1959). Predictable life events such as marriage and parenthood are traditionally accompanied by emotional upheaval.

Interest has also centered around accidental crises, accompanied by emotional and behavioral disturbances, precipitated by bereavement (Lindemann, 1944; Parkes, 1965), separation (Bowlby, 1969), threats to bodily integrity (Janis, 1958). Examination of these periods of disturbance shows that the period of upset is a turning point. On the one hand, those who solve the critical problems in a realistic way can be said to have used the opportunity for growth and maturation. On the other, those who fail, and whose adjustment is maladaptive to their life situation, can be said to have shielded themselves from the painful experiences of the crisis by well-known psychoneurotic evasions and defences, which may lead in the long run to psychiatric or psychosomatic illness.

A study of the case histories of many patients and family groups supports this way of conceptualizing, since we frequently find when we explore the past that there was a period when normal functioning suddenly deteriorated after an event of critical significance such as death, separation, etc. It is possible to speculate that during the period of upset something happens that changes the course of future development in the individual and the family group.

Studies of individuals and families in the throes of an emotional crisis (Lindemann, 1944; Kaplan and Mason, 1960) have revealed two phenomena important for both preventive and therapeutic work.

Firstly, there is greater fluidity of feeling at the time of the crisis associated with an increased willingness to accept help from others. Help may be actively sought and, when it is offered, more readily responded to. Less effort is needed to influence individuals in the family during the crisis than when they are in a stable state.

Secondly, access to unconscious material is greater during a period of upset; old problems which have laid dormant are revived in memory together with their affects and an opportunity to work at them again, together with the current issue, provides a chance to find new and better solutions.

It was with these ideas in mind that we decided to exploit the opportunity offered by a crisis in the B. family, with the aim of giving help in the current situation and in the hope of breaking an impasse in which a girl of 13 (who had been a school refuser for 1½ yr) and her multiproblem family had, up to that time, been totally resistant to help both from the community and from the clinic.

## THE B. FAMILY

This was a multi-problem family which had been involved with a variety of social and medical agencies throughout its history. Father (69 yr) had a congenital spinal deformity and other medical problems. He had not worked for many years and lived at home as a semi-invalid. During the time the family was known to the clinic, it was discovered that he had cancer. He was confined to bed at home and eventually died there. Mother (47 yr) also had a physical defect affecting her vision. She was a widow when she married Mr. B. 14 years ago, and brought her two children into the home—John who is now 23 yr, and Peter 25 yr. Both boys had been in approved schools earlier in their lives. Mother had worked as a charwoman until a few years ago when she developed an ulcerated leg. Mr. and Mrs. B. had two children, Susan 13 yr and Arthur 11 yr.

John married and left home four years ago. He returned with his wife and their first child after a year, after eviction from their own home. Another child was born but he made little effort to find new accommodation, and after much quarrelling the mother also had them evicted. Peter left at the same time. Shortly after this Susan refused to attend school, and the school authorities and the Children's Department became involved with the family.

The Children's Department and later the Clinic were unsuccessful in their attempts to get Susan back to school and after a year and a half of non-attendance the Children's Department was under strong pressure to receive Susan into care as a solution to the problem. It had become apparent, however, on the basis of our previous work with Susan and her parents, that this was a family problem involving the collusion of other members of the family in Susan's behavior. While professing to want Susan to attend school the mother encouraged Susan's dependence on her, and was in turn dependent on Susan for companionship. Arthur was jealous of his sister and provoked a good many quarrels. Susan appeared to be the family's representative in expressing its hostility to authority through her behaviour. Because we saw Susan's behaviour as symptomatic of a family problem we did not feel that separating her from her family was desirable. A clinic team composed of a psychiatrist (M.M.) and a caseworker (P.A.) arranged to visit the family along with the Child Care Officer (Mrs. X.) to see if there might be another way of helping them. While this was being planned, the father died, and our visit took place shortly after the funeral. Mrs. X. found that the mother received the idea of a visit unexpectedly well, and did not put it off on the grounds of her husband's death, as she might have done.

## Work with the family

The team's visit was for the purpose of assessing the family's readiness to accept help. Mrs. X. had arranged, at our request, that all three members would be present, to underline our view that the problem was a family one, and so that we could see something of their interaction.

At first the interchange between the team and the family consisted of bitter recrimination from mother towards Susan for not going to school: "Somebody will have to do something"; "I told her that she will have to be sent to boarding school"; and appeals to the team to make Susan attend—example, she told us that she had an ulcerated leg and would be going into hospital, and something would have to be done. Her tone of voice as she made this remark had a threatening quality. This led to a pouting obstinacy from Susan, and occasional retorts. During this part of the interview mother's face was hard and stony, but also had a look of abject misery. When one of us remarked on mother's unhappiness and our understanding of it in the circumstances, she talked with some bitterness about how lonely she felt, and as she said it she turned her face away from the children, who both giggled uneasily.

Mother had questioned the need for Arthur to be present as Susan was the "problem". We responded to this by referring to the signs of unhappiness and resentment that each member had shown in our presence, and emphasizing that we saw the problem as a family one in which all members were involved. Arthur was then able to express his feeling of wanting to help the family and to take his father's place by telling us about his paper round and

about how much he earned. Mother made no attempt to recognize or appreciate his desire to help, making instead a
rather sarcastic remark about the paucity of his earnings.
There were other times during the interview when we wit-
nessed examples of how each member of the family attempted to hide and deny feelings of depression and despair
from the others and from themselves, and anyone who
showed signs of revealing either depression or warm feelings, such as Arthur's desire to help his family, felt discom-
forted as their unrecognized feelings were discredited and
were forced out of sight again. Thus the children giggled
when mother said she was lonely and mother scoffed when
Arthur expressed a wish to help.

We pointed this out to them, recognizing at the same
time how anxious the children felt about mother; finally
they were able to agree that father's death had affected
them all and that they wanted help with their problems.
This was a much more positive response than we had had
in the past. They agreed to one of us (the caseworker) visiting them weekly, that all three of them would be present,
and that the focus of the meetings would be on how to improve relations between the members of the family.

The team had agreed that interviews should be conducted in the family's home because they had shown discomfort in attending the clinic in the past, and because of
the real problems which existed for this handicapped
mother in getting herself and two children to the clinic
regularly. Visiting was planned for a limited period (three
months) partly because of the pressure from authorities
over Susan's attendance and partly because of the family's
history of resistance to previous helping efforts.

During the caseworker's first visit, considerable time
was spent defining the *function* of the clinic and of the
caseworker. The voluntary nature of the relationship was
stressed because of the family's attitude to authority. The
caseworker presented himself as a person whose skills
could be drawn on to help them deal with some of their
problems if they chose to use him in this way. It was not
his function to get Susan back to school, although this
might be a result if they came to grips with the problems
which made it difficult for Susan to attend. The time-limit
was specified from the first and referred to in subsequent
sessions. It was established that the authorities would take
no action during this period in the hope that the family
would be able to deal with their problems in the time allotted. The regularity of the appointments was also emphasized, and the caseworker's expectation that they would all
attend if they were really committed to dealing with their
problems. They seemed to accept all of this as a genuine offer of help rather than an attempt to coerce them.

The first four or five weeks were spent exploring and testing the caseworker's definition of his function. Mother's
complaints quickly shifted from Susan's non-attendance to
the rivalry and quarrelling between the children. She tried
to cast the caseworker in the father's role, as an ally in her

criticism of and attempts to control the children. When this was interpreted, the children came to her defence and attempted to preserve the division between the angry parents and the naughty children. When this did not succeed, Arthur was able to express his resentment that he was always blamed by his mother for the quarrels (which was true) and his jealousy of Susan for being allowed to stay home. Teasing, quarrelling and chasing each other from the room took place when any uncomfortable topic was approached, and after many comments on this by the caseworker they were able to stay put for most of the sessions.

The caseworker took a very active role throughout. The subject of father's death was not broached by the family, but by the caseworker. The first time, Susan took a protective role towards her mother, saying it should not be discussed as it upset her. The second time it became clear that this was self-protection, because when mother was angry she would blame the children for their father's death, and imply that the same would happen to her if they continued their behavior. She also expressed anger with her husband for helping the children get round her instructions. Susan became angry with the caseworker and mother for the first time, saying, "Can't you let him rest?"

Frequent interpretations were made during this period of how family members acted out their feelings towards each other rather than expressing them in words. This led to a profitable discussion of John's eviction. The children revealed that their older brothers had taken a disciplinary role with them, and that they missed this. Mother also missed it and felt overwhelmed and bitter at having to take entire responsibility for her husband and the children. She admitted threatening the children with desertion, sometimes putting on her coat and leaving the house. It was apparent that she also used the possible hospital admission for treatment of her leg in the same way. The children retaliated with more defiance and bad behaviour.

During the next few weeks the mother became more depressed, and said that the caseworker's visits were a waste of time. Susan said it would be worth going back to school to get rid of the caseworker, and Arthur angrily defended his mother from the caseworker's upsetting remarks. This transfer of hostility from mother to caseworker was accompanied by an increased ability on the part of all family members to express positive feelings towards each other. Towards the end of this period Susan was absent from a session for the first time. It was learned that Arthur had been at home sick and that Susan had been attending school for several days. Arthur spoke of his fears of being deserted and of a death-bed promise to his father that he would be the man in the family and look after mother. When Arthur recovered, Susan again stayed home, and we were able to discuss the collusion between the children in "standing guard" over mother to make sure she did not desert them. It became apparent that this had been going on for a long time in a different way, Susan staying home in the daytime and going out with friends in the evening, Arthur going to school by day and staying home in the evening. Many of their quarrels took place when Arthur wanted to go out in the evening himself.

Mother became much more aware of the children's fears and began to see their behaviour based on these fears rather than a wish to torment her. The sessions became much more quiet and purposeful. Arthur was the most able to express his feelings and occasionally would do this for Susan as well.

During the month before the visits were to end, the family began to establish their independence of the caseworker. When Arthur came in during the eighth visit, it became clear that *both* he and Susan had attended school that day for the first time. He was very concerned about how his mother had managed by herself and she told him warmly what a pleasure it was to go about her housework and shopping knowing that the children were at school where they belonged. She had begun to care properly for her leg as well, and the ulcer was healing for the first time after several years.

Susan did not attend the sessions again. Her school attendance was not entirely regular as she avoided physical education days when she had to undress at school, but she managed 3-4 days per week.

On the second last visit, mother was occupied with another caller, and Arthur informed the caseworker that they could not be present the next week as they were all going away for a half-term holiday. Mother confirmed this when she came in and we said goodbye with the agreement that the caseworker would visit in a few months' time to see how they were getting along.

At the time of the follow-up visit 6 months later, mother looked much more presentable than before. She announced with much satisfaction that she had made contact with her married son again, and had seen three of her grandchildren for the first time. Her ulcer had cleared up completely, and she and Arthur were redecorating the flat while Susan was away for a vacation with relatives. Susan returned to school the following autumn and has attended more or less regularly since.

# DISCUSSION

The B. family presented many features characteristic of a disturbed pattern of family relating in which school refusal by one child occurs as a symptom (not necessarily the only one) of the family pathology (Hersov, 1960; Davidson, 1961). The family had many other problems of long standing, however, so this one was not singled out for special attention.

The main characteristic of the B. family was their denial of feelings, especially those of sadness and depression; because they could not tolerate expression of feelings in each other, they could not help each other. As
the most important caretaking figure in the family,
mother's depression was the most significant; this was
not admitted openly either by her or the children and
when it was elicited during the home visit the children's
way of dealing with it was "to laugh it off." Nonetheless
their awareness of her frailty was demonstrated by their
concern to keep an eye on her.

The caseworker's presence made it difficult for mother
and children to re-establish the ambivalent, alternately
clinging and rejecting relationship they had had before,
with the sick father as a convenient receptacle for the dis-
placed feelings of both anger and consideration which
they had for each other. Thus mother was able to move
from saying "You killed your father" to "I was angry
with him", and the children from "He was kind and you
were mean" to "We are afraid you will desert us too". In
the beginning mother would often imply in a menacing
way that if she let her feelings towards Susan go, she
would do her an injury. Later she was able to give up the
critical nagging approach to the children which she had
used to keep these feelings in check, and adopt a more
matter-of-fact kind of firmness with them. The children
were frightened by the power attributed to them to kill
their father and mother by their naughty behaviour and
were able later to reveal the source of their naughtiness:
their resentment over their mother's threats to desert
them.

A major difference between *family therapy* and individual therapy is that the therapist enters directly into
the interaction between the family members (Pollack,
1964). Even in the relatively passive role of listening, he
can often influence family members to listen to each
other both by identification with him and by introducing
a new feature into communication patterns in the family—members may feel "I am attended to, therefore I can
afford to attend". This mechanism can lessen tendencies
to projection and introjection among family members.
Pollak finds that family treatment is especially success-

ful where members exhibit character disorders, a common feature in multi-problem families. The therapist's presence also implies confidence in the family's ability to develop its adaptive capacities.

Although Mrs. B. clearly did not believe in any form of help other than that of "bringing Susan to her senses" and getting her back to school, or alternatively rejecting her by sending her away, the first visit showed that her feelings were not as inaccessible as before. Whilst maintaining our view that sending Susan away would not solve anything, we were able to secure her sanction to visit for a period to see if we could find another solution involving the whole family. Thus the family became the "patient" and no member was singled out as the "sick" one. This is an important principle in family therapy (Robinson, 1968; Langsley and Kaplan, 1968).

*Multi-problem families* have long been a concern of social agencies. The "hard core" of such families requiring help over long periods of time, often never becoming entirely independent, and giving rise to subsequent generations of families with the same characteristics, absorb a very high proportion of the resources of social agencies (Buell, 1952; Philp, 1963; Geismar and La Sorte, 1964). They have certain characteristics which must be taken into account in working with them.

One such characteristic is their mistrust of authority, and, through long association with authoritative agencies, their skill in manipulating them. Such agencies have the power to withhold money, remove their children, evict them from their homes. Multi-problem families know how to get what they want by saying and doing what is expected of them and by suppressing any information which might endanger their status. It was many weeks before Mrs. B. could allow the caseworker to know anything that could be interpreted as "neglect" of the children. This attitude is of course inimical to the formation of a helping relationship and must be overcome before any work can take place. In order to do this, the worker must establish and demonstrate that his function is not authoritative and that he and his agency are not accountable to the referring agency.

A second characteristic of multi-problem families is

their lack of ability to reflect on their feelings as individuals. Instead, they "act out" their feelings towards one another and towards the community, and this is related to their difficulty in accepting help from authorities. For this reason it is important to include the "healthier" members of the family in the work, even though they do not present a problem themselves. It was arranged that Arthur should attend the first and subsequent sessions for this reason. This reinforced our definition of the problem as a family one in the face of opposition from the mother and later revealed in what way Arthur was playing a role in the family pathology. He was more at ease with and able to reveal his own feelings, and was able to do this for his sister and mother as well. His presence allowed family relations to be observed and discussed without the possibility of denial.

A final characteristic of multi-problem families is their inability to sustain an "open-ended" commitment when they are offered this kind of help. The use of clearly defined and limited goals and a limited period of work is important in this connection. "Setting an ending can alleviate a client's feeling of being trapped in something that may go on forever, with his own will and self lost to the control of an outside force. It can serve as an incentive to him to use productively the present moment, out of the recognition that the relationship and service are not going to last indefinitely. In developing capacity and courage to enter on something, use it, let it go, he develops capacity and confidence in living with all things temporal . . ." (Smalley, 1967). There were many problems (such as Susan's sexual problems, the parents' deformities and their meaning) not touched upon. They were prepared to accept that family relations were not good and needed working on, but not to examine their own individual pathologies. It is possible, however, that a good experience like this may help individual members to seek help for themselves in future. They were able to accept visits from a team member and the discomfort which this caused for three months without identifying him with the "persecuting" authorities and erecting the same defences

against him. If they had seen him as a permament fix-
ture their reaction might have been quite different. Such
families are very jealous of the little autonomy they have
left, as their rejection of the caseworker towards the end
shows. On the other hand they were very proud to show
him their accomplishments on the follow-up visit.

Multi-problem families are painfully aware of their inadequacies, and if they are to be helped to change at all,
it must largely be on their own terms. It is necessary to
set goals and commitments well within their capacities,
and to be sure that they participate in setting them, otherwise the offer of help becomes a threat and is resisted as
such. They have seldom experienced any real engage-
ment between themselves and a helping person, with the
mutuality which this implies. They have experienced
"help" as being given to, with the strings of dependence
and the threat of withdrawal attached. The inadequacies
of such families are so apparent that it is difficult to "let
them be". A common reaction to such limited work as
this is : "Why didn't you carry on after having made such
a good start?". To do so would be to undermine the
sense of achievement they have developed in reaching
goals they have set for themselves, and to set oneself up
as knowing better what is good for the family. Much better to wait until they as a family or as individuals develop a sense that they want further help, and ask for it.
It will of course be important to make the asking easy,
and this is where the community agency with its ongoing contact with the family may be of further service
to them if it is sensitive to their needs.

Such a family's weaknesses are visible to all, and it is
important to look at their dilemma from their own point
of view. Erikson (1959) characterizes their difficulty as
one of *autonomy vs. shame and doubt*. Any helping effort which threatens the little autonomy they have left
(usually expressed in terms of being able to get round the
authorities) is bound to fail. They can only be engaged in
a helping process if it is acknowledged that they are the
ones who can make it work or scuttle it. This puts the relationship on what is for them a novel footing. Accepting

help then becomes a means of increasing their autonomy and not a further acknowledgement of their inadequacies.

## Relationship between community agency and mental health team

To be effective, crisis work of this kind requires a close partnership between a community agency (in this case the Children's Department) which has an on-going contact with numbers of multi-problem families, and a mental health team independent of the community agency (in this case a team from a child psychiatric clinic). The community agency must understand crisis work thoroughly, especially in the matter of timing, so that the team will be called in before defences and old patterns of family interaction are re-established. The mental health team must modify some of its traditional ways of working in order to respond to the crisis (Enzer and Stackhouse, 1968).

When the B. family were first referred to the clinic the family crisis that had precipitated Susan's refusal to go to school had, so to speak "gone cold" and the family did not wish to recall it by talking about it. In fact they were strongly motivated to avoid any work on the problem and, not surprisingly, traditional methods of psychotherapy failed to effect any appreciable change.

When the second crisis occasioned by the father's death occurred we were concerned to see them early, and we were heartened that they were willing to let us visit a day or so after the funeral.

With multi-problem families the goal is to make use of the crisis to affect chronic family problems which have been inaccessible in the past. Caplan (1961) sees crisis work as a way of raising the level of mental health in the community as a whole. He looks for natural crises such as birth or death which are known to put people at risk, and attempts by intervention to prevent maladaptive solutions to the problems created by these events. In a similar way, crisis work with multi-problem families, most of which are well known to social agencies, offers a way to raise the level of healthy family functioning in a "population" which is already identified as having difficulty in coping with the ordinary problems of living. Efforts concentrated in this area are therefore likely to produce even greater returns than a more diffuse approach.

The partnership between community agency and mental health team can be endangered unless each understands and respects the role of the other. The mental health team undertakes the crisis work not necessarily because it is more skilled, but because it is in a position to do so. It has no authority and is therefore perceived and responded to by the family in a way which facilitates their dealing with emotional rather than practical problems. The value of the referring agency's work is in sustaining the family in ordinary times. It has the resources and sanctions to do so, which the mental health team does not.

## SUMMARY

Multi-problem families can sometimes accept help during a period of crisis, even though they have resisted helping efforts in ordinary times. There are certain characteristics in such families which make it desirable to work within clearly defined limits to preserve their often uncertain sense of autonomy.

Crisis work depends on a partnership between the mental health team and a community agency which has consistent contact with a large number of families and which is prepared to call in the team when crises occur.

## REFERENCES

1. Bowlby, J. *Attachment and Loss,* Vol. 1. Hogarth Press: London, 1969.
2. Buell, B. *Community Planning for Human Services.* Columbia University Press: New York, 1952.
3. Caplan, G. Mental hygiene work with expectant mothers. *Mental Hygiene,* 1951, **35,** 41-50.
4. Caplan, G. *An Approach to Community Mental Health.* Tavistock Publications: London, 1961.
5. Caplan, G. *Principles of Preventive Psychiatry.* Tavistock Publications: London, 1963.

6. Davidson, S. School phobia as a manifestation of family disturbance: its structure and treatment. *J. Child Psychol. Psychiat.* 1961, 5, 270-87.

7. Enzer, N. B., & Stackhouse, J. A child guidance clinic approach to the multiproblem family. *Am. J. Orthopsychiat., 1968, 38, 527-38.*

8. Erikson, E. H. *Childhood and Society.* Imago Publishing Co.: London, 1951.

9. Erikson, E. H. Identity and the life cycle: selected papers. *Psychol. Issues, 1959, 1, No. 1, Monograph 1.*

10. Geismar, L. L., & La Sorte, M. *Understanding the Multi-Problem Family.* Association Press: New York, 1964.

11. Hersov, L. A. Persistent non-attendance at school. *J. Child Psychol. Psychiat., 1960, 5, 130-36.*

12. Hersov, L. A. Refusal to go to school. *J. Child Psychol. Psychiat., 1960, 5, 137-45.*

13. Janis, I. *Psychological Stress,* 1958, Chapman & Hall, London.

14. Kaplan, D. M., & Mason, E. A. Maternal reactions to premature birth viewed as an acute emotional disorder. *Am. J. Orthopsychiat., 1960, 33, 534-552.*

15. Langsley, D. G., *et al.* Family crisis therapy—Results and implications. *Family Process,* 1968, 7, 145-58.

16. Langsley, D. G., & Kaplan, D. M. *The Treatment of Families in Crisis.* Grune and Stratton: New York, 1968.

17. Lindemann, E. Symptomatology and management of acute grief. *Am. J. Psychiat.,* 1944, 101, 141-48.

18. Parkes, C. M. Bereavement and mental illness. *Br. J. Med. Psychol.,* 1965, 38, 1-12, 13-26.

19. Philip, A. F. *Family Failure.* Faber & Faber: London, 1963.

20. Pollak, O. Entrance of the caseworker into family interaction. *Social Casework,* 1964, 45, 216-220.

21. Robinson, M. Family based therapy. *Br. J. Psychiat. Soc. Work,* 1968, 8, 188-192.

22. Smalley, R. *Theory for Social Work Practice.* Columbia University Press: New York, 1967.

# 17. SHORT TERM FAMILY THERAPY

## Mordecai Kaffman, M. D.

Freud, in an often quoted paper published in 1919 (1), dealt with the impact of psychoanalysis on psychiatric needs of society and stressed the fact "that the therapeutic effects we can achieve are very inconsiderable in number. ... Against the vast amount of neurotic misery which is in the world, and perhaps need not be, the quantity we can do away with is almost negligible. ... At present we can do nothing in the crowded ranks of the people, who suffer exceedingly from neurosis." Freud raised the possibility that new simpler forms of psychotherapy based on psychoanalytic principle might be found. Almost half a century later, we still are searching for new psychotherapeutic tools allowing treatment of large masses of people.

Present methods of psychotherapy seem to be suitable to a limited group of people within our society. This is not only from an economic standpoint but also in view of their intrinsic content, which is connected with values and characteristics of the middle and upper class or our culture (2). Generally speaking, psychotherapy has remained an expensive, time consuming, and highly restricted therapy out of accord with the pressing needs of the community in the Mental Health Field. Israel by no means constitutes an exception. Practical shortcomings determine that only a negligible minority out of a large

Reprinted from *Family Process,* 1963, **2**, 216-234, by permission of the publisher and the author. Dr. Kaffman is Medical Director, Kibbutz Child and Family Clinic, Tel Aviv, Israel.

number in need of psychotherapy can get the necessary help. This is true, too, of the Israeli Workers Sick Fund, which maintains an efficient, low cost and modern provision of medical service covering all aspects of curative medicine for 70 percent of the total population. The search for a brief form of psychotherapy continues to be an urgent pragmatic problem, not only because of the scarcity and high cost of the present facilities for prolonged psychotherapy but also because of intrinsic advantages to be found in an available service of short term psychotherapy.

The simple fact that a large proportion of emotional disturbances, both in children and adults, can be dealt with satisfactorily without resorting to prolonged methods of treatment cannot be denied. This is usually ture for the vast majority of reactive emotional disorders and for acute and crisis situations leading to a breakdown of previous apparently "normal" behavior. Opportunely timed assistance can help to restore emotional homeostasis and prevent further impact of disorganizing anxiety which could determine progressive maladjustment, disintegration and serious psychopathology. Obviously, the sooner the required help is provided, the better are the expected results. However, clinical experience has shown repeatedly that even long established emotional disturbances might improve following short term psychotherapy. Not too rarely we witness in children outstanding clinical changes from previous abnormal behavior, or the dramatic disappearance of disturbing pathological symptoms as a result of brief therapeutic intervention destined to alleviate the pressure on a limited but sensitive area of conflict.

On the other hand, it appears (3) that certain shared expectations about the length of treatment as perceived by the therapist and the patient may determine much of the outcome of treatment. Patients of the lower social class in need of psychotherapy would hardly accept the fact already recognized by sophisticated members of the upper and middle class that emotional disturbances, unlike the usual physical complaints, require prolonged and intensive care to be continued for years. The different expectation regarding the length of treatment goes beyond the economic issue and seemingly could not be done away with even if increased psychotherapy services were created. At present, the shared expectation and conditioning of therapists and their patients of the lower class are in the direction of brief forms of psychotherapy. Now, one can assume that an agreement between expectancy and available services may constitute an important element to assure the continuance of treatment and influence positive outcome. Unindoctrinated patients of the labor class become genuinely surprised when told that more than one single interview is necessary to help solve their problems. They become suspicious and uncooperative if the prospect of long term psychotherapy is mentioned. From another angle, the sophisticated patient with a previous amount of knowledge about the complexities of mental life and the increased length of psychoanalytic treatment in order to get a "definitive cure" would be disappointed, skeptical and uncooperative, if short term psychotherapy were offered instead.

We may state, consequently, that short term psychotherapy is not only an urgent objective need, but also fits into the expectancies of a large mass of people. On these grounds, we consider it valuable to report on our own procedure for short term family psychotherapy (STFT) which has been in use throughout the years 1961 and 1962 at two separate clinical settings* devoted to the treatment of emotionally disturbed children. This preliminary report illustrates the rationale of the procedure, methodology, limitations and initial evaluation of the results of STFT in 70 consecutive cases referred to the clinics.

* This program of brief family therapy was initially carried out with Kibbutz children referred to "Oranim" Child Clinic of the Kibbutzim. Since the beginning of 1962, the same plan has been carried over to treat families of urban children at the Child Unit of the Haifa Mental Health Clinic of the Workers Sick Fund. The author serves at the latter Clinic as a Consultant Child Psychiatrist. Mention must be made of the understanding, cooperative attitude and invaluable assistance of the Director of the Haifa Clinic, Dr. S. I. Davidson, and the Psychiatric Social Workers, Mrs. Rosa Yiftah and Marianne Rusell.

## Focus on Family Interaction

Although the common reason for referral to the Child Guidance Clinic continues being some disturbing problem of the child, treatment in all our cases is family-centered. On theoretical and practical grounds the child cannot be seen isolated from the social unit to which his problems are etiopathogenically connected, especially if the dynamic interaction is still actively functioning (4). Continued osmotic interchange occurs between the intrapsychic and the interpersonal experience. Individual pathology cannot be separated, particularly in the case of a child, from family group psychopathology. Clinical evidence shows that changes in family dynamics may alleviate individual disturbances even in the absence of systematic individual therapy. On the other hand, skilled and intensive individual psychotherapy of a child may fail to elicit clinical improvement due to the absence of parallel changes in family psychopathology. Therefore, our clinical approach is neither child-centered nor parent-centered but focused on the integrated family interaction.

## Evaluation of Family Dynamics

As Alpern (5) has rightly pointed out, a clinical approach to brief therapy can only be adapted from the knowledge and experience of long term clinical psychiatric work with children and their parents. Short term family psychotherapy requires from the therapist skills and clinical judgment regarding the assessment of the central needs and conflicts of the child and parents' personality. The therapist should be able to reach, on the spot at the joint sessions with the family members, reliable conclusions on the essential characteristics of the parent-child relationship to enable him to interfere actively in the process of clarification and reorganization of family dynamics. Basically, one cannot conceive a different dynamic approach for short term psychotherapy than for prolonged psychotherapy.

## Goal and Purposes of Brief Family Therapy

It is not within the scope of a short service of family therapy to bring about basic and extensive alterations in character structure of family members. However, sustained changes in family dynamics and improvement of individual pathology can eventually be achieved. The therapist's help, to all the members of the family, in obtaining focused insight into the nature of conscious and preconscious conflicts is apt to lead to a readjustment and healthier family interrelationship, to goal modification and full use of potential possibilities.

No feasible resource leading to a healthier family adjustment should be dismissed by the therapist. We are not reluctant to make use of therapeutic counseling to eliminate obvious pathogenic factors, if we believe that this is a necessary step towards improvement and if we consider that the patient is ready to follow the advice. Certainly this is not the most refined therapeutic tool, but there is no logical reason to delay helpful counseling whenever evident detrimental factors can be quickly removed or reduced.

The aim in this form of therapy is to bring the family to an emotional equilibrium as rapidly as possible with improvement or elimination of symptoms. One may wonder how this goal can be obtained through restricted short term therapeutic intervention. Clinical experience shows what we call "the snowball phenomena." The beginning of healthy changes in behavior and attitudes both on the part of the child and the parents induces further mutual shifts in the parent-child relationship with additional positive achievements. Therapy has served to break a vicious circle, and from then on clinical changes do not run parallel to the intensity of therapy.

Any experienced therapist has seen more than once the steadily growing "snowball" of clinical improvement following a short therapeutic intervention. Doubtless, a number of operative factors are involved in the therapeutic process and clinical response. But we cannot dismiss the obvious fact that the change is mainly accomplished by direct or indirect interference on a stressful and pathogenic parent-child interaction. The therapeutic alliance with aim identification between the therapist and the patient is apt to determine a prompt symptomatic response. The initial symptomatic improvement might promote further acceptance and understanding of the child on the parental side, while the child ameliorates his chances to consolidate clinical gains with diminished anxiety, increased assertiveness and higher self esteem. Effective alleviation or removal of disorganizing pressure and anxieties may result in a sound resolving process of improved child-parent relationship.

# CLINICAL METHODOLOGY

Like any other therapeutic procedure, short clinical services for children and parents are not a panacea; they have a specific range of effectiveness and require adequate criteria for selection of patients.

## Selection of Cases

First, the quality and severity of family psychopathology, namely that of the child and significant family members, should be considered. Following an initial period of trial and error, we elaborated a diagnostic list which was sent to the eventual referral sources stating which cases should be regarded as inappropriate for short term family therapy. Among the categories to be excluded, the following ones were mentioned on the child side:

a) Long standing psychosis.

b) Sociopathic personality or cases in which institutional care is indicated.

c) Established neurological damage and/or mental deficiency being the essential clinical problem.

d) Chronic severe psychopathology in which the symptoms are highly structured and have been present and unchanged for several years.

On the parental side, we demanded the presence of a minimal amount of positive family ties and excluded the totally rejected, abandoned child. Complete lack of motivation on the part of both parents to be included in the therapeutic plan was also seen as contraindication for this form of therapy.

Suitable cases embraced all forms of child psychopathology up to the age of sixteen, provided that the emotional conflict was not totally internalized and the child had enough ego strength and anxiety to feel motivated in establishing object-relationship with the therapist.

Clinical experience with the first 70 cases referred for short term family therapy showed that in a large percentage of instances the above requirements were not met, although the amnestic data in the referral form appeared to fit the approved criteria of selection. This discordance between reported and actual facts seems to be related to different isolated factors. Usually, it was due to insufficient knowledge of the case on the part of the referral source, inadequate evaluation of the quality and intensity of the pathology, and last but not least, lack of clinical facilities to refer elsewhere a severe and pressing emotional problem. Therefore, a great many cases referred to us for STFT did not fit our criteria of selection and showed a more disturbed and long-standing psychopathology than we had intended to cope with. On the other hand, several chronic cases which at first glance did not appear to be suitable for short clinical service showed, however, such an evident and positive response to the initial family interview that continuation of treatment became a must. It was decided, therefore, to postpone the final decision about the nature of therapeutic intervention to be offered until direct contact with the family in the course of the first joint interview allowed a proper clinical assessment. STFT remained the most concrete available therapeutic possibility. Those cases seen as unsuitable for short clinical services were referred to long term psychotherapy, whenever feasible. Otherwise, the therapeutic procedure was restricted to the most practical advice to be given under the circumstances. In these cases, diagnostic work was completed in order to draw practical conclusions on the alternative treatment plan.

## History-taking Process

History-taking is a crucial part of the clinical procedure inasmuch as previous knowledge of significant objective data helps the therapist to assume an efficient
leading role. The intake interview is conducted by a
skilled Psychiatric Social Worker who meets with both
parents. The PSW is less interested in accumulating a
complete and detailed history than in gathering meaningful information on salient points. The interview is so
structured as to allow, in the first place, spontaneous
elaboration by the parents on the child's present behavior and problems. This is followed by specific questions
regarding cornerstone developmental features, medical
history, possible traumatic events and factual data on
family interaction. Whenever one of the parents in the
course of the joint interview requests overtly or tacitly a
separate interview to disclose information he finds difficult to bring up in the presence of his marital partner, the
demand is fulfilled.

At the end of the intake interview, concrete information is supplied to the parents concerning the steps to be
followed in the clinical procedure. An additional purpose
of the intake interview is to assist the parents in pre-
paring the child for the first family therapeutic interview. Most of the parents are badly in need of a clear-cut
explanation in order to avoid the usual approach of de-
ceiving the child regarding the aim of his visit at the clinic. Of course, the nature of the child's problems, his age,
the intelligence level of the parents and the quality of the
parent-child relationship will determine the kind of explanation given regarding the first therapeutic interview. In general terms, children over four years of age require a truthful explanation of the following facts: (a)
The parents have sought a "doctor's advice" on the ways
to help them and the child to get over the specific obvious
difficulties. The problems will be discussed with the doctor at an announced appointment. (b) An understand-
able description of the playroom setting seems helpful in
reassuring the young child or preventing an unpleasant
reaction of an adolescent youngster to the "kid stuff"
equipment.

We find it necessary to stress the fact that the preliminary contact with the family does not include the administration of psychological tests to the child. Clinical experience evidences that data gathered from the medical history, the intake process, and the psychiatric interviews with the child and his parents is sufficient for a trustworthy diagnostic psycho-dynamic assessment. It appears to us that we avoid confusion on the part of the child and allow for a more intensive focusing of the therapeutic process if the contact of the child with the clinical service starts immediately with the therapeutic interviews, which are, at the same time, of diagnostic nature.

### Single Therapist versus Team Work Approach

Traditionally, in most of the Child Guidance Clinics, the interdisciplinary team approach is used, not only for diagnostic purposes but also in the therapeutic procedure. The value and efficiency of the collaborative approach cannot be denied but, when applied to STFT, the method has obvious limitations and disadvantages. The single therapist approach allows for significant saving in time and effort, a cohesive view of family dynamics and, consequently, a consistent and uniform therapeutic intervention.

Collaborative work in therapy implies the need of additional time and appointments. Furthermore, even in the best staffed clinic and assuming an exceptionally similar theoretical and clinical approach of the members of the team, complete coordination is not possible. When time constitutes a crucial factor in therapy, and when immediate confrontation of the members of the family with the findings of the family-therapist interaction is designed to be one of the most important therapeutic elements, a team work approach does not seem to be feasible or adequate.

The following two family interviews, briefly summarized, illustrate this particular point of view. They show the effectiveness of a prompt direct intervention performed in a quasi-routine way by a single therapist in family therapy.

*Case I.* A girl, 11 years old, was brought to the clinic because of intense night fears lasting a couple of years, disturbing clinical manifestations of separation anxiety and
unrestricted aggressive behavior directed towards her
mother. In the course of the first joint interview (with parents, girl and therapist present), the girl complained about
her mother's oversolicitous interfering in all her activities,
continuously nagging about small things, and "treating
her like a baby". With the help of the therapist, the mother
and daughter were able to admit that the excessive contact
aroused mutual anger. However, the mother thought that
the aggressive responses of the daughter were exaggerated. She brought up examples of the girl's verbal and
physical aggressiveness to the point where even death
wishes were openly shouted in the course of the rift. The
girl showed confusion and obvious guilt feelings. The
therapist pointed out the ambivalent feelings of the child,
who felt encouraged to state that she really did not mean
the death of her mother. Then the father interfered, adding
that he had noticed some kind of relation between the quar-
rling during the day and the intense fears at night. When
everyone agreed with this observation and I suggested
that sometimes children are afraid that thoughts and
words may come true, the girl rushed to her mother, kissed
her and talked about her guilt feelings after the anger ex-
plosions.

The long standing night fears disappeared *after the
first therapeutic interview.* During the course of STFT,
which dealt with different pathogenic aspects of the interpersonal relationship, a striking improvement in the
family interaction was reached.

*Case II.* Naomi, a 15 year old girl, was referred to the
Clinic because of severe symptoms of emotional disturbance lasting several months. She was the youngest of
three children. Her older sister, 19, had an organic brain
condition which caused mental retardation, epileptic fits
and progressive blindness. The symptoms of our patient fitted into the picture of adolescent schizophrenia. Naomi
had marked persecutory delusions, ideas of reference and
pervasive anxiety. During the weeks preceding the treatment, she felt unable to attend school, did not leave her
room and demanded the constant presence of her mother.

The first joint interview with Naomi and both parents
yielded significant material regarding the sources of the delusional thoughts. A family pattern of denial of hostility
with reaction-formation defensive maneuver was soon recognized. The chronically sick sister was one of the objects
of repressed hostility. Naomi was able to express her feeling of deep guilt and her conviction that people were able
to perceive her awful "cruelty." She had started looking

around suspiciously to find the confirmation of her fear of being scrutinized by people because of her wrong doing and soon found that both strangers and her parents looked at her and talked secretively about her. She became convinced that people were plotting to send her to a mental institution. She was full of panic and was unable to leave home and go to school.

Actually, at the joint interview, the parents confirmed that they used to glance furtively, and talk secretively, about Naomi's strange behavior. They sought the advice of the family physician who suggested hospitalizing her in a psychiatric setting. All the arrangements were made by the parents to confine the girl without her knowledge.

To my surprise, after one single interview in which sufficient clarification of all these issues was attained, Naomi was able to go back to school and express sound criticism of her former delusional thought. Plans were made to institutionalize the sick sister instead of Naomi.

Undoubtedly, the same good clinical results and insight would be obtained with different therapeutic approaches, but the above integrated procedure in the hands of a skilled therapist seems to be less time consuming and at least equally rewarding.

Only in a few cases of extreme marital disharmony and hostility or complete absence of positive ties in the parent-child relationship was the joint therapeutic interview not possible, and the members of the family were seen separately. If we exclude these exceptional cases, no clinical contra-indication seems to exist for this integrative family approach. It was necessary, in a few cases, to exert some pressure on the mother to agree to the father's presence at the joint sessions, because she thought it was a waste of time, in that the father "has nothing to say at home" concerning the upbringing of the children. In most instances, which included a large percentage of patients of the working class, a good deal of cooperation and understanding of the essentials of family therapy was obtained on the part of both parents.

## First Therapeutic Interview

The initial joint family interview has paramount importance for the whole treatment process. Usually it is attended by both parents and the child, but not rarely other significant members of the family are also present. This is a prolonged interview, lasting from two to three hours, in which the therapist fills an active leading role that persists throughout the entire therapeutic process.

Free interaction of family members, including verbal communication and/or play activity of the child, is encouraged by the therapist in his attempt to assess the basic characteristics of family interaction and uncover the central conflict. Often the first emerging issue raised either by the parents or the therapist is the definition of the problems and difficulties. The verbal interchange that takes place regarding this point provides crucial clues on family dynamics, defense mechanisms and sensitive areas of conflict. The therapist should help structure this interview in such a way that every one, including the child, reaches a clear view and definition of the most distressing problems. Therefore, the first step should be to recognize the basic conflict and to avoid going astray with irrelevant issues. One should be sure that sufficient understanding of the problems under discussion has been gained by the child, and that he has formed a clear-cut picture of his own role as well as that of the parents in the treatment plan. Active interference of the therapist is needed to point out the central problem and overcome a parental approach of either overprotective secretiveness in the presence of the child or monopolizing moral lectures and accusations. He must dispel any deleterious implications that the therapist is the ally of the parents in stopping or curbing the child's misbehavior.

Once the essential issues have been exposed and defined, and a reasonable dynamic evaluation has been elicited through the joint interaction of the family and therapist, the different members of the family might be seen separately in the course of the same initial interview. No fixed formula can be established. Factors like the therapist's clinical assessment, the age of the child and the need to establish a closer individual relationship with him, the necessity for further clarification of marital issues, etc., will all determine the decision on separate interviews.

Individual short meetings with the child contribute to establishing a valuable positive relationship at the child's verbal level on the basis of whatever type of activity is selected by him. The essentials of the insight (but not the factual information) obtained in the separate interview are not kept sealed in the one-to-one relationship but are brought up and discussed in the most convenient way at the next joint family interview. Therefore, in every case, the initial therapeutic interview assembles the whole family at least at the beginning and the end of the interview process. In some cases, the need of separate interviews is not appreciated and treatment continues on an indivisible family basis. In most instances, the initial interview embraces four meetings: the whole family interview, the child alone, the parents, and again the entire family. The therapist should not feel under the pressure of time when getting the necessary clues to reach a sound preliminary dynamic evaluation of family interaction.

The understanding gained both by the therapist and the members of the family throughout the therapeutic interview is immediately utilized. The therapist is now able to help each member of the family make use of the insight gained. Surely enough, insight alone is worthless in the absence of parallel constructive support in the search for new ways of readjustment. Even if we succeed in uncovering how the self-assumed reasonable behavior is felt and interpreted by other members of the family, nothing would change in the course of STFT without additional reconstructive measurements encouraged by the therapist.

The search for a better understanding of the characteristics of family relationship and essential areas of conflict may lead to exposing in detail concrete recent incidents, but no premeditated effort is made to elicit or disclose historical data.

By the end of this initial interview, the therapist summarizes in a clear and concise way to all the members of the family whatever has become evident on the basic problems which are under discussion. He will add specific suggestions and recommendations if they are necessary and connected with the content of this interview. It is assumed that by the close of the first interview, the therapist is already aware of the therapeutic possibilities offered by a short plan of treatment and is capable of setting specific realistic goals, recognizing at the same time the inevitable limitations of the method. The goal of the treatment, including a tentative evaluation of the length of therapy and number and frequency of sessions, should be clarified to the members of the family. There are certain cases where it becomes apparent that STFT is unable in any way to help dissolve the family pathology. This forces an early decision to stop the clinical contact right at the first joint interview and to recommend other methods of treatment.

## Following Interviews

In subsequent meeetings, a flexible schedule persists regarding the length and distribution of the sessions, the number of participants, and the sequence of the separate and integrated talks within the framework of a whole interview. Again the child may be seen alone, or with one or all members of his family, for shorter or longer sessions, more or less frequently, all depending on the judgment of the therapist and the clinical course. The parents may also be seen separately or jointly.

In our view, a structured, fixed framework of treatment curtails the possibilities of a short term plan of family therapy. Thus, although on the average in our cases a total of ten weekly therapeutic sessions (each one lasting one to one-and-a-half hours) followed the initial prolonged interview, the distribution of these sessions varied considerably in the different instances. The procedure resembles chess variants to the extent that it is practically impossible to find two cases with the same distribution of the therapeutic interviews.

The following example may help to illustrate the point. Two children were referred separately because of seemingly identical complaints consisting of intense fear, temper tantrums and aggressive behavior. Both were included in the same diagnostic category (neurotic traits) and by mere coincidence each attended with his respective parents an identical number of therapeutic sessions. Both children showed considerable clinical improvement with total disappearance of the acute anxiety state. However, a quite different distribution of the allotted time of treatment was scheduled by the therapist. The first child was seen six times together with his parents, once with his father, three times alone, and the parents were seen separately once. The second child was seen only once with his parents, four times with his mother, four times alone; his parents were seen once together, and the mother was seen four times alone.

In most of the cases, the separate interviews with the child, based on play and/or verbal interchange, helped to build a very positive relationship between the child and the therapist, bringing forth useful elements of imitation and identification. Although Anna Freud does not seem to adhere anymore to her original view regarding the convenience of fostering a positive transference from the child to his therapist in the initial phase of analytic treatment, it seems to us that beyond any doubt the positive nature of the child-therapist connection constitutes an important factor influencing the success of the approach in short treatment plans.

Usually, after the first interview, children show a great deal of eagerness to return to the clinic. Parents tell us that their children await impatiently the next appointment and remind them of specific facets of the previous family interview. Young children often nominate the psychiatrist with all sorts of laudatory names or titles ("the wise doctor," "the good doctor," "my friend, the doctor,") while older children show elements of identification with the psychiatrist. A seven year old boy queried his parents on the requirements to become a psychiatrist, including financial questions on the matter, to be sure that he had selected the best choice.

For all the members of the family, each interview usually includes the following components which appear in a flexible changing order: redefinition of the problems and summary of what has been established during the preceding sessions, analysis of recent events to emphasize trends and changes in the family interrelationship, further scrutiny of factors determining failures and accomplishments in the treatment plan, realistic appraisal of the situation and expectations of the treatment, and specific acknowledgement of any gains or improvement.

### The End of the Treatment

Since length of STFT has been planned in advance and discussed with the whole family as early as the initial interview, one may assume that the close of the treatment does not arrive as a surprising move. In the vast majority of cases, the terminal closing phase of treatment can be implemented without particular difficulties. Only in a small minority of cases either the children or their parents do not seem to be ready for termination of treatment. The child may not want to give up the secondary gain of extra attention provided by the treatment, while parents may strive to maintain a relationship of further dependency based on continuous advice-seeking rapport.

Usually, termination of treatment comes as a natural and anticipated development. For all the cases which are not referred for further long term psychotherapy, provision is made to assure the possibility of additional isolated contacts according to clinical needs as felt by the child, the parents or the psychiatrist.

## CRITERIA AND EVALUATION OF IMPROVEMENT

A detailed report on the clinical material we dealt with, the type and duration of pathology, case presentation and results of treatment is beyond the scope of this paper and will be discussed in a subsequent article.

Although we tried to adhere to our original criteria of selecting disturbed families considered suited for STFT, in practice we felt both forced and entitled to enlarge the frame of our intervention. Thus, no few cases of chronically fixated neurotic conflicts, psychotic reactions, obvious parental rejection, broken homes, psychotic uncooperative parents, etc. were nevertheless accepted for treatment trial.

In our experience, the degree of positive change seems to be significantly related to the following factors:

1) Severity of present psychopathology in the child and family members.

2) Presence or absence of positive family ties.

3) Presence or absence of adverse environmental circumstances (broken homes, psychotic parents, extreme poverty).

4) Presence or absence of positive motivation for treatment, both on the part of the child and the parents.

All these factors should be appraised and weighed as early as the first interview.

Out of 70 families referred to us for STFT, 41 were considered unsuitable for this type of treatment, mainly in view of the degree and chronicity of family pathology. In most of the cases, the decision not to attempt short therapy was established in the course of the first exploratory family joint interview. However, even after a negative conclusion was reached, these families were often seen at two or three subsequent interviews and also referred for psychological evaluation in order to complete the diagnostic study and allow relevant advice on eventual therapeutic alternatives.

The following plan of treatment was proposed to these 41 families:

| | |
|---|---|
| Guidance with or without Environmental Changes | 22 |
| Residential Treatment | 10 |
| Prolonged Psychotherapy | 7 |
| Diagnostic Evaluation Only | 2 |

STFT was attempted with the remaining 29 families. The vast majority of the children of these families were six to 15 years of age, with a similar number of boys and girls. The referral symptoms showed a wide and varied distribution. The following problems were prevalent in the group of 29 children:

| | |
|---|---|
| Phobic Reactions with Incapacitating Fears | 11 |
| Repeated Acute Anxiety Attacks | 7 |

| | |
|---|---|
| Chronic Night Fears | 11 |
| Acute Separation Anxiety | 11 |
| Hyperaggressiveness | 10 |
| Severe School Discipline Problems | 6 |
| School Phobia | 2 |
| Stealing | 2 |
| Suicidal Threats | 2 |
| Long Lasting Enuresis and Encopresis | 3 |
| Anorexia Nervosa | 1 |
| Etc. | |

From a more general diagnostic point of view, the cases were classified as follows:

| | |
|---|---|
| Primary Behavior Disorders | 8 |
| Neurotic Traits | 9 |
| Psychoneuroses | 11 |
| Schizophrenic Reaction | 1 |

In 20 instances out of the total sample of 29, the symptoms had lasted several years, seemed to be organized and structured, and the chances appeared slim that short term treatment would be helpful. However, treatment was attempted after the initial clinical contact pointed out the possibility of positive influence on the family pathogenic interaction. Actually, in only five cases had the emotional disturbances existed a relatively short period of time. In all the remaining instances, we dealt with chronic, well-established symptomatology.

We devised a five point rating scale as a convenient evaluation method of therapeutic results. The following criteria were used:

1) No objective change in family dynamics. Subjective feeling that problems and symptoms are even worse.

2) No change. No objective evidence of symptomatic relief.

3) Moderate improvement as measured in objective and subjective positive changes. Manifest symptoms diminished in number and/or became milder in intensity.

4) Great improvement as evaluated by the family members and therapist. Obvious better family functioning. Most distressing symptoms and clinical problems disappeared.

5) Complete disappearance of referral problems. Complete absence of manifest clinical symptomatology. Ade-

quate insight positively used to modify or eradicate sources of former family difficulties.

Using this type of rating scale, the results given in Table 1 were obtained at the end of treatment. In most of the cases, a follow-up check six months after the end of treatment confirmed the initial evaluation.

It appears that in three quarters of the cases, a definite high degree of improvement (categories 4 and 5) was obtained as shown by the total disappearance of the central symptoms and referral problems. One may speculate about the significance of this high figure of clinical cure, especially in those instances of long standing emotional problems which constitute not not the exception but the prevalent case in our experience. The issue of "deep" versus "short superficial" therapy may be raised on theoretical grounds. But for those families who obtained the necessary help to cope with chronic distressing anxiety states or severe emotional disturbances or interlocked family conflict, the positive outcome of therapy and the stable achievements constitute the most convincing evidence.

Only one case dropped out of treatment in the beginning phase of STFT. In three cases, the need of prolonged psychotherapy for one or more members of the family was recognized at the end of the short therapy procedure and arrangements were made for its implementation. One additional case was referred for residential treatment.

## TABLE 1
### Degree of Clinical Improvement
### in 29 Families After
### Short Term Family Therapy

| Evaluation | Number |
|---|---|
| 1. Worse | 0 |
| 2. Unchanged | 3 |
| 3. Moderate Symptomatic Improvement | 4 |
| 4. Considerable Improvement | 9 |
| 5. Considerable Improvement (Still in Treatment) | 2 |
| 6. Total Symptomatic Improvement | 10 |
| 7. Unknown—Treatment Discontinued | 1 |

## SUMMARY AND CONCLUSION

I. The author discusses the rationale, indications and techniques of short term family therapy as practised by him at two different clinical settings (urban and rural areas). The paper is based on his clinical trial of this therapeutic procedure in 70 families referred to both clinics because of a distressing child-centered emotional problem. Instances of chronic severe psychopathology with highly structured and fixed symptomatology were considered out of the scope of a short therapeutic service. However, in view of the fact that in many cases with long standing internalized conflicts good results were obtained following the initial joint family appraisal interview, it was considered worthy to carry out, in many instances, the total plan of short term treatment.

II. Therapy is centered in the family interaction process. In all the cases the therapist meets several times with the integrated family. Additional meetings with separate members of the family are arranged according to a flexible schedule dictated by clinical needs. Duration of treatment is limited in advance and does not last more than three months. During this period of time, an average of ten family sessions take place. The therapist plays a very active role during both the family and separate interviews, helping to clarify the nature of conscious and preconscious family conflicts and utilizing any possible approach leading to a healthier family readjustment. Clinical evidence shows that effective alleviation or removal of a disorganizing stress situation and pervading anxiety may result in a sound continued process of improvement even in the absence of prolonged psychotherapy.

III. The procedure is based on a single therapist approach instead of the usual team approach. This allows a cohesive view of family dynamics and enables quick and uniform therapeutic interference. Emphasis has to be put upon the fact that short family therapy requires skills, clinical judgment and alertness in evaluation of parental-child needs and conflicts. The required skills can be acquired only through prolonged practice of traditional ways of dynamic psychotherapy.

IV. In 29 families in which the complete plan of short term family therapy was tried, clinical results were excellent. In more than three quarters of the cases a remarkable improvement was obtained as shown by the total disappearance of the central symptoms and referral problems.

The author's therapeutic procedure seems to be particularly suitable and useful in family psychopathology whenever there are still positive family ties, and enough ego strength, anxiety and motivation to establish a meaningful object relationship with the therapist.

# REFERENCES

1. Freud, S., "Turnings in the Ways of Psychoanalytic Therapy," *Collected Papers,* Vol. II, London, Hogarth Press, 1956, pp. 392-402.

2. Hollingshead, A. B. and Redlich, F. C., *Social Class and Mental Illness,* New York, Wiley, 1958.

3. Orne, M. T., "Implications for Psychotherapy Derived from Current Research on the Nature of Hypnosis," *Am. J. Psychiat.,* 118, 1097-1103, 1962.

4. Ackerman, N. W., *The Psychodynamics of Family Life,* New York, Basic Books, 1958.

5. Alpern, E., "Short Clinical Services for Children in a Child Guidance Clinic," *Am. J. Orthopsychiat.,* 26, 314-325, 1956.

# Behavior Modification Techniques

# 18. BEHAVIOR THERAPY
# WITH CHILDREN:
# A BROAD OVERVIEW

John S. Werry, M. B., F.R.C.P.(C) and
Janet P. Wollersheim, Ph.D.

Behavior therapy is a term coined by Eysenck (1959) to denote a system of psychotherapy of relatively recent origin (Wolpe, 1958) which is distinguished from other types of psychotherapy by its theoretical background and its points of emphasis in the clinical area.

Unfortunately, at least three factors have militated against a positive and inquiring attitude by child psychiatrists and other child therapists toward behavior therapy. The first of these is unfamiliarity with the terminology and concepts of behavior therapy, thus making it appear much more complex than it really is. The second deterrent has been the aggressive attitude of some of the protagonists of behavior therapy who have proselytized it as the only possible approach to therapy. The third and least defensible impediment is that of a conservatism resulting perhaps from some degree of institutionalization of present techniques of therapy. The aim of this review is to acquaint child therapists with some of the concepts and techniques of behavior therapy, to offer illustrative case studies, and to indicate what the

Reprinted from *Journal of the American Academy of Child Psychiatry,* 1967, **6**, 346-370. by permission of International Universities Press, Inc. and the authors. Copyright 1967, International Universities Press, Inc. Dr. Werry is Professor and Head, Department of Psychiatry, University of Auckland, School of Medicine, Auckland, New Zealand. Dr. Wollersheim is in the Department of Psychology, University of Missouri, Columbia, Missouri.

authors believe to be the pertinence of behavior therapy in the remediation of the psychopathology of childhood.

## THEORETICAL CONSIDERATIONS

The theoretical framework of behavior therapy is *learning theory* which, unlike earlier systems, did not grow out of the clinical situation but rather out of rigorously controlled laboratory experiments chiefly with animals. While differences between behavior therapy and more traditional approaches are in part due to its underlying theory, some appear merely to be semantic in nature.

One major difference between behavior therapy and more traditional approaches is the emphasis of the former upon overt behavior. In their enthusiasm to make psychology a legitimate science, early twentieth-century psychologists adopted a position of rigorous empiricism. It is therefore not surprising that behavior therapists have likewise shown themselves suspicious of elegant, hypothetical constructs like that of the ego, and have instead focused on more atomistic, more readily observable behaviors which in more common parlance might be described as "symptoms" or "ego functions" (Eysenck, 1959; Ullmann and Krasner, 1965). This difference is also partly attributable to the differing historical backgrounds of the two approaches: behavior therapy deriving from experimental psychology rather than from medicine. Behavior therapists, for example, do not talk about *psychopathology* but rather about *maladaptive behaviors*. Also, traditional psychotherapy had depended heavily on the medical disease model, in particular the concept of underlying unitary pathology (e.g., the unconscious conflict) producing a plethora of surface manifestations or symptoms. Experimental psychologists, on the other hand, have been interested largely in determining the functional relationships between environmental events or stimuli and organismic responses. Their interest, too, in pre-existing states within the organism has been limited, particularly since these organismic states were readily controllable in the laboratory setting.

The second major difference between behavior therapy and certain more traditional approaches is that, for the behavior therapists, maladaptive behavior (e.g., psychotic symptoms) is not seen as qualitatively different from what is arbitrarily defined as normal behavior. Both are acquired or *learned* and removed or *unlearned* in the same ways by essentially the same processes and are subject to the same general laws. The content of an individual's experience determines the specific kinds of behavior he exhibits or has learned, though organic factors may influence not only the range of potential behaviors but also the probability of certain classes of behavior being emitted and hence of becoming stabilized.

The third difference stems from behavior therapy's adherence to learning theory rather than to another theory such as that of psychoanalysis. Learning theory suggests two basic kinds of learning or conditioning (this latter term is essentially a synonym for learning). The first kind of learning, classical conditioning or *respondent learning*, was discovered by Pavlov and is probably the most familiar to child therapists. This is essentially the modification of a naturally occurring reflex arc usually involving the autonomic nervous system as effector, in which a neutral or conditioned stimulus is substituted for the natural or unconditioned stimulus. The simplest example of such learning in child psychopathology is Watson's little Albert who developed a rat phobia by being exposed to a naturally phobic stimulus, loud noise, every time he reached out to touch a white rat which had been initially an object of curiosity to the child (Watson and Rayner, 1920). The essential characteristics of this type of learning are the potency of environmental events or external stimuli in eliciting autonomic responses from a helpless and passive organism. Its pertinence to the human organism is probably paramount in all kinds of emotional reaction to external events.

The second type of learning has been emphasized by Skinner (1938) and is termed *operant conditioning*. Fundamental to the concept of the operant response is the idea, first, of choice and, second, of effecting or operating on the environment. Hence it usually involves the voluntary rather than the autonomic central nervous system. What makes the organism choose to perform one operant response rather than another in a nonnovel situation is considered to be determined by the consequences or *reinforcement* which followed the same act on previous occasions. In general, reinforcement is considered to follow the pleasure principle in which acts which are rewarded become more probable or learned, while unrewarded or punished acts become less probable or *extinguished.* The efficacy of a given reinforcer depends on several factors such the need state of the individual (food is unlikely to be effective if the subject has just satiated himself) and, in the human, a degree of idiosyncrasity stemming from the complex uniqueness of individual experience and our capacity for symbolism.

In operant learning, particularly in a higher organism, the stimulus is much less powerful than in respondent learning since, in operant learning, the stimulus represents a sign or cue indicating the possibilities of reinforcement, of reward or punishment which the organism may elect to heed or not, according to his own particular whim or need state. Nevertheless, the stimulus in operant learning does exhibit the characteristic of *stimulus generalization* as in respondent learning. This means that there is a range of environmental events which are likely to produce a learned response. The more similar these are to those of the learning situation, the greater is the chance of the learned behavior occurring. For example, it is assumed by parents that a child who learns certain modes of conduct at his own table will behave in a similar fashion when he eats with friends.

Of practical importance in therapy is the fact that the further along the stimulus generalization gradient a particular stimulus lies (that is, the more dissimilar it is to the original), the less likely it is to evoke the learned response, and also, in the case of the respondent behavior, the weaker the response will be. Also, no matter how much practice is undertaken, learning is never perfect. Thus, on some occasions, the presentatation of a stimulus will not evoke the learned response, but instead may evoke some other behavior. Further, it is possible to weaken the effect of a stimulus by presenting it in competition with another stimulus of antagonistic effect as typified by Miller's approach-avoidance conflict studies (1944). By utilizing this knowledge about the effect of the stimulus upon the response, behavior therapists can maximize the probability of occurrence of healthy behaviors and strengthen them at the expense of psychopathological alternatives.

Left to themselves, conditioned responses do not decay as a function of time or, in short, are not forgotten. They disappear in two ways. First, responses can be weakened through *extinction,* which means that the conditioned reflex is elicited without any presentation of the unconditioned stimulus, or, in the case of operant behavior, reinforcement does not follow the emission of the responses. Probably more common than extinction in the natural situation is the phenomenon of replacement or *counterconditioning* whereby the response to a given stimulus is changed to another response which is incompatible with the original one. Both extinction and counterconditioning are used extensively by behavior therapists in the treatment of already existing maladaptive responses. However, where no response exists or, in short, where the "symptom" is a sign of deficient functioning such as in the developmental type of enuresis (Barbour et al., 1963), *conditioning* is employed to develop the desired patterns of behavior.

## THE PRINCIPLES OF
## BEHAVIOR THERAPY

It is possible to delineate about seven phases in behavior therapy which are, with terminological modifications, equally applicable to other forms of psychotherapy.

*Problem Definition.* As mentioned above, behavior therapists have an atomistic approach to problem definition with the emphasis upon discrete observable behaviors (this includes verbalizations). Although theoretically one could construct a comprehensive list of all the symptoms and then proceed systematically to eliminate them, this procedure is seldom practicable. The usual procedure is to select the symptoms which are either most distressing to the patient or to those in his social environment, or most suitable for treatment. As such, problem definition is likely to be simple and practical.

*Problem Analysis.* Having isolated the symptoms which are both deserving and amenable to therapy, the therapist then attempts to determine the factors or stimuli which elicit the behavior, such as the feared situation in a phobia, and/or the factors which are perpetuating or reinforcing the problem behavior. This kind of information frequently requires some kind of observation of the child in a real-life situation such as at school or in the mother-child interaction. In respondent or emotional behavior, the therapist is likely to spend more time with stimuli; and in operant behavior, he is more likely to be concerned with determining the response-reinforcement contingencies in the child's natural environment.

*Mapping Out a Plan of Therapy.* From the diagnostic information gathered in the first two phases, the therapist plans his therapeutic program firm in the belief that he himself can control the patient's behavior in such a way as to maximize therapeutic effect rather than be guided by the patient himself as in play therapy or free association techniques.

*Motivating the Patient for Therapy.* This category requires no special description but is inserted only to indicate that though this point is seldom emphasized in papers on behavior therapy, it is no less important than in other approaches. After initial motivation, of course, the key to continued motivation lies both in the personality of the therapist and the proper structuring or *programming* of the plan of therapy.

*Behavior Shaping.* This is the first phase of actual treatment after initial motivation for therapy has been attained. Behavior shaping is a picturesque term which underlines the important principle of gradualism. Little by little, the therapist seeks to move the child's behavior closer to that behavior which is desired. The change is planned in gradual steps so that the behavior change can be relatively easily accomplished. Throughout treatment, the therapist assumes an active role, controlling both the stimuli and the response-reinforcement contingencies rather than waiting for an occasional *moment critique* so emphasized in other types of therapy. Because of this emphasis upon controlling environmental contingencies to alter the subject's response to stimuli, behavior therapy is as likely to be carried on in the child's own environment as in the therapist's office. Also because of the clarity and explicitness of the therapeutic program as designed by the professional behavior therapists, often it can be largely carried out by relatively unskilled persons such as the mother herself (Wahler *et al.*, 1965; Allen and Harris, 1966), the nurse (Ayllon and Michael, 1959), nursing assistants (Wolf, *et al.*, 1964), undergraduate students (Davison, 1964, 1965), or even machines (Werry and Cohrssen, 1965).

*Generalization of Behavior.*    Once the desired behavior has been achieved, and particularly where therapy has been carried out in the clinic rather than the child's natural setting, an active inquiry is made as to whether the behavior has *generalized* or is now manifest in all spheres of the child's natural environment where it should be. If the child is not performing the desired behavior in some situations, generalization must be produced directly by carrying therapy into other environments or by using as co-therapists persons such as parents who are with the child in many different environments.

*Stabilization of Behavior.*    It is also necessary to determine whether the behavior has acquired some degree of stability so that it will continue to be emitted once therapy has been discontinued. Studies with animals have shown that the quickest way to achieve desired behavior is to reinforce this behavior every time it occurs or is elicited (continuous reinforcement). However, resistance to extinction can be greatly increased by then moving on to a schedule of so-called intermittent or inconsistent reinforcement (Holland and Skinner, 1961). In a large number of cases, or course, stabilization of behavior should be ensured by naturally occurring reinforcement from significant persons in the child's environment or from the improved intrapsychic state of the patient. The general plan of the behavior therapist is to arrange for continuous and immediate reinforcement of the new behavior when this behavior is being acquired. The reinforcement is then moved to an intermittent schedule which approximates that occurring in the child's natural environment.

# TECHNIQUES OF BEHAVIOR THERAPY

Although the general principles of learning theory used in behavior therapy are relatively few (conditioning, counterconditioning, and extinction), the technologies of therapy or the practical methods of applying them in treatment are many. The following is a description of the major techniques used with children as reported in the literature up to the present time.[1] These methods have been grouped according to the principal point of focus in therapy: (1) the preceding environmental events or stimuli, (2) the response of the organism, (3) the environmental events consequent upon the response (reinforcement), and (4) the pre-existing intraorganismic state. Such a categorization is, of course, artificial since few techniques are completely pure, but it is offered in the hope that it will prove useful in the designing of individual therapeutic programs.

## Stimulus Manipulation

In view of the passive-reflexive response of the organism in respondent or classical conditioning, it is not surprising that attempts to deal with psychopathological conditions which typify this kind of learning (found

[1] July, 1966.

mostly in emotional reactions) try to overthrow the tyranny of the environmental stimulus by an attack directly on this stimulus.

*Systematic Desensitization of Stimuli.*    This is a method which capitalizes upon the weakness of the conditioned response and its lower probability of occurrence at the extremes of the stimulus generalization gradient. It was developed by Wolpe (1958) who usually simultaneously strengthens incompatible, alternative responses (*vide infra*) such as relaxation and assertion. In our experience, the simultaneous strengthening of an incompatible alternative response is by no means necessary for success, although Rachman (1965) has shown that it is more efficient to do so. The therapist constructs a scale of stimulus situations as, for example, in the treatment for a phobia, which are arranged hierarchically according to the intensity of the emotional reaction they provoke in the patient. Wolpe and Lang (1964) have recently constructed a fear survey schedule to facilitate this process. One then proceeds to expose the patient to the weakest of the stimuli either in fact (e.g., M. C. Jones, 1924a, 1924b) or in fantasy (Wolpe, 1958). Since the emotional reaction is relatively weak, the patient can, with some encouragement from the therapist or another person such as a parent, remain in this weakly phobic situation long enough to find that nothing terrible happens to him, thus extinguishing the anxiety associated with the situation. In this way, one moves progressively up the stimulus hierarchy until ultimately the most anxiety-provoking situations can be tolerated with minimal or no anxiety.

*Stimulus Attenuation.*    This technique is somewhat analogous to systematic desensitization and is usually used wittingly or not in combination with it. The technique relies on the interference by one stimulus with the effect of another when both are presented contemporaneously and has been used successfully by one of the authors (JSW) in the treatment of agoraphobia in an adolescent girl. The patient's mother who was very reassuring to the patient was instructed to accompany the girl on short, though ever-lengthening bus rides, thus attenuating the power of the phobic situations. Garvey and Hegrenes (1966) also used this technique in treating a case of school phobia.

*Cue Conversion.*   This method attempts to change the sign of a stimulus in terms of its capacity to signal pleasure or pain. In general, this method has been used mostly to convert positive signals of forbidden pleasures to negative or unpleasant ones by pairing them with noxious stimuli such as electric shock, emesis, etc. With some variations, this approach has been used extensively in the treatment of alcoholism and sexual perversions in adults, although the success of the results has been somewhat dubious except perhaps in fetishism (Raymond, 1956). One problem in using this technique in the treatment of addictions and perversions revolves around the difficulty of providing an alternative pro-social outlet for the instinctual drive. There is no reason why attempts should not be made to convert negative or neutral stimuli to positive ones. Examples of this strategy have appeared recently in the treatment of homosexuality (Thorpe, *et al.,* 1964) where the appearance of a scantily dressed female photograph is the signal that the shcok is about to be terminated, thus hopefully making the opposite sex a sign of relief and thus more attractive. A similar approach has been used by Lovaas, *et al.* (1965b) in the treatment of autism where the act of moving toward an adult was the means of terminating a mildly unpleasant electric shock. This procedure ultimately resulted in a significant increase in spontaneous display of affection by the children toward adults.

Obviously, the use of noxious stimuli in children presents serious ethical problems, and it really can be justified only where the condition is so severe that no other technique can reach the child or where the physical or social consequences of a given behavior are likely to be extremely serious (see Lovaas, *et al.,* 1965a, 1965b). Child therapists often make the mistake of assuming that inasmuch as society itself already punishes most of these conditions, the application of noxious stimuli is completely futile. Such a point of view fails to recognize the crucial importance of timing since punishment by society or parent is usually quite distant and the immediate consequences of the forbidden act are highly pleasurable.

*Interference with Sensory Feedback.* This technique has been used principally in the treatment of speech disorders such as stuttering where it seems that the patient's perception of his own speech is somehow important in the pathogenesis. Various techniques have been employed such as the shadowing technique (Cherry and Sayers, 1956) where the therapist reads and the patient repeats this back two syllables behind the reader. Under these conditions stuttering is much reduced or even absent, and in this way proper speaking habits can be strengthened. Other recent developments are the metronome method of Meyer and Mair (1963) in which the patient adjusts the cadence of his speech to a metronome rate of between 70 and 80 beats per minute. Under these conditions most patients immediately begin to speak without stuttering. One of the advantages of this particular technique is that with the development of a portable hearing aid type of metronome (Meyer and Mair, 1963) the patient can then proceed to expose himself to increasingly more anxiety-provoking talking situations, and thus carry out systematic desensitization of the anxiety component of his stuttering.

*Modeling.* The elegant studies by Bandura and Walters (1963) have demonstrated that children can learn a great deal simply by observing the behavior of others. Factors which facilitate the potency of the models are the consequences of the response to the model, how rewarding the model has been to the child, the competence and status of the model, and the power the model has to reward or punish the child. The experiments of Bandura and Walters indicate how some of these factors may actually be used in the therapeutic situation to enhance the potency of the therapist if he is interested in promoting identification with himself. Modeling is also likely to prove to be one of the more efficient ways of producing new patterns of complex behavior in children, particularly in younger age groups who are less amenable to verbal instruction.

## Response Manipulation

*Reciprocal Inhibition.* In this technique, largely attributable to Wolpe (1958), the therapist strengthens responses which are incompatible with the undesirable behavior and which thus *reciprocally inhibit* the maladaptive responses (usually anxiety or withdrawal). Thus, it is essentially counterconditioning. The inhibiting responses which have been used are muscular relaxation and assertive responses (Wolpe, 1958) and pleasure associated with the gratification of various biological drives. For example, Mary Cover Jones (1924b) was able to cure a two-and-a-half-year-old boy of a phobia by presentation of phobic objects while the child was eating his favorite food. The technique of reciprocal inhibition is unlikely to be successful unless it is used in conjunction with systematic desensitization since, as discussed above, the situation must be arranged such that the adaptive behavior has a higher probability of occurring than does the maladaptive behavior. Where the aim is to teach assertive responses, as, for example, in treating an overly timid child, the modeling techniques of Bandura and Walters (1963) should be helpful in initiating this type of behavior, but modeling would not likely be successful without systematic presentation of opportunities for successful display of assertion. The technique would involve having the child practice assertion in simple situations and then in increasingly more difficult situations.

*Contrived Responses.* Here, a response is made to occur but in an artificial form or situation so that, if maladaptive, it can be attenuated or its normal response-reinforcement contingencies altered. Where a child simply lacks skills, he can be taught them (e.g., Quay, *et al.,* 1966). Usually this involves acting out threatening or traumatic situations in play therapy or in carefully controlled play acting (Lazarus and Abramovitz, 1962). By such means, the child can gradually develop adaptive alternative behaviors for certain situations, or extinguish maladaptive behavior or the vivid emotional components of certain traumatic memories.

Differences in the behavior therapy approach in this type of therapy are probably less than with other techniques described in this review. Nevertheless, traditional approaches have probably relied too much upon the power of verbal conceptualization or interpretation rather than on the behaviors themselves as vital instruments in extinction or conditioning processes. There probably also has been too little faith in the utility of the therapist's playing an active role in promoting and controlling the child's behavior in the therapeutic situation which is an essential component of the behavior therapy approach. The technique of emotive imagery (Lazarus and Abramovitz, 1962) illustrates some of these important differences.

*Successive Approximation.* This is analogous to systematic desensitization except that the emphasis is on the response rather than on the stimulus. Where the desired behavior is complex in terms of the child's ability to achieve it, or where modeling or verbal instruction are relatively ineffective because of autism or low mental age, a hierarchy of responses in terms of their closeness to the desired behavior can be constructed so that each step is relatively easily achievable, whereas the distant goal may of itself be quite inaccessible initially. Moving from readiness tasks to learning letters and thence to words is an example of the principle of successive approximation applied to the learning of reading. Successive approximation requires for its success an understanding of important principles of reinforcement (*vide infra*). However, in the example of learning to read, reinforcement factors are usually ignored since they are assumed to be intrinsic to the successful solution of the task or ubiquitous in the natural approbation which comes with progress toward a socially approved goal (see Hunt, 1965).

*Negative or Massed Practice.* In this technique, the

symptom, usually a motor habit such as a tic, is repeated voluntarily for several periods each day. The complicated theoretical explanation (Yates, 1958) is less pertinent here than the several clinical demonstrations (Yates, 1958; H. G. Jones, 1960a; Rafi, 1962; Walton, 1961; and Agras and Marshall, 1965), of the efficacy of this treatment method especially with tics.

## Reinforcement Manipulation

Here we are concerned with strengthening or weakening particular behaviors by manipulating their environmental consequences or reinforcement. These techniques are particularly relevant to operant or choice learning. It should be emphasized at this point that reinforcement depends for its success not only on its capacity to appeal to the individual child (Bijou and Baer, 1963) but also on close temporal proximity (within a few *seconds*) to the behavior which is the subject of therapeutic attention (Holland and Skinner, 1961). It is surprising how this extremely important principle of immediacy of reinforcement is so little understood and so frequently violated by child therapists and parents alike. Also important is the so-called scheduling of reinforcement as discussed above, with consistency being desirable in the early stages and deliberate inconsistency being desirable to ensure permanence in the behavior once it is achieved.

*Withholding Reward.* Many undesirable behaviors in children are maintained because parents or others are unwittingly reinforcing these behaviors through attention or granting the object of the undesirable behavior (e.g., Lovaas, *et al.*, 1965a; Allen and Harris, 1966). Teaching the parent or other adult figure such as the teacher who is reinforcing this kind of behavior to ignore it instead, often results in its prompt extinction (Brown and Elliot, 1965). Sometimes it will be necessary to instruct or actually to demonstrate to these adults what they may have already felt they should do but which they do not carry out for a variety of personal reasons (Wahler, *et al.*, 1965).

*Instituting Reward (Positive Reinforcement).* In order to use this successfully, the therapist must know: (i) the type of behavior he wishes to develop in the child; (ii) how to get the child to exhibit this behavior; and (iii) what is rewarding or reinforcing to this particular child (Bijou and Baer, 1963). The first of these requires accurate problem definition before therapy is commenced. The second requires a knowledge of stimulus generalization gradients, successive approximation, and modeling techniques; and the third, a willingness to experiment with a wide variety of possible rewards, some of which, for example, candy, trinkets, etc., may require the overcoming of considerable prejudice on the part of the therapist himself and the parents of the patient.

However, in the majority of situations, the type of reinforcement to be applied will generally prove to be conditioned or symbolic such as attention or approbation from another human being. Much attention has been given in the traditional psychotherapeutic literature to the importance of the therapist-child relationship. Looked at in terms of learning theory, the importance of this lies in the reinforcing quality the therapist acquires for the child. What is lacking in the traditional approach is probably lack of emphasis on the therapist's improving his reinforcing value by using concrete rewards if necessary and in systematically using his charismatic value in reinforcing pro-social behavior. Recently, ingenious and apparently successful attempts have been made to use the peer group as an important source of reinforcement by making some kind of group reward contingent upon the amount of adaptive behavior exhibited by a deviant pupil (Patterson, 1965a). One of the important unpremeditated outcomes of this particular study was the movement of the patient from a very low to a very high status position in the peer group. In another study (Straughan, *et al.,* 1965), peer reinforcement was utilized in treating elective mutism in a 14-year-old boy.

Another method of applying positive reinforcement is the implementation of Premack's Principle (1959), which states that a preferred activity can be used as a reinforcement for a less popular one if the former is made contingent upon the latter. Homme and his colleagues (1963) described the use of Premack's Principle in a nursery school situation where desirable behavior such as sitting quietly in a chair and looking at the blackboard were greatly increased in frequency by instructing the children that if they sat quietly for what was initially quite a short period, they would then be permitted to get up and run around and make as much noise as they liked for a short period. An interesting feature of this particular study is that it was possible quickly to increase the time required for sitting and to decrease and eventually to omit altogether the running around time except at recess. Again, this approach, like all other applications of reinforcement, depends for its success upon the *immediate* application of the reinforcement *after* the adaptive behavior rather than application of the reinforcement at a time remote from the performance of the adaptive behavior or antecedent to it.

One final point in the application of reinforcement needs emphasizing, namely, selectivity. In certain types of behaviors such as attention-seeking, the parent is likely to reward only high intensities of this behavior (Bandura and Walters, 1963) so that a very ignored child may find that his only way of attracting attention is to scream and shout. Such intense behavior may of course produce punishment, but a very deprived child may consider even this kind of attention rewarding. What the parent should be doing, or course, is rewarding more moderate demands for attention and ignoring the intense levels.

*Deprivation and Satiation.* Sometimes it will prove necessary to strengthen or attenuate natural reinforcers rather than to institute reinforcers *de novo*. For example, eating in Western civilization is mostly a function of social custom rather than hunger, and the reinforcing value of food can be greatly strengthened by judicious deprivation of food (Ayllon, 1963; Wolf, *et al.,* 1964). Conversely, on occasion, the best approach to maladaptive behavior may be to weaken the reinforcer by giving the patient an overabundance of it. This is well illustrated in the treatment of a towel-hoarding patient by permitting her to hoard as much linen as she wished (Ayllon, 1963). Satiation may, on occasion, work against the therapist as can be seen in the remark of one of the pupils in a class for emotionally disturbed children who stated that he was not going to pay attention in class for a mere ten candies when he could get about a hundred in a fifteen-minute individual conditioning session after class (Quay *et al.*, 1966).

*Punishment.*   As used in this context, punishment is defined as the application of an aversive or noxious stimulus which may be indirect or symbolic (e.g., castigation) as well as physical (e.g., spanking). In general, though punishment obeys many of the same laws as reinforcement, particularly that of immediate contingency upon the response, its effects are somewhat more complex (Bandura and Walters, 1963). First, punishment suppresses rather than eliminates responses so that they have a tendency to reappear when the child is sure that the punishment is unlikely to occur. Second, in susceptible children, generalized inhibition may result, extending to include healthy as well as punished behaviors. Finally, what appears to be punishment may in fact, in a very deprived child, be rewarding; nor can one entirely discount the possibility of genuine masochism. Nevertheless, punishment has a definite role to play particularly in combination with reward for incompatible, adaptive, alternative behavior where it may greatly facilitate the course of therapy (Lovaas, *et al.*, 1965b; Wahler, *et al.*, 1965) and in the cue conversion method mentioned above.

## Manipulation of Intraorganismic Drive States

There is already much evidence to show that drive state greatly influences the behavior of an organism. One important effect is simply that of energizing behavior where the relationship, like most biological functions, is curvilinear. Thus, at lower levels of arousal, an increment in drive will facilitate performance, but at the higher levels performance will be impeded by an increment in drive (Duffy, 1957). More complex or less well learned functions tend to be first impaired, making primitive or chronic behaviors like psychopathological, emotional reactions more probable (Bindra, 1959; Yates, 1961). In addition to purely quantitative elements, drive also has a qualitative or directional component such as pain avoidance, restitution or homeostasis, sexual satisfaction, or reduction of cognitive dissonance (Hunt, 1965). This qualitative dimension of drive will make certain classes of behavior which in the past have successfully lowered the particular emotional tension more probable (Holland and Skinner, 1961, pp. 235-240). Hence, in behavior therapy, it may be of great advantage to manipulate both the *level* and the *type* of emotional state in order to maximize the probability of appearance of certain adaptive behaviors (e.g., Feldman and Werry, 1966). Psychopharmacological agents seem to have important quantitative effects on drive states, although the evidence for a qualitative effect is relatively unconvincing except in the case of antidepressant drugs. One of the great weaknesses of psychopharmacological studies is that drugs have been used as an end in themselves instead of as an important tool with which to facilitate the learning of new behaviors. The deliberate manipulation of drive state by pharmacotherapy in a 13-year-old tiqueur by Walton (1961), the use of dextroamphetamine in conjunction with the conditioning treatment of enuresis by Young and Turner (1965), and the use of drugs to induce relaxation in the successfuly desensitization of a three-and-a-half-year-old child by Lazarus (1960) are milestones in both behavior therapy and psychopharmacology research. Other possible ways in which drive state might be deliberately manipulated are through hypnosis, muscular relaxation, environmental structuring, food deprivation, and paying close attention to sex and personality in the selection of a therapist for individual children.

# TYPES OF PROBLEMS TREATED

This section of the review is essentially nothing more than a bibliography. This is so, not only in the interests of conciseness, but also because most of the reported literature of behavior therapy to this date consists of detailed individual case studies. Child therapists who would be interested in investigating the possibilities of behavior therapy in specific conditions would gain most by reading the case studies themselves. The authors hope that some of the terminological problems will have been obviated by previous sections of the review.

In categorizing the clinical conditions, the authors have tried to strike a balance between current nosology and the symptom-oriented approach of behavior therapists.

## Neurotic Symptoms

*Anxiety Symptoms (phobias, fears, school phobia, etc.).* Possibly because it is relatively easy to identify the eliciting stimuli, children's fears and phobias have received a great deal of attention from behavior therapists and reportedly with considerable success. The techniques employed have generally been systematic desensitization to the stimulus often with concomitant strengthening of alternative responses antagonistic to anxiety such as affectionate, feeding, and social responses. Authors who report successful cases are Mary Cover Jones (1924a, 1924b), Eysenck and Rachman (1965, pp. 209-210), and Lazarus (1960) in children with animal phobias; Lazarus and Abramovitz (1962), Kushner (1965), and Lazarus (1960) in children with specific situational anxiety such as separation anxiety, agoraphobia, etc.; Patterson (1965b), Lazarus, *et al.* (1965), Eysenck and Rachman (1965, pp. 218-222), and Garvey and Hegrenes (1966) in children with school phobias.

Rachman and Costello (1961) offer a general theoretical review of the etiology and treatment of children's phobias from the behavior therapy point of view.

*Conversion Symptoms.* Because of their well-known capacity to attract positive environmental reinforcement or "secondary gain," conversion symptoms are eminently suitable to the behavior therapy approach. The principle technique used to treat conversion syptoms is withdrawal of reward for the conversion behavior and the instituting of reinforcement for pro-social alternative behavior. Harris and her colleagues (1964; Allen and Harris, 1966) were able to treat regressive crawling and severe scratching in this fashion. More traditional conversion symptoms such as blindness have as yet been treated mostly in adults (Eysenck and Rachman, 1965, pp. 93-104), though Straghan et al. (1965) treated elective mutism in a fourteen-year-old boy by using peer approval and material reinforcement.

*Obsessive-Compulsive Symptoms.* Published reports thus far concern only the treatment of adults, though there is no reason why the techniques used such as reciprocal inhibition should not be applied to children. As might be expected, however, the therapeutic effect in treating obsessive-compulsive symptoms has been of somewhat limited extent (Walton and Mather, 1963).

## Psychophysiological Reactions

Enuresis has been the target of a large number of studies using the bed-buzzer or "conditioning" apparatus (DeLeon and Mandell, 1966; H. G. Jones, 1960b; Werry, 1966), the exact *modus operandi* of which is at the moment unclear, but is most likely reinforcement manipulation using mild punishment (Lovibond, 1963a). Cure rates have ranged from as high as 90 percent (H. G. Jones, 1960b) to as low as 30 percent (Werry and Cohrssen, 1965). Recent approaches have improved the results of therapy by simultaneous administration of drugs (Young and Turner, 1965), by the use of intermittent rather than continuous reinforcement (Lovibond, 1963b), and by a modification of the apparatus to make cessation of the punishment (i.e., the loud noise produced by the buzzer) more nearly contingent upon cessation of the act of micturition (Lovibond, 1963a).

Encopresis has yielded good results principally with the combination of successive approximation and application of reward (Neale, 1963; Gelber and Meyer, 1965; Keehn, 1965; Peterson and London, 1965). The latter paper is remarkable in that the authors demonstrate how a cognitive or insight approach can be used *in conjunction with* the behavior therapy approach.

Wolf and his colleagues (1965) were successful in treating vomiting by withdrawing the reinforcement which usually followed the vomiting. White (1959), using successive approximation, and Hallsten (1965) using systematic desensitization and positive reinforcement, successfully treated eating problems.

Cherry and Sayers (1956) and Meyer and Mair (1963) report success in treating stuttering using stimulus feedback interference. Maclaren (1960) used auditory retraining and removal of punishment (criticism) in treating stammering, while Kerr, *et al.* (1965) used application of reinforcement to develop voaclization in a mute child.

Walton (1961) successfully treated multiple tics in a child using the negative practice technique in combination with chemotherapy. Feldman and Werry (1966) were unsuccessful using the negative practice technique because of the development of severe anxiety, which, however, might possibly have been obviated by prior treatment with systematic desensitization techniques.

## Psychotic Symptoms

To date, most published reports on behavior therapy with psychotic children have consisted of isolated experiments rather than complete treatment programs. In terms of the assumptions of behavior therapy, the principles of learning theory should apply equally to psychotic as to normal children. This assumption is supported by the experimental studies of Ferster and DeMyer (1962), Davison (1964, 1965), Eysenck and Rachman (1965, p. 238), Hingtgen, *et al.* (1965), Marr, *et al.* (1966), Metz

(1965), Lovaas, *et al.* (1965a, 1965b, 1966), and Wolf, *et al.* (1964). These findings all demonstrate how normal behavior can be increased at the expense of psychotic behavior by direct application of learning theory principles. Thus, techniques which have proved fruitful in manipulating the behavior of normal children should hold great promise for the treatment of childhood psychosis. Of particular interest in this context are the procedures aimed at developing social interaction and cooperation (Azrin and Lindsley, 1956; Allen, *et al.*, 1964; Davison, 1964, 1965).

## Conduct Disorders

Williams (1959), Wahler, *et al.* (1965), and Boardman (1962) have all successfully treated temper tantrums and other kinds of oppositional behavior by instructing parents in the manipulation of reinforcement particularly the withholding of reward. Hart, *et al.* (1964), Bijou and Baer (1963), and Zimmerman and Zimmerman (1962) were able greatly to reduce the frequency of a wide variety of conduct problems in the school situation by similar techniques using teachers as co-therapists. Rickard and Dinoff (1965) were successful in treating rebelliousness in a summer camp by using camp counselors as therapists. Capitalizing on some experimental work by Levin and Simmons (1962a, 1962b) which demonstrated superiority of material rather than social reinforcement for conduct problem children, Schwitzgebel and Kolb (1964), Slack (1960), and Burchard and Tyler (1965) were able successfully to treat a wide variety of antisocial behavior. Quay, *et al.* (1966) significantly improved classroom attention in conduct problem children by immediately reinforcing the desired behavior with light flashes followed by candy.

Patterson (1965a) and his coworkers (1965) successfully treated two hyperactive boys in the classroom through immediate reinforcement by an experimenter of sitting-still behavior. An untreated hyperactive child in the same classroom did not improve.

# CONCLUSIONS

In this review, the authors have attempted to review behavior therapy as it has been, or might be, applied to the treatment of the psychopathology of childhood. Wherever possible, techniques, theoretical concepts, and clinical conditions have been described in familiar terms without having eliminated some of the essential differences in the new approach. Principally, behavior therapy rests upon a functional and empirical orientation, adherence to a well-formulated experimentally derived theory, and an active, systematic manipulation of patients' behavior, environmental stimuli, environmental consequences or reinforcement and even of the therapist himself. Those who, like Glover (1959), in recognizing the familiar in the new would deny any substantive difference thereto, fail to understand that a new approach may, indeed *should,* build on the foundation of existing knowledge, or to recognize that a new approach may be more heuristically cast. Nor does the new necessarily preclude the continuance of the old. A more meaningful question is to ask where the proper place for behavior therapy lies among the *therapies* of child psychopathology.

In the authors' opinion, behavior therapy is most likely to be the treatment of choice: (a) where there are discrete, easily recognizable symptoms or problem behaviors, (b) where the patient or his parent is symptom-rather than insight-oriented (Yamamoto and Goin, 1965); (c) where, because of clinical conditions or mental age, the patient is unamenable to conflict-insight-verbalization approaches (e.g., Goldfarb, 1965); (d) where child therapists are scarce since, because of its systematic and concrete nature, behavior therapy is readily able to be executed by relatively unskilled therapists with some degree of supervision (Allen and Harris, 1966; Ayllon, 1963; Brown and Elliot, 1965; Davison, 1964, 1965; Wahler, *et al.,* 1965; Wolf, *et al.,* 1964).

By means of reference to a now not inconsiderable bibliography, the growing number of therapeutic successes attributable to behavior therapy have been indicated. Unfortunately, most of these reports have been by psychologists and have appeared in books (e.g., Eysenck and Rachman, 1965; Ullman and Krasner, 1965) and in scientific journals not usually read by child therapists. At the moment there is only a small number of studies which have attempted to compare behavior therapy with more traditional approaches, and the evidence for the superiority of the new technique (DeLeon and Mandell, 1966; Land and Lazovik, 1963; Paul, 1966; Rachman, 1965; Werry and Cohrssen, 1965) seems about equaled by that which shows it to have no advantage (Cooper, 1963; Koenig and Masters, 1965; Marks and Gelder, 1965). Significantly, perhaps, Koenig and Masters showed that the *therapist* was more important than the *therapy*. Nevertheless, it would be unwise for child therapists to ignore this important development in therapy. Failure to take cognizance of developments in this area will not only lead to compartmentalization of child therapy between psychology and the other disciplines, but could also lead to an unnecessary limitation in the therapeutic spectrum offered by child psychiatric facilities. Even if behavior therapy does not prove ultimately to be superior to traditional techniques in the areas where it is most appropriate, because of its ability to utilize relatively unskilled therapists, it merits serious consideration. Further, its theoretical preciseness and its emphasis on the scientific method may open avenues to research in certain areas of psychotherapy which are presently methodologically insoluble.

Thus, behavior therapy with children, though no panacea, seems likely to bring limited but significant relief at least to certain patients presently unamenable to, or unreachable by, traditional techniques and holds a potentiality for enlarging the theoretical horizons of child psychiatry.

# REFERENCES

1. Agras, S., & Marshall, C. (1965), The application of negative practice to spasmodic torticollis. *Amer. J. Psychiat.*, 122:579-582.
2. Allen, K. E., & Harris, F.R. (1966), Elimination of a child's exces-

sive scratching by training the mother in reinforcement procedures. *Behav. Res. Ther.,* 4:79-84.

3. Allen, K. E., Hart, B., Buell, J. S., Harris, F. R., & Wolf, M. R. (1964), Effects of social reinforcement on isolate behavior of a nursery school child. *Child Develpm.,* 35:511-518.

4. Ayllon, T. (1963), Intensive treatment of psychotic behaviour by stimulus satiation and food reinforcement. *Behav. Res. Ther.,* 1:53-61.

5. Ayllon, T., & Michael, J. (1959), The psychiatric nurse as a behavioral engineer. *J. Exp. Anal. Behav.,* 2:323-334.

6. Azrin, N. H., & Lindsley, O.R. (1956), The reinforcement of cooperation between children. *J. Abnorm. Soc. Psychol.,* 52:100-102.

7. Bandura, A., & Walters, R. H. (1963), *Social Learning and Personality Development.* New York: Holt, Rinehart, & Winston.

8. Barbour, R. F., Borland, E. M., Boyd, M. M., Miller, A., & Oppe, T. E. (1963), Enuresis as a disorder of development. *Brit. Med. J.,* 2:787-790.

9. Bentler, P. M. (1962), An infant's phobia treated with reciprocal inhibition therapy. *J. Child Psychol. Psychiat.,* 3:185-189.

10. Bijou, S. W., & Baer, D. M. (1963), Some methodological contributions from a functional analysis of child development. In: *Advances in Child Development and Behavior,* ed. L. P. Lipsitt & C. S. Spiker. New York: Academic Press, Vol. I, pp. 197-231.

11. Bindra, D. (1959), *Motivation: A Systematic Reinterpretation.* New York: Ronald Press, pp. 210-257.

12. Boardman, W. K. (1962), Rusty: a brief behavior disorder. *J. Consult. Psychol.,* 26:293-297.

13. Brown, P. & Elliot, R. (1965), Control of aggression in a nursery school class. *J. Exp. Child Psychol.,* 2:103-107.

14. Burchard, J. & Tyler, V., Jr. (1965), The modification of delinquent behaviour through operant conditioning. *Behav. Res. Ther.,* 2:245-250.

15. Cherry, C. & Sayers, B. (1956), Experiments upon the total inhibition of stammering by external control, and some clinical results. *J. Psychosom. Res.,* 1:233-246.

16. Cooper, J. E. (1963), A study of behaviour therapy in thirty psychiatric patients. *Lancet,* 1:411-415.

17. Davison, G. C. (1964), A social learning therapy programme with an autistic child. *Behav. Res. Ther.,* 2:149-159.

18. ———(1965), The training of undergraduates as social reinforcers for autistic children. In: *Case Studies In Behavior Modification,* ed. L. P. Ullmann & L. Krasner. New York: Holt, Rinehart, & Winston, pp. 146-148.

19. DeLeon, G. & Mandell, W. (1966), A comparison of conditioning and psychotherapy in the treatment of functional enuresis. *J. Clin. Psychol.,* 22:326-330.

20. Duffy, E. (1957), The psychological significance of the concept of "arousal" or "activation." *Psychol. Rev.,* 64:265-275.

21. Eysenck, H. J. (1959), Learning theory and Behavior therapy. *J. Ment. Sci.,* 105:61-75.

22. ——— & Rachman, S. (1965), *The Causes and Cures of Neurosis: An Introduction to Modern Behavior Therapy Based on Learning Theory and the Principle of Conditioning.* San Diego: Knapp.

23. Feldman, R. & Werry, J. S. (1966), An unsuccessful attempt to treat a tiqueur by massed practice. *Behav. Res. Ther.,* 4:111-117.

24. Ferster, C. B. & DeMyer, M. K. (1962), A method for the experi-

mental analysis of the behavior of autistic children. *Amer. J. Orthopsychiat.*, 32:89-98.

25. Garvey, W. P. & Hegrenes, J. R. (1966), Desensitization techniques in the treatment of school phobia. *Amer. J. Orthopsychiat.*, 36:147-152.

26. Gelber, H. & Meyer, V. (1965), Behaviour therapy and encopresis: the complexities involved in treatment. *Behav. Res. Ther.*, 2:227-231.

27. Glover, E. (1959), Critical note on "Wolpe's Psychotherapy." *Brit. J. Med. Psychol.*, 32:68-74.

28. Goldfarb, W. (1965), Corrective socialization: a rationale for the treatment of schizophrenic children. *Canad. Psychiat. Assn. J.*, 10:481-493.

29. Hallsten, E. A., Jr. (1965), Adolescent anorexia nervosa treated by desensitization. *Behav. Res. Ther.*, 3:87-91.

30. Harris, F. R., Johnston, M. K., Kelley, C. S., & Wolf, M. M. (1964), Effects of positive social reinforcement on regressed crawling of a nursery school child. *J. Educ. Psychol.*, 55:35-41.

31. Hart, B. M., Allen, K. E., Buell, J. S., Harris, F. R., & Wolf, M. M. (1964), Effects of social reinforcement on operant crying. *J. Exp. Child Psychol.*, 1:145-153.

32. Hingtgen, J. N., Sanders, B. J., & DeMyer, M. (1965), Shaping cooperative responses in early childhood schizophrenics. In: *Case Studies in Behavior Modification,* ed. L. P. Ullmann & L. Krasner. New York: Holt, Rinehart, & Winston, pp. 130-138.

33. Holland, J. G. & Skinner, B. F. (1961), *The Analysis of Behavior: A Program for Self-instruction.* New York: McGraw-Hill.

34. Homme, L. E., DeBaca, P. C., Devine, J. V., Steinhorst, R., & Rickert, E. J. (1963), Use of the Premark principle in controlling the behavior of nursery school children. *J. Exp. Anal. Behav.*, 6:544.

35. Hunt, J. McV. (1965), Intrinsic motivation and its role in psychological development. In: *Nebraska Symposium on Motivation,* ed. D. Levine. Lincoln: University of Nebraska Press, pp. 189-282.

36. Jones, H. G. (1960a), Continuation of Yates' treatment of a tiqueur. In: *Behaviour Therapy and the Neuroses: Readings in Modern Methods of Treatment Derived from Learning Theory,* ed. H. J. Eysenck. Oxford: Pergamon, pp. 250-258.

37. ———(1960b), The behavioural treatment of enuresis nocturna. In: *Behaviour Therapy and the Neuroses: Readings in Modern Methods of Treatment Derived from Learning Theory,* ed. H. J. Eysenck. Oxford: Pergamon, pp. 377-403.

38. Jones, M. C. (1942a), The elimination of children's fears. *J. Exp. Psychol.*, 7:382-390.

39. ———(1924b), A laboratory study of fear: the case of Peter. *Pedagog. Sem.*, 31:303-315.

40. Keehn, J. D. (1965), Brief case-report: reinforcement therapy of incontinence. *Behav. Res. Ther.*, 2:239.

41. Kerr, N., Meyerson, L., & Michael, J. (1965), A procedure for shaping vocalizations in a mute child. In: *Case Studies in Behavior Modification,* ed. L. P. Ullmann & L. Krasner. New York: Holt, Rinehart, & Winston, pp. 366-370.

42. Koenig, K. P. & Masters, J. (1965), Experimental treatment of habitual smoking. *Behav. Res. Ther.*, 3:235-243.

43. Kushner, M. (1965), Desensitization of a post-traumatic phobia. In: *Case Studies in Behaviour Modification,* ed. L. P. Ullman & L. Krasner. New York: Holt, Rinehart & Winston, pp. 193-196.

44. Lang, P. J. & Lazovik, A. (1963), Experimental desensitization of a phobia. *J. Abnorm. Soc. Psychol.,* 66:519-525.

45. Lazarus, A. A. (1960), The elimination of children's phobias by deconditioning. In: *Behaviour Therapy and the Neuroses: Readings in Modern Methods of Treatment Derived from Learning Theory,* ed. H. J. Eysenck. Oxford: Pergamon, pp. 114-122.

46. ——& Abramovitz, A. (1962), The use of "emotive imagery" in the treatment of children's phobias. *J. Ment. Sci.,* 108:191-195.

47. ——Davison, G., & Polefka, D. (1965), Classical and operant factors in the treatment of a school phobia. *J. Abnorm. Pscyhol.,* 70:225-229.

48. Levin, G. R. & Simmons, J. J. (1962a), Response to praise by emotionally disturbed boys. *Psychol. Rep.,* 11:10.

49. —— ——(1962b), Response to food and praise by emotionally disturbed boys. *Psychol. Rep.,* 11:539-546.

50. Lovaas, O. I., Berberich, J. P., Perloff, B. F., & Schaeffer, B. (1966), Acquisition of imitative speech by schizophrenic children. *Science,* 151:705-707.

51. —— Freitag, G., Gold, V. J., & Kassorla, I. C. (1965a), Experimental studies in childhood schizophrenia: analysis of self-destructive behavior. *J. Exp. Child Psychol.,* 2:67-84.

52. ——Schaeffer, B. & Simmons, J. Q. (1965b), Building social behavior in autistic children by use of electric shock. *J. Exp. Res. Pers.,* 1:99-109.

53. Lovibond, S. H. (1963a), The mechanism of conditioning treatment of enuresis. *Behav. Res. Ther.,* 1:3-15.

54. ——(1963b), Intermittent reinforcement in behaviour therapy. *Behav. Res. Ther.,* 1:127-132.

55. Maclaren, J. (1960), The treatment of stammering by the Cherry-Sayers method: clinical impressions. In: *Behaviour Therapy and the Neuroses: Readings in Modern Methods of Treatment Derived from Learning Theory,* ed. H. J. Eysenck. Oxford: Pergamon, pp. 457-460.

56. Marks, I. M. & Gelder, M. G. (1965), A controlled retrospective study of behaviour therapy in phobic patients. *Brit. J. Psychiat.,* 111:561-573.

57. Marr, J. N., Miller, E. R., & Straub, R. R. (1966), Operant conditioning of attention with a psychotic girl. *Behav. Res. Ther.,* 4:85-87.

58. Metz, J. R. (1965), Conditioning generalized imitation in autistic children. *J. Exp. Child Psychol.,* 2:389-399.

59. Meyer, V. & Mair, J. M. M. (1963), A new technique to control stammering: a preliminary report. *Behav. Res. Ther.,* 1:251-254.

60. Miller, N. E. (1944), Experimental studies of conflict. In: *Personality and the Behavior Disorders,* ed. J. McV. Hunt. New York: Ronald Press, pp. 431-465.

61. Neale, D. H. (1963), Behaviour therapy and encopresis in children. *Behav. Res. Ther.,* 1:139-149.

62. Paul, G. L. (1966), *Insight versus Desensitization in Psychotherapy.* Stanford: Stanford University Press.

63. Patterson, G. R. (1965a), An application of conditioning tech-

niques to the control of a hyperactive child. In: *Case Studies in Behavior Modification,* ed. L. P. Ullmann & L. Krasner. New York: Holt, Rinehart, & Winston, pp. 370-375.

64. ————(1965b), A learning theory approach to the treatment of the school phobic child. In: *Case Studies in Behavior Modification,* ed. L. P. Ullmann & L. Krasner. New York: Holt, Rinehart, & Winston, pp. 279-285.

65. ————Jones, R., Whittier, J. & Wright, M. (1965), A behaviour modification technique for the hyperactive child. *Behav. Res. Ther.* 2:217-226.

66. Peterson, D. R. & London, P. (1965), A role for cognition in the behavioral treatment of a child's eliminative disturbance. In: *Case Studies In Behavior Modification,* ed. L. P. Ullman & L. Krasner. New York: Holt, Rinehart, & Winston, pp. 289-295.

67. Premack, D. (1959), Toward empirical behavior laws: I. Positive reinforcement. *Psychol. Rev.,* 66:219-233.

68. Quay, H. C., Werry, J. S., McQueen, M., & Sprague, R. L. (1966), Remediation of the conduct problem child in the special class setting. *Except. Child,* 32:509-515.

69. Rachman, S. (1965), Studies in desensitization. I: The separate effects of relaxation and desensitization. *Behav. Res. Ther.,* 3:245-251.

70. ————& Costello C. G. (1961), The aetiology and treatment of children's phobias: a review. *Amer. J. Psychiat.,* 118:97-105.

71. Rafi, A. A. (1962), Learning theory and treatment of tics. *J. Psychosom. Res.,* 6:71-76.

72. Raymond, M. J. (1956), Case of fetishism treated by aversion therapy. *Brit. Med. J.,* 2:854-857.

73. Rickard, H. C. & Dinoff, M. (1965), Shaping adaptive behavior in a therapeutic summer camp. In: *Case Studies in Behavior Modification,* ed. L. P. Ullmann & L. Krasner. New York: Holt, Rinehart, & Winston, pp. 325-328.

74. Schwitzgebel, R. & Kolb, D. A. (1964), Inducing behaviour change in adolescent delinquents. *Behav. Res. Ther.,* 1:297-304.

75. Skinner, B. F. (1938), *The Behavior of Organisms: An Experimental Analysis.* New York: Appleton-Century-Crofts.

76. Slack, C. W. (1960), Experimenter-subject psychotherapy: a new method of introducing intensive office treatment for unreachable cases. *Ment. Hyg.,* 44:238-256.

77. Straughan, J. H., Potter, W. K, Jr., & Hamilton, S. H., Jr. (1965), The behavioral treatment of an elective mute. *J. Child Psychol. Psychiat.,* 6:125-130.

78. Thorpe, J. G., Schmidt, E., Brown, P. T., & Castell, D. (1964), Aversion-relief therapy: a new method for general application, *Behav. Res. Ther.,* 2:71-82.

79. Ullmann, L. P. & Krasner, L., Eds. (1965), *Case Studies in Behavior Modification.* New York: Holt, Rinehart, & Winston, pp. 1-63.

80. Wahler, R. G., Winkel, G. H., Peterson, R. F., & Morrison, D. C. (1965), Mothers as behavior therapists for their own children. *Behav. Res. Ther.,* 3:113-124.

81. Walton, D. (1961), Experimental psychology and the treatment of a tiqueur. *J. Child Psychol. Psychiat.,* 2:148-155.

82. ————& Mather, M. D. (1963), The application of learning principles to the treatment of obsessive-compulsive states in the acute and chronic phases of illness. *Behav. Res. Ther.,* 1:163-174.

83. Watson, J. B. & Rayner, R. (1920), Conditioned emotional reactions. *J. Exp. Psychol,* 3:1-14.

84. Werry, J. S. (1966), The conditioning treatment of enuresis. *Amer. J. Psychiat.,* 123:226-229.

85. ——& Cohrssen, J. (1965), Enuresis: an etiology and therapeutic study. *J. Pediat.,* 67:423-431.

86. White, J. G. (1959), The use of learning theory in the psychological treatment of children. *J. Clin. Psychol.,* 15:226-229.

87. Williams, C. D. (1959), The elimination of tantrum behavior by extinction procedures. *J. Abnorm. Soc. Psychol.,* 59:269.

88. Wolf, M., Risley, T., & Mees, H. (1964), Application of operant conditioning procedures to the behaviour problems of an autistic child. *Behav. Res. Ther.,* 1:305-312.

89. ——Birnbrauer, J. S., Williams, T., & Lawler, J. (1965), A note on apparent extinction of the vomiting behavior of a retarded child. In: *Case Studies in Behavior Modification,* ed. L. P. Ullmann & L. Krasner. New York: Holt, Rinehart, & Winston, pp. 364-366.

90. Wolpe, J. (1958), *Psychotherapy by Reciprocal Inhibition.* Stanford: Stanford University Press.

91. —— & Lang, P. L. (1964), A fear survey schedule for use in behaviour therapy. *Behav. Res. Ther.,* 2:27-30.

92. Yamamoto, J. & Goin, M. K. (1965), On the treatment of the poor. *Amer. J. Psychiat.,* 122:267-271.

93. Yates, A. J. (1958), The application of learning theory to the treatment of tics. *J. Abnorm. Soc. Psychol.,* 56:175-182.

94. ——(1961), Abnormalities of psychomotor functions. In: *Handbook of Abnormal Psychology : An Experimental Approach,* ed. H. J. Eysenck. New York: Basic Books, pp. 52-53.

95. Young, G. C. & Turner, R. K. (1965), CNS stimulant drugs and conditioning treatment of nocturnal enuresis. *Behav. Res. Ther.,* 3:93-101.

96. Zimmerman, E. H. & Zimmerman, J. (1962), The alteration of behavior in a special classroom situation. *J. Exp. Anal. Behav.,* 5:59-60.

# 19. PARENT THERAPISTS: AN OPERANT CONDITIONING METHOD

## Mervyn K. Wagner, Ph.D.

Most efforts with operant conditioning procedures have been with hospitalized clients and have generally produced dramatic results. A few of the most prominent are the work of Lovaas and associates[1] with autistic children, Bijou[2] with retardates, Ayllon and Azrin[3] and Atthowe and Krasner[4] with psychiatric patients, and Burchard[5] with delinquents. The reinforcement principle, utilized within the context of an operant conditioning paradigm, can be applied to most types of behavior, particularly deficient behaviors, using as a model the basic approaches made practical by Skinner.

There have been some attempts using this approach[6-8] at training parents as "therapists," but only in a very formalized, experimenter-oriented setting. This paper outlines an approach that the author has found to be useful in an outpatient setting and that has considerable general application. The procedure can best be described through a clinical case study, but a great deal of clinical material will be omitted since the case itself is irrelevant.

The client here described was an 11-year-old girl who was referred by a pediatrician for severe school and home problems. The emphasis in this illustration is on a

Reprinted from *Mental Hygeine,* 1968, 52, 452-455, by permission of the publisher and the author. Dr. Wagner is Associate Professor and Director, University of South Carolina Psychological Service Center, Columbia, South Carolina.

reinforcement program for the child's home setting, though a teacher-directed plan was also initiated at her school to help with her short attention span, periodic hypomanic behavior, poor peer relations, and masturbation in the classroom.

The client had a WAIS I.Q. of 90 (school group test I.Q. of 101) and was in the sixth grade. She quite probably had had encephalitis when she was about three years old, though this had not been diagnosed medically. The child was of middle-class background and had two older brothers. At home she was dependent upon her over-protective and overcritical mother to the point where she frequently needed to be dressed in order not to be late for her school bus. She was aggressively dependent in many other ways and successfully manipulated her parents through considerable crying, whining, and demanding behavior. At the dinner table she ate voraciously, using her hands instead of the utensils, despite her mother's constant criticism. She spent a great deal of time in self-depreciating behavior, crying and telling her parents that she was "dumb" and "ugly" and that no one liked her. She would cry and have temper tantrums when she did not get something she wanted.

The decision to use an operant conditioning approach with this child was predicated on a number of factors: (1) The parents were motivated. (2) The etiology seemed to be more closely related to the interaction precipitated when she was ill for a long period of time and less involved with the adjustment of the parents *per se*. (3) Her two older brothers seemed reasonably well adjusted. (4) The parents did not have the financial means to become involved in long-term psychotherapy. (5) I thought it might work and wanted to try it.

Initially, I spent about one-and-a-half hours obtaining a history and told the parents that for our next interview I wanted them to observe the child, the home situation, and each other and bring me a list of any types of behavior that needed to be changed. I also wanted them to list things that could serve as rewards for the child. At the second session, two days later, more history material was gathered, particularly relative to the observations

compiled by the parents. These were discussed, and the
proposed reinforcement procedures were described to the
parents. At this session I also spent some time with the
child and gave her some brief psychologic tests.

At our third session, a few days thereafter, the outline
shown on page. 295 - 297 was given to the parents and discussed in detail with them.

The parents were interviewed once a week for the next
four weeks in order to iron out any difficulties they might
be having with the procedure. However, the greatest advantage of these interviews was to reinforce their efforts
at reinforcement. Actually, in this case they did not need
much in the way of reinforcement since the changes that
occurred in their daughter were sufficient. They were
seen for the last time about two months after the initial
interview. However, there was, and continues to be, very
frequent telephone contact.

Within four months, the girl had stopped eating with
her hands and had almost completely stopped the
whining, crying, and having temper tantrums. She had
also improved considerably in the other behaviors that
were part of the program and in some that were not. This
girl had by no means become an average, "normal," 11-
year-old; but, with only eight professional contacts, she
had begun to move steadily in that direction.

Considerable space could be devoted to discussing the
parent-child dynamics in this case, but focusing on them
directly was unnecessary. Even with respect to elements
of the parent-child relationship that are considered dynamic (e.g., the mother's unconscious hostility toward
her daughter), changes may occur in this type of program. Three factors, in the process of development, are
tending to decrease the mother's hostility: *(1)* The mother
is deriving pleasure from being able to serve as a positive
reinforcer, for a change. *(2)* The interpersonal relationship is becoming more of a reciprocal arrangement, i.e.,
the daughter does things to get rewards that are rewarding to the mother, and the mother rewards her. *(3)* The
mother is beginning to feel that she has some control
over her daughter's behavior.

The limitations of this method that have been most obvious are reinforcement consistency and parent motivation. The parents have tended to slack up on the plan when definite changes have been observed. For example, after the daughter had eaten an entire meal with her utensils, the parents expected her to continue doing so from then on and resumed the old method of criticizing when she slipped back to her previous ways of eating.

This approach to "therapy" is markedly less effective when the parents represent a continuing source of psychologic irritation to the child; but, when the motivation is there, the changes can be effected. If we are to use our manpower in the mental health field with maximum effectiveness, it is necessary for us to put the therapy where the problem is—in the home.

# REINFORCEMENT PROCEDURES FOR PARENTS

## General Instructions

1. The most important principle for your daughter to learn is that positive behavior makes a difference, and that what happens to her in the way of rewards is dependent upon a certain kind of behavior.

2. Reinforcement or reward must follow regularly and consistently behavior tending in a certain direction or of a certain kind. These reinforcements should be given as soon as possible after the behavior has occurred and should be as consistent as possible.

3. Your daughter must learn that negative behavior achieves nothing (not even punishment, in most cases).

4. We can have her achieve the behavior we want only by short steps in the right direction. It is important that these short steps be rewarded.

Parents must work together at noticing what the other is doing. Reinforce each other when a good reinforcement of daughter's behavior is seen. Ask each other how to reinforce a particular behavior (if stuck, write it down and we'll go over it). Father: Note particularly mother's criticism. Comment positively when she could have been critical and wasn't. Mother: Note particularly when father is giving in to whining. Make a friendly comment or praise when he doesn't. Both: Reinforce each other's efforts to let her do things on her own. Talk to brothers about what to do and the need for their active co-operation. (Remember, reinforce behavior as it moves in the direction you want. Don't wait until it becomes what you want.)

| What we want to occur | Reinforcement | What we want to stop | Non-reinforcement or punishment |
|---|---|---|---|
| More independent, self-sufficient behavior | Reinforce with praise and rewards the behavior you desire. Look for evidence or signs of behavior you want. Don't just see that it's not there and criticize. Look for when the behavior changes in the direction of the behavior you wish. Reward small changes in the positive direction. (Don't expect changes too fast.) Let her do things on her own. If she makes some progress, reinforce with praise. | Whining, crying, demanding | Ignore most of what we want to stop. Never, never give in to whining or excessively demanding behavior. When she wants something reasonable, however, be quick to give it to her before she cries. Punish only severe breaches of discipline (not after you lose your temper). I prefer depriving her of positive things, such as television, or sending her to her room; but spanking may sometimes be necessary. Do not threaten. If you say that a particular thing will happen if she does such and such, mean it and do it (or don't say it). |
| Improved eating behavior | Praise her when she uses her utensils. For now, at least, ignore her when she doesn't. Reinforce when she eats slowly. Make comments such as, "It pleases me to see you eat more slowly." Help her in eating slowly by interrupting her speed with questions and comments, and try to make mealtime as pleasant as possible. (I think that the probable reason for her eating so rapidly is that the criticism she has experienced at mealtimes has made her want to get it over with.) | Poor table manners | Mostly just ignore poor manners; but it may be necessary, if the poor manners occur so frequently that you can't reinforce good manners, to comment occasionally to her about "eating more slowly," etc. |

296

| Goal | Behavior | Procedure | Comments |
| --- | --- | --- | --- |
| Increased self-esteem | "Nobody wants me." | When she is crying about how dumb she is, don't argue with her; ignore it. Reinforce her self-esteem by commenting positively when she does things more positive. Tell her she is capable, etc., often, but not when she is moaning about how she's not. | This is pretty much handled by reinforcement procedure. Just ignore this kind of behavior. |
| Ability to accept criticism and not have her way all the time | Crying when criticized; getting angry or crying when she doesn't get her way | Don't say "don't"; say "do" whenever possible; then praise her when she does. Do your best to give her what she wants when she is reasonable in both her request and her manner.<br><br>Notice general positive improvement in her behavior. For example, if she has gone all day without whining, tell her that because of this you'll take her bowling Saturday. | You are not going to be criticizing nearly as much. Don't give in when she cries, but make a real effort to give in when she asks without crying. |

297

# REFERENCES

1. Lovaas, O. I., Freitag, G., Gold, V. J., and Kassorla, I. C. *Journal of Experimental Child Psychology,* 2:67, 1965.

2. Bijou, S. W. *Psychological Record,* 13:95, 1963.

3. Ayllon, T., and Azrin, N. H. *Journal of Experimental Analysis of Behavior,* 8:357, 1965

4. Atthowe, J., Jr., and Krasner, L. *Journal of Abnormal Psychology,* 73:37, 1968

5. Burchard, J. D. *Psychological Record,* 17:461, 1967.

6. Bijou, S. W. Experimental Studies of Child Behavior, Normal and Deviant. In: Krasner, L., and Ullmann, L. P. (Eds.) *Research in Behavior Modification.* New York, Holt, Rinehart and Winston, 1965, pp. 56—81.

7. Patterson, G. R., McNeal, S., Hawkins, N., and Phelps, R. Programming the Social Environment. Paper presented before the Western Psycological Association, Long Beach, Calif., 1966.

8. Wahler, R. G., Winkel, G. H., Peterson, R. F., and Morrison, B. C.: *Behavior Research and Therapy,* 3:113, 1965.

# Pharmacotherapy

# 20. THE USE OF PSYCHOACTIVE DRUGS IN THE OUTPATIENT TREATMENT OF PSYCHIATRIC DISORDERS OF CHILDREN

Irvin A. Kraft, M.D.

The use of psychopharmacological agents in the treatment of children and adolescents differs in some ways from their use with adults. This paper describes a framework in which to view these differences and the over-all patterns of drug treatment of nonadults. Pharmacological and psychological aspects have been well described by Fish[1] and others,[2] but one aspect has not been emphasized—the setting of drug therapy with children.

By legal definition and by the practicalities of administration, outpatient psychopharmacotherapy for nonadults involves three or more persons. The triad comprises the child, a parent, and the physician. Often in a nuclear family situation more than one parent becomes involved, for the other parent and siblings also are affected by drug administration.

## The Human Context

The utilization of a psychoactive agent by the physician places the act deeply into a biosocial matrix. Psycho-

Reprinted from *The American Journal of Psychiatry*, 1968, **124**, 1401-1407, by permission of the publisher and the author. Copyright 1968, the American Psychiatric Association. Dr. Kraft is Associate Professor of Pediatrics and Psychiatry, Baylor College of Medicine, Houston, Texas and Medical Director of the Texas Institute of Child Psychiatry, Texas Children's Hospital, Houston.

pharmacotherapy, perhaps more intimately than other forms of drug treatment, occurs in a group-dominated setting: i.e., group dynamic transactions intervene to influence drug effects. This does not gainsay intrinsic pharmacological activity, but it does suggest that a drug's effect in children becomes difficult to determine in and of itself.

The human context of psychopharmacotherapy is interdigitated with complex biological, social, chemical, and psychological factors. The interactional patterns, while probably typical of the fabric of medical care, have some unique characteristics of their own.

The family in our culture has been reduced to the nuclear family as the operating unit. As such, it has lost many of its original functions but retains a sexual (reproductive) and a psychological one. The latter consists of providing its offspring with a productive emotional climate for growth and development.

The treatment of the sick has been delegated to the institutions of the doctor and the hospital[4]. Thus in our society various agencies, such as the schools, tell the parents that their child is disturbed. The family physician or psychiatrist then is asked to determine whether the degree of deviancy from the norm is pathological, and, if so, what care-taking process to follow. Once so diagnosed, the family unit is confronted with a failure in one of its major functions. This often means a reassessment by parents and even siblings, as well as the patient, at some level of awareness of their performance and roles.[5,6] It is within this context that drug therapy usually takes place. It occurs as part of the doctor-patient relationship and the roles implicit for physician, patient, and family.

This treatment modality, in whatever manner used, occupies a part of the doctor-patient role relationship. Legally, it involves a minimum of three persons and their roles. It partakes of the flavor and functions the therapist sees as his role vis-a-vis the family. In such circumstances, the essential pharmacological actions of the compound undergo modifications of diminution or potentiation amid the complexities of the various forces then at work.

## Treatment Choices

The psychiatrist follows one or more of three patterns, depending on his therapeutic orientation to the restoration of family homeostasis: 1) directed drug therapy; 2) drug therapy as primary and counseling as secondary; 3) psychotherapy as primary and medication as secondary.

Before these are described in detail, it will be helpful to outline the procedures and information basic to making the decision which path to follow. A fundamental and crucial factor is the attitude of the psychiatrist. If he considers drug therapy to be a lower order procedure, the child's mother or, in the case of an adolescent, the patient himself, will sense it. Unbounded enthusiasm is not a basic requirement, but a thoroughly passive approach helps little.

A thorough anamnesis serves as the basis for deciding which path to follow. This historical review should include the gestation and neonatal period and the developmental sequences of the child. In effect, a life chart emerges with reference to dates, incidents, the patient's reactions to them, and the circumstances surrounding the events. School records, usually available, give a sequential picture of the child's group testing of intelligence and his educational progress via the annual standardized achievement tests. Specialized psychological testing, including the Bender-Gestalt and other perceptual tests, often helps significantly in evaluating minimal brain dysfunction. Projective testing may be included, especially in late latency and older children. Depending on the therapist's viewpoint, an electroencephalogram might aid in reaching a diagnosis.

Especially with younger children, the psychiatrist's estimate of the effects of drug administration is strongly influenced by parental reports. Unless he is conducting a specific study in which school reports and other collateral data are collected at selected frequent intervals, the practicing psychiatrist relies heavily on what the mother relates. In the third pattern of secondary drug therapy perhaps the child's appearance and behavior as well as his productions afford information on drug-induced changes. Yet if reliance is placed on parental reports of home observations and of school performance, the mother's personality traits can well influence the selection of facts and impressions given to the psychiatrist. Her dynamics color the reports in obvious ways that must be considered by the clinician in his impression of the drug's effects, but her covert omissions and shadings also alter her observations. For example, if she is compliant and wishes to please the authority figure, she senses and gives the answers the therapist desires. Or, if oppositional, she adjudicates and tempers responses to suggest a picture of drug failure.

What criteria hold for choice of treatment? What are the results of the work with drugs to date? Here the philosophy of the psychiatrist enters, for his own perception of himself as a person, as a physician, as a scientist, as a clinician, and as a therapist often determines his path. Levitt[3] suggests that ". . . available evaluation studies do not furnish a reasonable basis for the hypothesis that psychotherapy facilitates recovery from mental illness in children." Similarly, no clear-cut evidence supports such a hypothesis regarding psychopharmacotherapy for children. Thus the therapist, as with any instrument of therapy, decides how drug treatment fits his own conceptualization of the doctor-patient relationship. In that context, considering many accessory factors such as available time, energy, and finances, the therapist decides how to utilize pharmacologic agents in his therapeutic responsibilities to the patient and family.

The psychiatrist can with equanimity utilize psychotropic agents with most difficulties of childhood, but usage depends on how he does it, in what context, and with what goal. Certainly he sees psychopharmacotherapy not as a panacea but as an additional instrument of the physician's own individualized approach to the doctor-patient relationship. We assume in medical care that the physician uses all modalities that help him aid the human organism in its process of recovery. Since in most of medicine treatment is not a guarantee against recurrence, except in organ removal, the utilization of psychotropic agents fits in with that premise. The major goal of such a spectrum of usage is straightforward: the relief of suffering.

## Directive Drug Therapy

To return to the three patterns of drug administration, the first, directive drug therapy, is based upon the psychiatrist's authority implicit in the doctor-patient relationship. The psychiatrist adds the medication with its real and magical properties to his own potent capacity as a caretaker. He accepts the role delegated to him by the family, and he authoritatively asserts that the drug will help the patient and the situation. This implicit omnipotence pervades other directions and remedies he proposes for altering the conditions diagnosed as a form of illness or deviancy from health. Two illustrations of this technique might be helpful.

> *Case 1.* George, a bright-eyed six-year-old first grader, had done well in school until the second semester, when his mother underwent abdominal surgery. His grades dropped shortly thereafter, he fidgeted constantly, sleep patterns changed for the worse, and he began to exhibit a winking tic.
> The principal suggested to his parents that they consult their pediatrician, who then referred George to a child psychiatrist. After a diagnostic evaluation, the psychiatrist prescribed chlorpromazine for a three-week period. He firmly stated to the parents that the problem was a temporary aberration which would respond to the drug and the mother's full resumption of her family duties.
> George soon slept better and quieted down in school. At the brief follow-up visit three weeks later, George no longer showed symptoms and his schoolwork had returned to its former levels. A telephone check a year later revealed continued satisfactory progress and no return of disturbance.

This therapeutic intervention coupled the drug's calmative qualities with the psychiatrist's powerful assurance that the child would reassume his healthy developmental patterns.

> *Case 2.* Mary, a 13-year-old high-achieving adolescent, had refused to attend school for several months. Her mother and stepfather permitted this and arranged for a tutor. Mary was still restless, however, and she complained of headaches and vague abdominal pains. Her physician

recommended psychiatric consultation, in which it was found that Mary had been trapped in the interpersonal marital cross-fire of her parents. Her mother, quite deeply concerned about her own maternalism to Mary and the sons by her second husband, channeled much of this anxiety and stress through Mary.

Mary was told that she must return to school the next day and that the medication would ease her symptoms until other matters were corrected. She took chlordiazepoxide for three weeks, with a complete remission of her school refusal and somatizations.

The "I'll take over now" attitude of the therapist, reinforced by the chemical agent, relieved Mary of her responsibility, reduced her need to be rageful, and allowed her to resume her age-adequate, peer-directed behavior. During the ensuing year of discord and severe acting-out by her parents, Mary persisted in regular school attendance and accomplishment without recurrence of symptoms.

## Drug Therapy with Counseling

In the second mode of drug usage the psychiatrist continues to be directive, but he utilizes supportive psychotherapy as well. The clinician maintains the medication in varying dosages, changing it often if necessary. He functions steadily and constantly in his chosen framework of the authority figure who has assumed continuing, significant responsibility for the patient. He anticipates family upsets and events which will alter the patient's equilibrium, and he manages them by a readjustment of drug dosage as well as suggestions for different living maneuvers.

Case 3. Tracy, a nine-and-one-half-year-old peculiar fourth grade student, had been under medical surveillance since the age of 18 months, when a neurologist suspected a disorder of lipoid metabolism. At age eight a competent clinical psychologist suggested childhood schizophrenia. Tracy vomited at school routinely and acted in a bizarre manner with his peers, yet he stayed marginally at grade level in a regular class. His father had committed suicide by hanging when Tracy was five days old.

The psychiatrist placed Tracy on a phenothiazine compound and saw him briefly twice a week for three months.

The vomiting stopped within a week, and the unusual behavior diminished at home and in the neighborhood. He
made the Little League team and played regularly. He
handled without regression the sudden death of his very
close grandfather. Special education was recommended.

This second mode of drug usage also finds application
with adolescents. The psychiatrist or general physician
manipulates drug dosage and timing to control anticipated upsets and to manage the aftereffects of those
events that occur unexpectedly.

Case 4.    Judy, a tense, preoccupied 15-year-old, had undergone treatment a year previously with good results. She
was now uneasily anticipating her first formal dance.
Judy called her psychiatrist, asking for reassurance and a
brief renewal of the medication she had taken before. She
took the amitriptyline a day or so before the dance, which
proved highly successful for her, and then, after reporting
her good time to the therapist, she stopped the medication.
Subsequent social adventures transpired without her re-
course to medication.

## Psychotherapy with Medication

In the third modality, with psychotherapy primary
and medication secondary, the psychiatrist emphasizes
the psychodynamic factors and interpersonal relationships as they emerge in weekly or more frequent therapeutic meetings. At times a medication can be inter-
polated into the treatment pattern to help control depres-
sive episodes, rage reactions, or other special vicissi-
tudes. The compound to be used should manifest specifici-
ty, but it mainly augments a special phase of the doctor-
patient relationship that has been carefully nurtured and
constructed in psychotherapy.

Case 5.    Madeline, a 16-year-old girl of very superior intelligence, feared she would fall heir to the cancer from which
her father had died. After seeing a movie on venereal disease, she insisted on several blood tests, expecially after
dates during which intensive petting occurred. At times
her transferential feelings toward her male therapist became
threatening, and she would be given small amounts of
chlordiazepoxide. The calmative effect aided her, and she
could then continue her therapeutic work. Because she
could become very upset on certain kinds of dates and at
special events, medication was started several days ahead

and seemed to lessen the stress and strain of these incidents.

As with any utilization of the adolescent's environment, the medication functions within the framework of the doctor-patient relationship. It augments and extends the dependency phase in a way that produces immediate, positive consequences for the patient. Whatever works well finds acceptance in the youth, augmenting the dynamic therapeutic relationship.

The foregoing assumes that the symptomatology of the child or adolescent often represents the emotional radar of the nuclear family. Thus diagnostic and treatment interventions offer the family an opportunity to examine and to reconstitute itself. Obviously, rearrangement of such facets of the multiple roles and power relationships within the family takes time. Psychopharmacotherapy for the putative patient often affords temporary balm to him and his family.

> *Case 6.*   Roger, an 11-year-old boy of average intelligence and potential, had been pushed by his parents to bring home high grades, to star in Little League, and to play with the most socially acceptable boys his parents could maneuver for him. This pressure, more consistent with the needs of his parents than with Roger's requirements for growth, culminated in bedwetting, nightmares, and a sullen defiance.
>
> The psychiatrist pointed out the interparental dynamics, a disclosure quite unexpected and discomforting to them, and prescribed nortriptyline for Roger's enuresis and other behavior. After a month's time, during which his parents consulted further with the psychiatrist about their own patterns, Roger no longer bedwet, and his presenting picture disappeared.

In this case the medication augmented the role of the psychiatrist as a pathfinder for the parents and a rescuer for Roger. It gave them all an opportunity to examine an intolerable situation with intermediate help available to the family's emotional transmitter.

At times a family finds itself off balance when a gradual trend culminates in a near-crisis. This not infrequently occurs with a child, usually a boy, who had done poorly in school for several years and whose activity level begins to present socialization and acceptance problems outside the home. After the diagnostic process is over, there often remains a time gap before remedial educational and psychotherapeutic measures can be started. Drug therapy spans this interval by slowing down the child and by offering the family an opportunity to establish a new rhythm of intrafamilial relationships.

> *Case 7.* Jim was an alert, quickly moving third grader. When he was not charming the teacher with his warm smile, he exasperated her with his inability to read well and to do his schoolwork. His parents underwent nightly trauma over homework. Jim's inability to sit still, even before a television set, no longer seemed cute and only mildly annoying. The whole matter assumed serious proportions in the face of impending school failure. The family was referred to a child psychiatrist, and a diagnostic evaluation pieced the puzzle together as minimal brain dysfunction. Treatment began with dextroamphetamine sulfate. This quieted Jim down, and the family used this time to regroup and to reconstitute its views of Jim and of themselves.

Sometimes a child's problems fail to yield to routine diagnostic procedures, and a trial of pharmacotherapy brings to a focus the key factors.

> *Case 8.* Ellen, the pretty five-year-old daughter of an auto mechanic, was brought in for consultation after five months of unremitting nightmares and stereotyped daily mumblings about Philip, her dead brother. Ellen, the last of six siblings and 12 years younger than her next sibling Philip, had seen him struck by an errant car as he tried to fix their auto, which was parked off the road. Ellen suffered facial injuries in the accident. In the midst of the turmoil, as her mother sought help nearby, Ellen was seized by a stranger who took her away. When the ambulance arrived, Ellen's mother rescued her from the stranger and took her to the hospital with her brother, who died on the way. Philip's death abruptly halted his pending appointment to a service academy and terminated his mother's use of him as a substitute father for Ellen.
> As Ellen's dreams of the death scene repeated themselves nightly, she also talked incessantly of her brother to whoever would listen. When placed on chlorpromazine, she began to sleep without dreams and to cease her daytime talking about Philip. As soon as she was better, her father underwent psychiatric hospitalization and her mother's bitterness and rage increased. Neither parent, despite 26 years of marriage, could face the intensity of their hostile feelings. Keeping Philip alive by Ellen's symptoms served them both. As Ellen improved, they worsened and had to be seen for therapy.

Under some circumstances there may be no community resource available for treatment of a child. Pharmacotherapy, initiated by a psychiatrist and carried through by the family physician, may be the only therapy possible. When used directively, this method can be helpful to lower anxiety levels.

> *Case 9.*  Cathy had been reluctant to attend school for the first three semesters, and she then refused to go to school at all. Her father, a truck driver, was hostile to psychiatric intervention and refused to cooperate in the consultation. Nevertheless, Cathy was seen and diagnosed as having minimal brain dysfunction with auditory integration defi-. cits. She was placed on medication. Her mother, under mandatory directions, was able to return her to school and work out with the principal some remedial tutoring arrangements. As her mother refocused on the cerebral dysfunction rather than on Cathy's needs for overprotection, the child continued to attend school regularly. Thus pharmacotherapy and remedial education altered a severe school phobia situation.

Certain kinds of behavioral abnormalities are termed target signs and symptoms. They comprise the ones with a definable individuality. They may, however, fit into different diagnostic categories: enuresis, for example, can be a neurotic trait at one age and a minor adjustment phenomenon at another. Encopresis, school refusal, facial tics, cough tics, and sometimes hyperkinesis can be target symptoms. The behavioral patterns that might be termed socialized, such as stealing and fire setting, do not readily lend themselves to this grouping.

Target symptoms can and do respond to drug therapy, but once again the total therapeutic situation and doctor-patient relationship must be considered. Enuresis, for example, responds differently to placebo and active substance when administered in a child psychiatry clinic by a child psychiatrist than when placebo and drug are given in a pediatrician's office by him or his nurse. Hyperactivity has been shown to respond to dextro-amphetamine and to chlorpromazine.[7]

Thus childhood psychopharmacotherapy operates in a context of role theory, the doctor-patient relationship, and in three major patterns of usage. When applicable, it also serves several different goals. Some additional fac-

tors in the practical aspects of outpatient psychopharmacotherapy will be described below.

## Dosage and Administration

Dosage traditionally is stated in terms of body weight,
but, practically, it is simpler to use the medication without reference to body weight. For example, a three-year-
old average-size child can readily tolerate 30 to 50 mg. of
chlorpromazine before sleep. The psychiatrist can use
alert clinical judgment to titrate and to rearrange dosages when indicated, rather than being restricted by arbitrary criteria.

Another factor affecting dosage is the attitude and manner of the physician. In one circumstance the psychiatrist used his currently favorite compound in his custom-
arily forceful and enthusiastic manner, and the patients,
as he evaluated them, improved considerably. The same
active agent in the hands of a nihilistically inclined,
quiet, nonforceful psychiatrist failed to achieve similar
results.

The time of day in which the patient takes the medication affects results, for the traditional three-times-a-day
and twice-a-day arrangements fail to take into account
the child's life pattern. We have found that a major intake of chlorpromazine, chlordiazepoxide, or amitriptyline one-half to one hour before expected sleep time produces calmative effects far into the next day. A smaller
morning dose seems to sustain the drug effect satisfactorily. Unless the child accelerates late in the day to
become difficult in the "witching hours" of four to seven
p.m., no additional doses are needed until bedtime. Con-
trarily, the energizers, such as dextroamphetamine, tend
to affect sleep patterns adversely and are better given in
the morning and perhaps later afternoon upon return
from school.

It often works more effectively not to have medication
given during school hours, especially for the younger
children. The after-school, mid-afternoon administration
avoids possible difficulties for the child taking a drug

during classes. Similarly, in the summer vacation time, a camping experience might present obstacles to the continued intake of a psychotropic agent.

Especially in the directive use of drugs, the popular and current notions about the active agent may influence the parental attitudes and their subsequent reporting. Articles in the lay press about addiction or dangers with a given compound add to this. Parents should be told honestly about the drug and their cooperation solicited. The hypochondriacal, fearful mother can instill corresponding fears and concerns in the child. Sometimes a covertly hostile, angry mother hopes to prove her point to her husband that the child is bad by the way she slants her observations and reports on the child's responses to the drug. Or, a not uncommon comment is, "That same pill didn't help my husband, so how can it help my little girl?"

Keeping track of the patient, once he has been placed on a drug in either of the first two treatment paths, becomes a practical problem. In our experience most mothers find biweekly reporting by telephone to an office assistant quite satisfactory. They know a written report of the conversation will be read by the psychiatrist and changes suggested, if needed. Periodic brief visits aid in observing drug effects and in maintaining the directive aspect of the doctor-patient relationship.

Side effects tend to be minimal in children; they are often an exaggeration of the agent's intended effect, such as drowsiness. Photosensitivity to chlorpromazine occurs, and anorexia sometimes accompanies dextroamphetamine usage. Large doses of phenothiazines can produce parkinson-like signs. By and large, the standard drugs do not show significant side effects that contraindicate their usage when judiciously applied and followed. Addiction to them in children also seems to be rare.

## REFERENCES

1. Fish, B. Drug Therapy in Child Psychiatry: Pharmacological Aspects, *Compr. Psychiat.* 1:212-227, 1960.

2. Grant, Q. Psychopharmacology in Childhood Emotional and Mental Disorders, *J. Pediat.* 27:1-9, 1963.

3. Levitt, E. E. Psychotherapy with Children: A Further Evaluation, *Behav. Res. Ther.* 1:45-51, 1963.

4. Parsons, T., and Fox, R. C. Illness, Therapy and the Modern Urban American Family, *J. Soc. Issues* 13 (4):31-44, 1952.

5. Spiegel, J. P. "The Resolution of Role Conflict Within the Family," in Greenblatt, M., Levinson, D. J., and Wilhaus, R. H., eds. *The Patient and the Mental Hospital.* New York: The Free Press of Glencoe, 1957, pp. 545-564.

6. Vogel, E. F, and Bell, N. W.: "The Emotionaally Disturbed Child as the Family Scapegoat," in Bell, N. W., and Vogel, E. F. *A Modern Introduction to the Family.* New York: The Free Press of Glencoe, 1960, pp. 382-397.

7. Weiss, G., Werry, J., and Minde, K. Studies on the Hyperactive Child: The Effects of Dextroamphetamine and Chlorpromazine on Behavior and Intellectual Functioning, read at the 123rd annual meeting of the American Psychiatric Association, Detroit, Mich., May 8-12, 1967.

# 21. DRUG USE IN PSYCHIATRIC DISORDERS OF CHILDREN

## Barbara Fish, M. D.

Drugs serve as important a function in the treatment of distrubed children as they do in the treatment of adults. If appropraite drugs are chosen they can control symptoms that do not respond readily to other measures. Drugs do not interfere with leaning if the dose is regulated properly. They need not disrupt the psychotherapeutic relationship if the psychological meaning of the medication to the child and his parents is treated with skill and understanding. Used properly, drugs can actually facilitate the educational and psychotherapeutic aspects of treatment.[7]

## GENERAL INDICATIONS FOR DRUG THERAPY

With children, as with adults, one prescribes psychotropic drugs for susceptible target symptoms. The classical diagnostic categories are even less useful as a guide to treatment than they are in adults, since so many children's disorders present undifferentiated and variable pictures. Drugs are most effective in reducing psychomotor excitement. Optimally, the reduction of impulsiv-

Reprinted from *The American Journal of Psychiatry,* 1968, **124** (Feb. Supp.), 31-36, by permission of the publisher and the author. Copyright 1968, the American Psychiatric Association. Dr. Fish is Psychiatrist-in-charge of Children's and Adolescent Services, Bellevue Hospital, Psychiatric Division and Associate Professor of Psychiatry, New York University School of Medicine, New York.

ity and irritability is accompanied by lessened anxiety, improved attention span, and more organized behavior.

To a lesser extent drugs can increase spontaneous activity and affective responsiveness in states of apathy and inertia. The latter symptoms occur much less frequently before puberty than after. The younger the child, the more is psychiatric disturbance of any type expressed in hyperexcitability, hyperactivity, and disorganized behavior which can respond to medication.

In many psychotic children drugs may also reduce psychotic thought disorder and improve contact with reality.[8,10] Drugs can modify a child's responsiveness to his experiences, but chemicals alone cannot undo learned behavior, character patterns, or neurotic attitudes. For instance, aggressive behavior responds to drugs only if it is associated with affective or motor outbursts. Less explosive negativistic children often experience little subjective discomfort and may resent the physiological changes produced by drugs, feeling that these are a threat to their autonomy.

Whether drugs can improve learning and intellectual functioning and, if so, in which types of children is still to be determined.[9,13] Children with severe mental retardation and fragmentation of functioning associated with organic brain disease or schizophrenia are the most likely to retain residual defects. However, in the absence of effective drug treatment they respond mimimally to educational and milieu therapies and psychotherapies.

## TIMING THE INITIATION OF DRUG THERAPY

A trial of drug therapy is indicated for appropriate target symptoms if psychotherapeutic and environmental measures do not quickly relieve the child's subjective distress and restore optimal functioning. This judgment differs from adult therapy to the extent that children are more dependent upon the adults who care for them and more responsive to environmental changes. The psychiatrist must observe the interaction of the child and his symptoms with his family before introducing drugs.

Since children's symptoms usually change more rapidly than those of adults, one can often evaluate a child's response to outpatient or residential treatment within two to four weeks.

If his symptoms disappear completely when the child is in his usual environment and he is able to resume normal social and academic activities with the use of social manipulation and psychotherapy alone, then obviously the addition of drug treatment is not warranted. However, if symptoms or a restriction in function persist after four weeks, one should not withhold drugs which might accelerate recovery just because the child is responding slowly to other measures. Months, or even weeks, of exclusion from normal experiences at critical periods in a child's life may leave irreversible deficits.[9]

A school phobia is an outstanding example of a situation which should be treated as a medical emergency. A prompt return to school can prevent chronic disability and drugs should be added quickly to the total treatment program is they are needed to accomplish this. Even when the damage from delayed recovery is less obvious, one must weigh the slight chance of harm from drugs against the limitation in the child's function and the strain imposed on his family if drugs are withheld. If an acute crisis demands immediate medication, drugs should be withheld later on to evaluate the child's own capacity for reintegration and to determine whether medication must be continued.

## SELECTION OF SPECIFIC DRUGS

In general, as with adults, more potent drugs are required for more severe disorders, but the standard diagnostic categories provide only a gross guide to severity. In children, severity within a diagnostic group increases with greater intellectual, perceptual, and neurological impairment and with greater affective and motoric disturbance.[8,9]

It is necessary to define subgroups of the classical diagnostic categories which have comparable responses to treatment. We have developed a descriptive typology for this purpose which classifies the spectrum of children's psychiatric disorders on the basis of typical behavior on psychiatric examination. This typology has proved to be significantly related to the responses of children to both psychologic and pharmacologic therapies.[10] In schizophrenic children under five years, we found that the response to drug treatment or to placebo was related to the degree of language impairment.[11,12]

Hyperactive and hypoactive children may react differently to drugs. There are also individual differences in relative sensitivity to the sedative and stimulating properties of different drugs. These must be determined by exploring the dose-response curve for each child.

The clinician should become familiar with a few representative minor and major tranquilizers and stimulants which span the spectrum of potency and differential effects. Additional drugs may be used if sensitivity to previous drugs makes substitution necessary.

The following discussion of the most useful drugs in the treatment of children's psychiatric disorders will be limited to instances in which children's behavioral and central nervous system responses differ from those of adults (children's toxic and allergic systematic reactions are the same as those of adults).

## Minor Stimulants

Amphetamines relieve anxiety and stimulate overly inhibited neurotic children, especially those with constricted speech and affect, with learning difficulties, with school phobias, or with disturbing sexual preoccupation.[1,8]

Bradley reported that in addition to these effects, doses of up to 40 mg. per day also "quieted" many hyperactive children. Most of these had "behavior disorders of psychogenic origin," but a number had convulsive disorders. Children with "structural neurologic" disorders did not improve.[2,3] Others have also found that amphetamines are more effective for children, hyperactive or otherwise, when their disorders are in the neurotic range of severity. Amphetamines are less effective and may even increase the symptoms of children with schizophrenia or chronic brain syndromes.[1-3,8,14] These authors limited the diagnosis to chronic brain syndrome to relatively severe disorders.

A confused and contradictory literature on the effectiveness of minor stimulants in children has arisen, because hyperactive children with a wide variety of diagnoses and degrees of severity are often considered as if they were a uniform group. Hyperactivity is a common symptom in children. Whether it responds to minor stimulants or tranquilizers or whether it requires potent neuroleptics depends on the severity of the underlying disorder.[8-10] The unproven assumption that all hyperactive children have "minimal brain damage" only adds to the confusion, since the use of this term varies enormously from one center to another.

We still need a well-controlled study comparing the effectiveness of amphetamines with mild and major tranquillizers in hyperactive children, a study in which the severity and type of the children's initial disorders and the criteria for chronic brain syndromes are spelled out in terms that everyone can recognize. Precise measures are needed to distinguish the "quieting" and decreased restlessness that accompanies increased interest and persistence in academic tasks[2,3] from a true decrease in the force and speed of motor activity and excitement if we are to learn which children can be helped by minor stimulants.

In the author's experience, children complain of subjective discomfort and frequently show anorexia and weight loss in doses over 15 mg. per day. Bradley also reported a fairly high incidence of increased tension and irritability, anorexia, and insomnia in his patients.[2] In Eisenberg's controlled study, a significant improvement in seven adolescent delinquent boys given dextroamphetamine occurred when they received 30 or 40 mg. per day, but during this period their average weight loss was 4 to 6 lbs.[6]

## Minor Tranquilizers

These drugs have a somewhat wider application in

children than in adults, since mild drugs are frequently effective even for children with moderately severe organic or schizophrenic reactions. These drugs are primarily useful in mild to moderately severe neurotic and "primary" behavior disorders, comparable to their use in adults. Unlike adults and adolescents, prepuberty children do not tend to become addicted to medication.

*Diphenhydramine* (Benadryl) has been used for over 15 years to treat disturbed children.[1,8,14] It is most effective in disorders associated with hyperactivity, but also reduces anxiety in very young children who are not hyperactive. It may even be helpful in moderately severe organic or schizophrenic disorders, although it is not potent enough for the most severely disturbed of these children.[8,10] Unlike the other drugs, diphenhydramine decreases in effectiveness at puberty. Young children tolerate doses two to four times higher by body weight than do adults, and the drug reduces symptoms before producing drowsiness or lethargy. After 10 to 11 years of age, children respond like adults: the drug frequently produces malaise or drowsiness and is most helpful as a bedtime sedative.[8]

*Meprobamate* (Equanil, Miltown) appears to be less effective for hyperactivity than diphenhydramine in the same subjects, but unlike diphehydramine it continues to be effective in neurotic children into adolescence.[8]

*Chlordiazepoxide* (Librium) has a sedative action in some children comparable to the most effective minor tranquilizers. In other children it stimulates speech and thought associations, like the amphetamines, but produces a more prominent euphoria. This is therapeutic for some depressed, hypochondriacal, and inhibited children. In susceptible children, however, this stimulant action produces toxic excitation, with disorganization of thought and behavior, before any therapeutic effect occurs.

To date the large number of other minor tranquilizers have shown no special actions which differentiate them from the three drugs described above; in fact, many appear to be weaker (even totally ineffective) and more variable in their action in the same patients.

## Major Tranquilizers: The Phenothiazines and Rauwolfia Alkaloids

Extensive experience has demonstrated that the pheno-thiazine compounds are highly effective in moderately to severely disturbed children with "primary" behavior disorders, schizophrenia, or organic brain syndromes.[1,8,13,14]

*Dimethylamine Series.* The major difference between the use of these drugs in children and adults is that extra-pyramidal reactions are rare in children and can be terminated promptly by reducing the dose. The relative potency of different members within this group is the same for children as it is for adults.

*Piperazine series.* These drugs are especially useful in hypoactive schizophrenic or neurotic children who require drugs as potent as the phenothiazines but who tend to be depressed by therapeutic doses of chlorpromazine. Severely apathetic schizophrenic children with IQs under 70 may require and tolerate larger doses or trifluopera-zine by body weight, as compared to adult patients, with no signs of dystonia. In these children the drug may have useful stimulating effects, increasing alertness and motor drive. If they are very young and responsive to the drug, it may even increase motor skills, social responsive-ness, and language.[8,11]

Less impaired children tend to be more sensitive than adults to the stimulating effects of these drugs; small doses may produce irritability, agitation, and dyskine-sia. The adult dose, adjusted strictly for body weight, may be two to five times too high for such a child. This may well account for the high incidence of dystonic effects reported in the pediatric literature.[4,5,15,19]

Trifluoperazine (Stelazine) may be 20 to 100 times as potent as chlorpromazine in the same child, in all but the most retarded schizophrenic children.[8] Fluphenazine (Permitil, Prolixin) is more potent per unit dose than tri-fluoperazine. Prochlorperazine (Compazine), perphena-zine (Trilafon), and thiopropazate (Dartal) are about five to ten times as potent as chlorpromazine in the same child.[8]

*Piperidine series.* Since chlorpromazine-induced extra-pyramidal symptoms are not a problem in children, thioridazine (Mellaril) does not appear to have any advantage for children over chlorpromazine that outweighs its additional systemic toxicity. Since mepazine (Pacatal) has a relatively high incidence of toxicity in adults, its use is not advised for children.

*Rauwolfia alkaloids* have a less reliable action than the phenothiazines and are reserved for severely schizophrenic children who have not responded to phenothiazines.

## Antidepressants

Antidepressants are indicated in the depressions of adolescence, comparable to their use in adults. Psychotic retarded depressions are rare before mid-adolescence and virtually nonexistent under 10 to 11 years of age.

Pouissant and Ditman demonstrated in a controlled study that 25 to 50 mg. of imipramine (Tofranil) at bedtime significantly reduced the frequency of enuresis when compared to placebo. Individual regulation of dosage, longer duration of treatment, and gradual withdrawal of medication after a child was dry for two months increased the number of improvements. The children who improved the most were those who showed the most central nervous system stimulation. They were somewhat irritable and they awakened at night to urinate.[18] This suggests that a lower threshold for awakening may have been the effective component in the drug's action rather than its anticholinergic action or its effect on mood. Whether imipramine has any advantages over the older drugs used for enuresis, especially amphetamine and atropine, has not yet been tested.

## Anticonvulsants and Hypnotics

Early reports of the effectiveness of hydantoin compounds in the treatment of children whose behavior disorders were associated with nonspecific electroencephalographic abnormalities[16,20] have not been confirmed by later workers.[14,17] The author's experience agrees with this latter impression.

Hypnotics have not been demonstrated to be effective in psychiatric disorders of prepuberty children. Barbiturates may actually increase anxiety and disorganization in severely disturbed children. Chloral hydrate or mild tranquilizers usually suffice as nighttime sedation unless insomnia is associated with a severe disorder requiring major tranquilizers.

## REGULATION OF DRUGS

As with adults, drug therapy should start with the mildest drug which might be effective. The dose should be increased regularly until symptoms disappear or until the first signs of excessive dose appear (mild headache, fatigue, irritability, etc.). This must be done to insure that the useful dose range has been fully explored.

However, young children rarely report such symptoms. One must ask and look for malaise, anorexia, weight loss, or sudden behavioral deterioration which are associated with increases in dose, since these may indicate that the dose is too high for the particular child. The child's alertness, attention, and performance in school must be followed as carefully as the adult's performance on his job to determine whether the dose is insufficient or too high.

The child's response to medication may indicate that a more sedative or a more stimulating mild drug is required. Otherwise, one should explore more potent drugs in the same manner and not try a haphazard succession of drugs of similar type when symptoms persist with the highest tolerated dose of a mild drug. The optimal dose is the level which maximally reduces symptoms and increases function without causing discomfort.

In mild disorders, where symptoms disappear with mild medication, drugs need be continued only for a brief period to give the child and his family sufficient time to establish a new level of adaptation in the absence of symptoms. In severely disturbed children who do not obtain complete relief from symptoms even with potent medication, drug therapy may have to be maintained, just as it is with chronic adult patients.

## DRUG THERAPY COMBINED WITH PSYCHOTHERAPY

Drug therapy can very readily be combined with psychotherapy in treating children, and it should be, if both aspects of treatment are indicated. Young children generally accept medication in a matter-of-fact fashion as something doctors give them to make them better. Adolescents tend to regard medication more suspiciously as an interference with their autonomy. This attitude requires the same sensitive and skillful handling as other aspects of adolescent therapy.

Parents should be told that, at best, drugs produce only quantitative changes and that the child will not be cured or "made over." Discussions of all the other measures needed to help the child will emphasize this point.

In patients of any age, the therapeutic meaning of biologic measures, verbal interpretations, or environmental manipulations depends upon the conscious and unconscious attitudes of all the participants. In treating children, parents must also be involved. The many ramifications of the therapeutic management of the attitudes of parents and children around drug therapy cannot be dealt with here. In the author's experience, if drug therapy is put into its proper perspective by the physician, medication itself can then be accepted readily by parents and child as simply another way in which the doctor is trying to help the child.[7]

## REFERENCES

1. Bender, L., & Nichtern, S. Chemotherapy in Child Psychiatry, *New York J. Med.* 56:2791-2796, 1956.

2. Bradley, C. Benzedrine and Dexedrine in the Treatment of Children's Behavior Disorders, *Pediatrics* 5:24-37, 1950.

3. Bradley, C., & Bowen, M. Amphetamine (Benzedrine) Therapy of Children's Behavior Disorders, *Amer. J. Orthopsychiat.* 11:92-103, 1941.

4. Cleveland, W. W., & Smith, G. F. Complications Following the Use of Prochlorperazine (Compazine) as an Antiemetic, *Amer. J. Dis. Child.* 96:284-287, 1958.

5. Ehrlich, R. M. A Neurological Complication in Children on Phenothiazine Tranquilizers, *Canad. Med. Ass. J.* 81:241-243, 1959.

6. Eisenberg, L., Lachman, R., Molling, P. A., Lockner, A., Mizelle, J. D., & Conners, C. K. A Psychopharmacologic Experiment in a Training School for Delinquent Boys: Methods, Problems, Findings, *Amer. J. Orthopsychia.* 33:431-447, 1963.

7. Fish, B. Drug Therapy in Child Psychiatry: Psychological Aspects, *Compr. Psychiat.* 1:55-61, 1960.

8. Fish, B. Drug Therapy in Child Psychiatry: Pharmacological Aspects, *Compr. Psychiat.* 1:212-227, 1960.

9. Fish, B. "Evaluation of Psychiatric Therapies in Children," Hoch, P., and Zubin, J., eds.: *The Evaluation of Psychiatric Treatment.* New York: Grune & Stratton, 1964, pp. 202-220.

10. Fish, B., & Shapiro, T. A Typology of Children's Psychiatric Disorders: I. Its Application to a Controlled Evaluation of Treatment, *J. Amer. Acad. Child Psychiat.* 4:32-52, 1965.

11. Fish, B., Shapiro, T., & Campbell, M. Long-Term Prognosis and the Response of Schizophrenic Children to Drug Therapy: A Controlled Study of Trifluoperazine. *Amer. J. Psychiat.* 123:32-39, 1966.

12. Fish, B., Shapiro, T., & Campbell, M. A Classification of Schizophrenic Children Under Five Years, *Amer. J. Psychiat.,* to be published.

13. Fisher, S. (ed.) *Child Research in Psychopharmacology.* Springfield, Ill.: Charles C. Thomas, 1959.

14. Freedman, A. M. Drug Therapy in Behavior Disorders, *Pediat. Clin. N. Amer.* 5:573-594, 1958.

15. Jabbour, J. T., Sheffield, J. A., & Montalvo, J. M. Severe Neurological Manifestations in Four Children Receiving Compazine (Prochlorperazine), *J. Pediat.* 53:153-159, 1958.

16. Lindsley, D. B., & Henry, C. E. Effect of Drugs on Behavior and Electro-encephalograms of Children with Behavior Disorders, *Psychosom. Med.* 4:140-149, 1942.

17. Pasamanick, B. Anticonvulsant Drug Therapy of Behavior Problem Children with Abnormal Encephalograms, *Arch. Neurol. Psychiat.* 65:752-766, 1951.

18. Poussaint, A. F., & Ditman, K. S. A Controlled Study of Imipramine (Tofranil) in the Treatment of Childhood Enuresis, *J. Pediat.* 67:283-290, 1965.

19. Shaw, E. B., Dermott, R. V., Lee, R., Burbridge, T. N. Phenothiazine Tranquilizers as a Cause of Severe Seizures, *Pediatrics* 23:485-492, 1959.

20. Walker, C. F., & Kirkpatrick, B. B. Dilantin Treatment of Behavior Problem Children with Abnormal EEG's, *Amer. J. Psychiat.* 103:484-492, 1947.